Loeb Classical Monographs

In Memory of
James C. Loeb

GREEK DIALECTS

and the Transformation of an Indo-European Process

Gregory Nagy

HARVARD UNIVERSITY PRESS

CAMBRIDGE, MASSACHUSETTS

1970

The Loeb Classical Monographs are
published with assistance from the
Loeb Classical Library Foundation

Distributed in Great Britain by Oxford University Press, London

Library of Congress Catalog Card Number 69–12730

SBN: 674–36226–8

Printed in the United States of America

ACKNOWLEDGMENTS

I wish to thank generally all my colleagues and friends at Harvard University for their encouragement, and especially Wendell Clausen, Chairman of the Classics Department. For their advice on specific problems, I am grateful to Henning Andersen, Bruce Boling, Donald Cooper, Ives Goddard, Jay Jasanoff, Antanas Klimas, D. G. Miller, H. A. Roe, J. L. St. John, and Roy Wright. I owe special thanks to Warren Cowgill and F. W. Householder for their scrutiny of this work at various stages, and I am equally grateful to Jerzy Kuryłowicz for his gracious advice. Of course this list does not necessarily imply assent by these men to any of the ideas here presented. I also thank Mrs. Katryna Jacobsen for her kindness in helping me with the manuscript. What I value most of all is the sustained interest and counsel of my teacher and friend Calvert Watkins. To him I dedicate these lucubrations, or at least whatever may be wholesome in them; and I hope that the reader will not find too much chaff to winnow.

G. N.

CONTENTS

GENERAL ABBREVIATIONS

$>$/$<$	(is) phonologically changed to/from
$\rightarrow$/$\leftarrow$	founds or presupposes/ (is) founded or presupposed by
$\Rightarrow$/$\Leftarrow$	(is) transformed into/from
( )	contains optional elements
[ ]	contains phonetic elements
/ /	contains phonemic elements
⟨ ⟩	contains graphemic elements
{ }	used to set off any symbolized process or relationship so that the contingent syntax will not be disrupted
‖	marks a morpheme-boundary
#	marks absolute word-initial and word-final positions
ø	zero
V	vowel
R	r l m n
C	consonant, including R, unless the latter is separately indicated
C' or Ĉ	palatalized C
ə	laryngeal; the symbol is simply traditional, with no implication intended here regarding actual articulation
i̯ u̯	non-syllabic i u

*   marks conjectured forms; when an entry starts with *V C X Y etc., the asterisk is generally canceled; conversely, an asterisk generally cancels italics

:   versus; though vs. is also used when clarity seems at stake

IE   Indo-European

BIBLIOGRAPHICAL ABBREVIATIONS

Bechtel, *GD* I, II, III = F. Bechtel, *Die griechischen Dialekte* (Berlin 1921, 1923, 1924); when this work is cited for dialectal entries, the specific epigraphical locus and classification can be consulted therein.

Benveniste, *Origines* = E. Benveniste, *Origines de la formation des noms en indo-européen* I (Paris: Adrien-Maisonneuve, 1935).

Buck, *GD* = C. D. Buck, *The Greek Dialects* (Chicago 1955).

DGE = *Dialectorum Graecarum exempla epigraphica potiora*, ed. E. Schwyzer (Leipzig 1923); when epigraphical forms are cited from Schwyzer's and Bechtel's collections, their practice of supplying conjectured accentuations will not be followed here.

Evidence for Laryngeals,[2] ed. W. Winter ('s-Gravenhage 1965).

Frisk, *GEW* = Hj. Frisk, *Griechisches etymologisches Wörterbuch* I/II (Heidelberg 1960/1961ff.).

GLK = *Grammatici Latini* I–VII, ed. H. Keil (Leipzig 1857–1888).

IE Dialects = *Ancient Indo-European Dialects*, ed. H. Birnbaum and J. Puhvel (Berkeley and Los Angeles 1966).

R. Jakobson, *Selected Writings* I: *Phonological Studies* ('s-Gravenhage: Mouton, 1962).

Kuiper, *Vedic noun-inflexion* = F. B. J. Kuiper, *Notes on Vedic noun-inflexion* (Medede{e}lingen der [Koninklijke] Nederlands{ch}e Akademie van Wetenschappen, Afde{e}ling Letterkunde, Nieuwe Reeks 5.4 [Amsterdam 1942]).

Kuryłowicz, *Accentuation* = J. Kuryłowicz, *L'accentuation des langues indo-européennes*[2] (Wrocław/Kraków 1958).

—— *Apophonie* = *L'apophonie en indo-européen* (Wrocław 1956).

—— *Études* = *Études indoeuropéennes* (Kraków 1935).

—— *Inflectional Categories* = *The Inflectional Categories of Indo-European* (Heidelberg: Winter, 1964).

—— "Procès analogiques" = "La nature des procès dits 'analogiques'," *Acta linguistica* 5 (1945–1949) 15–37; reprinted in Kuryłowicz's *Esquisses linguistiques* (Wrocław/Kraków 1960) 66–86; also reprinted in *Readings in Linguistics* II, ed. E. P. Hamp, F. W. Householder, R. Austerlitz (Chicago: University of Chicago

Press, 1966) 158–174. Because at the time of this writing the third version was most readily available, its pagination will regularly be cited for reference.

Lejeune, *Traité* = M. Lejeune, *Traité de phonétique grecque*[2] (Paris: Klincksieck, 1955).

Leumann, *LG* = M. Leumann, *Lateinische Laut- und Formenlehre*, vol. I of F. Stolz/J. H. Schmalz, *Lateinische Grammatik*,[5] rev. M. Leumann/J. B. Hofmann (München 1926–1928).

Meillet, *Dialectes* = A. Meillet, *Les dialectes indo-européennes*[2] (Paris 1937).

—— *Introduction* = *Introduction a l'étude comparative des langues indo-européennes*[8] (Paris 1937).

Schwyzer, *GG* I = E. Schwyzer, *Griechische Grammatik* I (München 1939).

Thumb/Kieckers, *GD* I = A. Thumb and E. Kieckers, *Handbuch der griechischen Dialekte* I[2] (Heidelberg 1932).

Thumb/Scherer, *GD* II = A. Thumb and A. Scherer, *Handbuch der griechischen Dialekte* II[2] (Heidelberg 1959).

J. Wackernagel, *Kleine Schriften* I, II (Göttingen 1953).

Watkins, *Celtic Verb* I = C. Watkins, *Indo-European Origins of the Celtic Verb* I. *The Sigmatic Aorist* (Dublin: Dublin Institute of Advanced Studies, 1962).

van Wijk, *Genetiv Singular* = N. van Wijk, *Der nominale Genetiv Singular im Indogermanischen in seinem Verhältnis zum Nominativ* (Zwolle 1902).

GREEK DIALECTS
and the Transformation of an
Indo-European Process

INTRODUCTION

At a time of accumulating evidence for traces of more than one Greek dialect in the texts of Linear B,[1] it becomes especially important to refine the dialectal criteria that can be extended all the way back from the classical to the Mycenaean era. Such criteria are relatively few—so few, in fact, that E. Risch's well-known "Übersichtstabelle"[2] offers only eight dialectal features which can be considered applicable to that early a period. At the head of this list is the contrast {-τι- : -σι-}, an isogloss which principally distinguishes the classical idioms of Dorian and West-Aiolian (with e.g. δίδωτι) from Arcadian, Cypriote, Attic/Ionic, and East-Aiolian (with δίδωσι). An important difficulty, however, is that in the assibilation of *-τι- to -σι-, the precise phonological conditions involved have not adequately been formulated. Until such a formulation is found, the very occurrence of this assibilation, as well as its distribution, remains a crux.[3] Only on one point is there general agreement: that {*-τι- > -σι-} was prevented when -σ- preceded *-τ-. Otherwise, from a synchronic evaluation of the dialects where change from *-τι- to -σι- did occur, no intrinsic feature seems evident which could motivate this innovation in all its attested manifestations.

[1] Cf. e.g. E. Risch, "Les différences dialectales dans le mycénien," *Proceedings of the Cambridge Colloquium on Mycenaean Studies*, ed. L. R. Palmer and J. Chadwick (Cambridge 1966) 150–157.

[2] Cf. "Die Gliederung der griechischen Dialekte in neuer Sicht," *Museum Helveticum* 12 (1955) 61–76.

[3] The problem is conveniently outlined by Lejeune, *Traité* 53–55, and by Schwyzer, *GG* I 270 f. For a useful critical survey of submitted solutions, cf. J. Holt, "Remarques sur l'assibilation grecque," *Mélanges linguistiques offerts à M. Holger Pedersen* (Aarsskrift for Aarhus Universitet 9.1 [København 1937]) 176–182.

An inference to be drawn, then, is that the phonological conditions which had originally prompted {*-τι- > -σι-} became significantly altered by e.g. the period of classical Attic. I hope to demonstrate that the attested ι in -σι- had been endowed with different phonological properties in preclassical times: to wit, that there was once an alternation {-i̯-/-ι-}, conditioned by (1) accentual patterns and (2) prevocalic/preconsonantal position. An attempt to sketch the specific environment of this alternation {-i̯-/-ι-} is submitted in chapter III; but before reaching that stage of the argument, we have to account for this basic question: why is IE *-i̯- in the context -Ci̯V- reflected by Greek sometimes as etymological *-i̯-, sometimes as -ι-? This issue in turn raises a still broader one: how was the IE feature known as "Sievers' Law" operative on inherited *-i̯- in Greek and in other IE dialects? I propose that a formulation of these conditions from the IE standpoint leads to a precise understanding of the Greek alternation {-i̯-/-ι-}, which in turn has a direct bearing on the prehistoric innovation {*-τι- > -σι-}. Once we discern how this innovation was motivated, the dialectal contrast {-τι- : -σι-} becomes a more significant criterion for distinguishing the very earliest dialectal divisions in the Greek language.

CHAPTER I

POSTCONSONANTAL/PREVOCALIC
*-i̯- IN IE GRAMMATICAL
CATEGORIES

§1. At an early period of IE when *ə was still functionally consonantal, *i̯ and *i had been combinatory variants—the former predictably occurring adjacent to a vowel, the latter elsewhere.[1] The same distribution holds for *u̯/*u, *r/*r̥, *l/*l̥, *m/*m̥, *n/*n̥: hence

(V)i̯V	Vi(C)	(C)i̯V vs.	(C)i(C)
(V)u̯V	Vu(C)	(C)u̯V vs.	(C)u(C)
(V)R̂V	VR(C)	(C)RV vs.	(C)R̥(C).

Between C and V, however, a split developed, the resulting patterns of which have come to be known as "Sievers' Law";[2] applied specifically to *i̯/*i, the formulation is this: *-i̯- after light syllable, *-i- after heavy syllable: hence -V̆Ci̯V- vs. -V̄CiV- and -V̄C₁C₂iV-.[3] For representational

---

[1] F. Edgerton, "The Indo-European Semivowels," *Language* 19 (1943) 83–123: here conveniently summarized, from previous works, are the formulations commonly known as "Sievers' Law" (more appropriately "Sievers' Rule"—the designation which I will use throughout) and "Edgerton's Converse"; J. Kuryłowicz, "Zur altpersischen Keilschrift," *Zeitschrift für Phonetik, Sprachwissenschaft und Kommunikationsforschung* 17 (1964) 563–569 (for an earlier version, cf. Kuryłowicz's *Esquisses linguistiques* [Wrocław/Kraków 1960] 274–280).

[2] Named after E. Sievers; cf. his "Zur Accent und Lautlehre der germanischen Sprachen," *Beiträge zur Geschichte der deutschen Sprache und Literatur*, ed. H. Paul, W. Braune, and E. Sievers, 5 (1878) 63–163, esp. 129 ff.

[3] The Sanskrit metrical terms *laghu-* ("light") and *guru-* ("heavy") provide precedent for such syllabic designations.

3

convenience, this opposition can be symbolized in the simplified form of -V̄Ci̯V- vs. -V̄CiV-. So also -V̄Cu̯V- vs. -V̄CuV-, -V̄CrV- vs. -V̄Cr̥V-, -V̆ClV- vs. -V̄Cl̥V-, -V̆CmV- vs. -V̄Cm̥V-, -V̆CnV- vs. -V̄Cn̥V-. Thus far, these distributions at such a posited stage of IE are strictly within the realm of combinatory variants, and to this extent, Sievers' formulation is justifiable.

But there then arises at least one new crucial circumstance which disrupts the original pattern: to wit, *-iəV- > *-iV-, *-uəV- > *-uV-, -R̥əV- > -R̥V-.[4] (The combinations *-iV- and *-uV- will henceforth be represented with their subphonemic off-glides: *-ii̯V- and *-uu̯V-; thus the relationship of *-ii̯- and *-uu̯- to *-i̯- and *-u̯- respectively can be described as additive in the order here given [plus i or u] or subtractive in the reverse [minus i or u].) In the IE period preceding the disappearance of *-ə- in the slots just described, the existence of a morpheme-boundary (‖) before e.g. *-(i)i̯V- did not prevent obligatory phonological transformations depending solely on the quantity of the preceding syllable:

  1. -V̄C + (i)i̯V- ⇒ -V̄C‖ii̯V-
  2. -V̆C + (i)i̯V- ⇒ -V̆C‖i̯V-;

likewise

  1. -V̄C + (u)u̯V- ⇒ -V̄C‖uu̯V-
  2. -V̆C + (u)u̯V- ⇒ -V̆C‖u̯V-

and

  1. -V̄C + (R̥)RV- ⇒ -V̄C‖R̥RV-
  2. -V̆C + (R̥)RV- ⇒ -V̆C‖RV-.

In essence, the synchronic rules 1 and 2 are Sievers' Rule and Edgerton's Converse respectively.

---

[4] Cf. Kuryłowicz, *Apophonie* 171 n. 12, 341.

§2. But once structures like -VCiəV- and -VCuəV- undergo a phonological shift to -VCii̯V- and -VCuu̯V-, then a constraint like that symbolized by 2 can cease to be obligatory. That is, -Cii̯V- and -Cuu̯V- are now possible after both light and heavy syllables, and thus *-ii̯- and *-uu̯- become morphologically reappraised as redundant configurations after light syllables, in contrast with the previously obligatory *-i̯- and *-u̯-. While e.g. *-i̯- and *-ii̯- may survive just so in inherited forms from the IE standpoint, there follows a drastic extension in productive categories constituting the mold for new formations. For example, let a morpheme-boundary occur just before *-(i)i̯- of an IE-inherited nominal formant *-‖(i)i̯o-, henceforth represented simply by the nominative singular *-‖(i)i̯os: so long as a given nominal with such a suffix is appreciated as a derived form, the morpheme-boundary of its formant *-(i)i̯os will continue to be perceived, and the suffixal ensemble itself will remain productive. Thus when the process {*-iəV- > *-ii̯V-} entails a disruption of the phonological opposition {-V̆Ci̯V- : -V̆Cii̯V-}, it thereupon happens, as posited, that *-ii̯- becomes a formally redundant variant of *-i̯- after light syllables. Here the factor defined by Kuryłowicz as polarization[5] can become operative. In e.g. -V̆C(i)i̯os, the redundant configuration *-ii̯- becomes generalized over the essential *-i̯-, so as to polarize a productive, marked category from unmarked counterparts where productivity ceased or was felt as never having existed. In other words, there evolves (after *-iəV- > *-ii̯V-) a contrast of productive -V̆C‖ii̯os vs. unproductive -V̆Ci̯os; likewise -V̆C‖uu̯os vs. -V̆Cu̯os. In postconsonantal/prevocalic

---

[5] Axiom I: "Un morphème bipartite tend à s'assimiler un morphème iso-fonctionnel consistant uniquement en un des deux éléments, c'est-à-dire le morphème composé remplace le morphème simple." Cf. Kuryłowicz, "Procès analogiques" 162.

position, then, *{-i- : -i̯-} and *{-u- : -u̯-} cease to be combinatory variants, becoming autonomous entities instead. But what of the former combinatory variants *{-r̥- : -r-}, *{-l̥- : -l-}, *{-m̥- : -m-}, *{-n̥- : -n-}? Here too, with the development {-R̥əV- > -R̥V-}, Edgerton's Converse ceases to be obligatory. As for the actual manifestation of -CR̥V-, it is reflected as e.g. Indic -CirV-/-CurV-, -CamV-, -CanV-; Avestan -CaRV-; "South European" -CaRV- (Celtic, Italic, Greek, Armenian); "North European" -CuRV- (Germanic) and -CiRV-/-CuRV- (Baltic and Slavic).[6] Granted, there was widespread morphological extension, in e.g. the "European" languages, of *-aR(V-) and *-iR(V-)/ *-uR(V-) as the productive replacement of -R(V-) even after light syllables;[7] the detailed demonstration of this circumstance remains one of the most important accomplishments of Kuryłowicz's *Apophonie*. But there is a signal difference between a morphologically productive *-aR(V-) or *-iR(V-)/*-uR(V-), polarized from a corresponding unproductive -R(V-), and the originally kindred opposition of likewise productive *-ii̯(V-) or *-uu̯(V-) to residual *-i̯(V-) or *-u̯(V-) respectively. Although both types involve the opposition {syllabic : non-syllabic}, only the *-ii̯- and the *-uu̯- show homorganic components for the

---

[6] Clear summary by Kuryłowicz, *Apophonie* 394 f.

[7] E.g. Greek στεγ-νός "waterproof" vs. στεγ-ανός "covering, covered, waterproof"; λίχ-νος "gluttonous" vs. λιχ-ανός "licking" (or "licking finger" = "forefinger"); etc. Cf. Schwyzer, *GG* I 489. It is noteworthy that the more archaic forms have a more restricted semantic range than the newer forms; this distribution illustrates Kuryłowicz's axiom IV: "Quand à la suite d'une transformation morphologique une forme subit la différenciation, la forme nouvelle correspond à sa fonction primaire (de fondation), la forme ancienne est réservée pour la fonction secondaire (fondée)." Cf. Kuryłowicz, "Procès analogiques" 169. In this case the differentiation is lexical, not derivational or inflectional.

For similar evidence in verbs with -ν-ειν and -αν-ειν, cf. Schwyzer, *GG* I 700 f.

syllabic member; on the other hand, once prevocalic -R̥-
becomes *-aR-, *-iR-, *-uR- and the like, these syllabic
opposites of simplex prevocalic -R- are now characterized
by constituents which are distinctly not homorganic;
indeed, the latter circumstance tends to deactivate even
Sievers' Rule,[8] since what used to be -R̥- after heavy
syllable and is now *-aR- in e.g. Greek may no longer be
perceived synchronically as syllabic combinatory variant
of non-syllabic -R-, but rather, as the separate phonemes
*-a- and -R-, capable of existing in positions where they are
independent of each other. As for the constituents of *-ii̯-,
however, the *-i- and the *-i̯- are by themselves mere
combinatory variants in every slot other than postcon-
sonantal/prevocalic; so also the constituents of *-uu̯-.
Thus it is conceivable that Sievers' Rule could continue
to be operative on postconsonantal/prevocalic *-i̯- and
*-u̯- (hence ⇒ *-ii̯- and *-uu̯- after heavy syllable), but no
longer on -R- in the same slot. Yet with such a limited
application, so that *-r-, *-l-, *-m-, *-n- no longer afford a
structural parallel, the chances for the survival of Sievers'
Rule are that much more weakened. Then too, even if it
finally happens that e.g. -V̆Cii̯V- becomes -V̆Ci̯V-, such a
development would merely mean the leveling of an allophonic variation, whereas a morphological opposition could
persist: -V̆C‖ii̯V- vs. -V̆Ci̯V-, as also -V̆C‖ii̯V- vs. -V̆Ci̯V-.

§3. Given an inherited morphological opposition between
e.g. productive nominals in (-V̆C)‖ii̯os and unproductive
counterparts in (-V̆C)i̯os, there still remains the question of
what could happen if the morpheme-boundary in the former
were to be eroded. In other words, what if a particular
word with a configuration -V̆Cii̯os were to lose its status as a
synchronically derived form? The expected consequence is

---

[8] Hence e.g. θέρηγ-νον "wicker body of the harvest-cart" (vs. the variant
θερήγ-ανον); also τερπ-νός, σπερχ-νός, ἰσχ-νός, etc.; cf. Schwyzer, *GG* I 489.

that *-iios in this instance could no longer be perceived as productive suffixal formant, so that the given form in -V̆Ciios would become relegated from a productive (marked) nominal category into its unproductive (unmarked) counterpart. Accompanying this relegation is the loss of the formal mark of productivity, syllabic *-i- (= *-ii-); that is, marked and syllabic *-i- (as in -V̆Ciios) reverts to unmarked and nonsyllabic *-i̯- (as in -V̆Ci̯os). Such formal enactment of a functional attrition, of course, can occur only when the productive marker is still homorganic with the unproductive marker, as in the case of *-i(V-) = *-ii(V-) vs. *-i̯(V-), or *-u(V-) = *-uu̯(V-) vs. *-u̯(V-). In the case of *-R̥(V-) vs. *-R(V-), however, once *-R̥(V-) becomes *-aR(V-) in e.g. Greek, reversion of this *-aR(V-) to *-R(V-) is no longer possible. Thus even though e.g. suffixal -ανος is no longer a productive formant in classical Greek, it cannot revert to -νος because the markers -an(V-) and -n(V-) are not homorganic variants. Hence the survival of both the newer type στεγανός (reflecting the original morphological extension of prevocalic *-n̥- after light syllable) and the older στεγνός.[9] In sum, the factor of morphological attrition from e.g. -V̆C‖i̯os to -V̆Ci̯os in a given IE language makes it an elusive task to determine whether a given word with an attested nominal suffix *-i̯o- had ever belonged to a productive category with suffix *-ii̯o-. If the latter suffix is no longer productive anywhere in the specified language, then we may even expect the universal attestation of -V̆Ci̯os to the exclusion of -V̆Cii̯os. Nevertheless, certain phonological developments could have arrested the morphological attrition of e.g. -V̆C‖i̯os to -V̆Ci̯os. If at a certain period there arise such irrevocably divergent phonological developments as *-ii̯o- > X and *-i̯o- > Y, then the very distribution of suffixal

---

[9] Cf. n. 7 above.

X and Y in given words of the attested language will determine which of these words had belonged to productive or unproductive nominal categories respectively during the unattested period of the phonological transformations yielding X and Y. Even if X, the reflex of *-iio-, is no longer synchronically productive in the attested language, it still reveals that any surviving word with suffixal X had indeed belonged to a productive nominal category at the unattested period of the phonological transformation *-iio- > X.

§4. In the Brittonic branch of Celtic (as distinct from the Goidelic branch), there are clear reflexes of a pristine morphological opposition between productive nominals with the configuration -V̆C‖iio-/-V̆C‖iiā- and unproductive counterparts with -V̆Cio-/-V̆Ciā-; on the other hand, there is no trace of Sievers' Rule and Edgerton's Converse (i.e., preceding heavy syllables do not generate prevocalic *-ii- as opposed to *-i-), as the evidence assembled below will show. Thus a Brittonic language like Welsh provides an ideal example of morphological extension (whereby the presence of ‖ requires *-iio-/-iiā-) and of morphological retention (whereby the absence of ‖ allows *-io-/-iā-), without other inherited factors involved. The crucial circumstance which preserves the prehistoric opposition of -V̆C‖iio-/-V̆C‖iiā- vs. -V̆Cio-/-V̆Ciā- is the irrevocable divergence in phonological development between the former and the latter. In Welsh, the relevant reflexes are these:

from *-io- vowel-infection[10]
from *-iā- vowel-infection
from *-iio- vowel-infection + suffix -ydd
from *-iiā- vowel-infection + suffix -edd.

[10] For a survey of vowel-infection in Brittonic, cf. H. Lewis and H. Pedersen, *A Concise Comparative Celtic Grammar*[2] (Göttingen 1961) 106–112. Cf. also K. Jackson, *Language and History in Early Britain* (Edinburgh 1953) 579–618.

The phonological development of Welsh *-ydd* and *-edd* is to be explained thus:

En brittonique, le traitement le plus général, ou pour mieux dire celui dont les exemples sont le plus nombreux consiste à maintenir le *i* en hiatus avec une valeur vocalique, si bien que devant la voyelle suivante il développe après lui un *y* [= -*i̯*-]. Ce *y* à son tour se renforce au point de devenir un *d*, en sorte qu'après la chute de l'ancienne voyelle finale, il subsiste simplement une finale *i* + *d*. Cette finale est en gallois *-ydd* ou *-edd*, suivant que la voyelle tombée était un *ŏ* ou un *ā*. C'est-à-dire que l'ancien suffixe *-io-* [= -*i̯o*-] est représenté par *-ydd*, et l'ancien suffixe *-iā-* [= -*i̯ā*-] par *-edd*.[11]

The suffix *-ydd* is formant of (a) adjectives, (b) agent-nouns,[12] (c) object-nouns, (d) abstract nouns,[13] while the suffix *-edd*, of (d') abstract nouns likewise;[14] hence the following examples from Welsh:[15]

(*a*) *newydd* "new" < *nou̯-i̯o-; cf. Old Breton *nouuid*, Breton *nevez*, Old Irish *nuae*. Morphological parallels: Sanskrit *návyaḥ*, Gothic *niujis*, Oscan *Nouios*.

(*b*) *prydydd* "poet" < *k^wr̥t-i̯o-; for the base, cf. the residual Irish noun *creth* "art of poetry" < *k^wr̥t-o-; cf. also Vedic *kr̥ṇóti* "makes," Old Slavonic *čaro-dějь* "magician," Lithuanian *ker-ěti* "bewitch," etc.[16]

[11] J. Vendryes, "Sur le traitement brittonique de *i* en hiatus," *Bulletin de la Société de Linguistique de Paris* 47 (1951) 2.

[12] For instances of agent-nouns with *-i̯o- in Baltic, etc., cf. chap. ii § 9, esp. n. 47.

[13] Vendryes, "Le traitement brittonique" 3, proposes that abstract nouns with *-i̯o- were inanimate; hence Brittonic nominative/accusative singular *-i̯on. Type (c) is probably a semantic specialization of type (d), arising after the period when the latter became unproductive. (For a discussion of the process whereby abstract nouns become concrete nouns, cf. chap. ii § 9, § 11.) If so, there is no need to ascribe both functions (c) and (d) to the original suffix *-i̯o-; the latter of the two will suffice.

[14] Cf. the Greek type κακίᾱ (← κακός), discussed in chap. ii § 12.

[15] For an ampler list, from which the present selection was made, cf. Vendryes, "Le traitement brittonique" 3 f.

[16] On the Baltic and Slavic attestations of *k^wer-/k^wor-/k^wr̥-: "The association with magic in this group of derivatives, which recurs in Vedic *kártram* "spell, charm" ([*Atharva-Veda*]), would make it likely that the image underlying

(c) *mynydd* "mountain"[17] < *mon-i̯o-; cf. Old Breton *monid*, Cornish *meneth*, Breton *menez*.

(d) *riydd*[18] "royal splendor" < *rēg-i̯o-; cf. Old Irish *ríge* "royalty" < *rēg-i̯on*.

(d') *riedd*[19] "royal splendor" < *rēg-i̯ā-.

These forms, then, are reflexes of the type -V̆C‖i̯o-/-V̆C‖i̯ā-. But wherever a particular word with this pattern loses its status of derived form bearing a specific function in its suffix *-i̯o-/-i̯ā-, the morpheme-boundary (‖) is then eroded; as a consequence, the marked syllabic *-i-, the sign of productivity, reverts to unmarked non-syllabic *-i̯-; hence -V̆Ci̯o-/-V̆Ci̯ā-. In the Brittonic languages, the phonological reflex of the latter pattern is different from that of the productive counterpart -V̆Ci̯o-/-V̆Ci̯ā-. For example, Welsh, as already noted, has transmitted the configurations *-i̯o-/-i̯ā- in the guise of vowel-infection alone, without accessory suffixal *-ydd/-edd*. Hence such examples as the following:

caill "testicle" < *kall-i̯o- or *kall-i̯ā-; cf. Gaulish *epo-call-io-n* "equī testiculus."

ceirch "oats" < *kork-i̯o- (to be noted is the unmistakably heavy syllable preceding *-i̯o- here); cf. Breton *kerc'h*, Old Irish *coirce*.

dyn "man" < Celtic *don-i̯o-, cognate of Greek χθόνιος; cf. Old Irish *duine*.

[Old Irish] *creth* is one of magically transforming something into something, rather than the simple notion of craftsmanship in Greek ποίησις; ποιέω."— C. Watkins, "Indo-European Metrics and Archaic Irish Verse," *Celtica* 6 (1962) 214 f.

[17] The original meaning of *mynydd* was probably "Gebirge" rather than "Berg" (cf. n. 13). The epigraphical MONEDORIGI (*Corpus Inscriptionum Insularum Celticarum* 413, fifth century) probably contains Late British *monido-; if so, the name would mean "Mountain King": Jackson, *LHEB* (n. 10) 355.

[18] Spelled *rihyd* in e.g. *The Red Book of Hergest;* other orthographic variants: *rihit, rihyt*. For a detailed list of attestations, cf. Vendryes, "Le traitement brittonique" 4.

[19] Spelled *riet* in e.g. *The Black Book of Carmarthen;* other orthographic variants: *ried, rihed, rhiedd*. Cf. Vendryes, "Le traitement brittonique" 4.

eil "other, second" < **al-i̯o-; cf. Old Irish *aile*, Latin *alius*, etc. *haid* "swarm" < **sat-i̯ā-; cf. Old Irish *saithe*.

We have reason, then, to expect that in borrowings of Latin words with *-ius*, *-ia* (as also with original *-eus*, *-ea*), the morphological force of these alien suffixes is likewise not perceived. Thus even though e.g. the *-eus* of Latin *cuneus* "wedge" would already show **-i̯o-* at the time of borrowing, the absence of a synchronically-perceived morpheme-boundary nonetheless excluded the Welsh development of a potential form with productive suffix **-‖i̯o-*; instead, what is *cuneus* in classical Latin ultimately yields Welsh *cyn*, without the suffixal *-ydd*. Likewise *bēstia* "beast" > ... > *bwyst* (without *-edd*), etc.[20]

§5. Phonological developments in Goidelic, unlike Brittonic, have obliterated the original opposition of productive nominals with the pattern -V̆C‖i̯o-/-V̆C‖i̯ā- vs. unproductive counterparts with -V̆Ci̯o-/-V̆Ci̯ā-. From all four of these patterns, **-i̯o- *-ii̯o- *-i̯ā- *-ii̯ā-*, the uniform Old Irish reflex is *-e*.[21] Thus even such a synchronically unmotivated configuration as **al-i̯o-/al-i̯ā-*, with no surviving morpheme-boundary between etymological root and suffix, yields Old Irish nominative singular masculine/feminine *ail-e* "other," with the same *-e* as seen in any reflex of once-productive **-i̯o-/-ii̯ā-*. The phonological circumstances leading to such a leveling of the opposition between productive -V̆C‖i̯V- and unproductive -V̆Ci̯V- will be outlined presently;[22] it is more important, however, to note first of all that whereas Goidelic does not preserve reflexes of

[20] Cf. Vendryes, "Le traitement brittonique" 5; also Jackson, *LHEB* (n. 10) 363, § 42.
[21] Cf. R. Thurneysen, *A Grammar of Old Irish*, rev. and enl. ed., trans. D. A. Binchy and O. Bergin (Dublin: Dublin Institute for Advanced Studies, 1946) 60 f.
[22] Cf. § 5.9 *infra*.

such an opposition in nominals, it does in verbals. The relevant facts can be analyzed as follows:

(1) There are two kinds of *i*-verbs in Old Irish: Thurneysen's class B II (a "strong" conjugation) and class A II (a "weak" conjugation),[23] otherwise known as *i*-stems and *ī*-stems respectively.[24] Constituents of the former class are deverbative (or primary) from the Celtic standpoint,[25] while those of the latter are either deverbative or denominative. In Old Irish the denominative verbs of class A II are still synchronically productive (in the deponent diathesis, when reinforced by the accessory suffix *-agi-/-igi-*),[26] whereas deverbatives of both classes A II and B II are residual. We can compare the kindred distribution in Latin, where *i*-verbs are in either the 3rd or 4th conjugation if deverbative from the Italic standpoint, but exclusively in the 4th if denominative; here again, deverbative *i*-verbs are residual, and only denominative *i*-verbs retained productivity.[27]

(2) The crucial distinction between the present stems of these two types of Old Irish *i*-verbs is found in the endings of the active conjunct 3rd singular:[28]

A II *-i* < *-īt*; e.g. (*fo*)·*dáli* "distributes" < *dāl-īt*; Thurneysen's paradigmatic exemplar: ·*léici* "leaves"

B II *-ø* < *-it*; e.g. (*fo*)·*daim* "endures" < *dam-it*; Thurneysen's paradigmatic exemplar: ·*gaib* "takes."

---

[23] Cf. Thurneysen, *Grammar* § 523, § 549.

[24] Cf. H. Pedersen, *Vergleichende Grammatik der keltischen Sprachen* II (Göttingen 1911) 839 f: s.v. "Präsensbildung" in the *Sachindex*, there is an invaluable list classifying all the *i*-verbs found in the *Verbalverzeichnis* (450–658) into *i*-stems and *ī*-stems, wherever possible.

[25] In fact, strong verbs cannot be denominative in Old Irish: cf. Thurneysen, *Grammar* 336.

[26] E.g. *béo* "living" → ·*béoigedar* "vivifies," *follus* "clear" → ·*foilsigedar* "clarifies," *debuith* "strife" → ·*debthigedar* "fights," *ainm* "name" → ·*ainmnigedar* "names," etc.; cf. Thurneysen, *Grammar* 337 f.

[27] Cf. § 6.

[28] From here on, the reconstruction of desinences as well as stems will become a factor affecting the arguments offered. For an appraisal of the problems involved in tracing back the desinential system of the Celtic verb, I have had

I propose that *-īt and *-it in these instances are at best transitional, and as such must be traced back further to *-ii̯et[29] and *-i̯et respectively.[30] The second reconstruction is especially controversial, but the basic argument supporting it can be postponed[31] until we weigh the implications. The most fundamental of these is that if not only -i is from *-ii̯et but also -ø from *-i̯et, then we see in the contrast between conjunct 3rd singular (present) -i and -ø of A II and B II verbs respectively a reflex of the IE-inherited opposition between productive -V̆C‖i̯iV- and unproductive -V̆Ci̯V-. And the vehicle whereby this morphological opposition

---

the benefit of reading a preliminary copy of C. Watkins' forthcoming book, *A History of Indo-European Verb Inflexion* (Part I of *Indo-European Grammar* III: *Morphology*; English-language version). In this invaluable work, we find convincing evidence to show that the earliest layer of inherited thematic-stem verbs in Celtic had no 3rd singular *t*-desinence: hence e.g. Old Irish 3rd singular conjunct ·*beir* is ultimately derived from IE *bhere; the type *bheret, by contrast, is an innovation which can be motivated in terms of Celtic.

[29] There is also a residual stative-intransitive A II type with inherited formant *-ē- (rather than *-ii̯e-/-ii̯o-); for a list of probable and possible Old Irish constituents, cf. J. Vendryes, "Restes en celtique du thème verbal en -ē-," *Mélanges linguistiques offerts à M. Holger Pedersen* (Aarsskrift for Aarhus Universitet 9.1 [København 1937]) 287–292. For the reconstruction of *-ii̯et, cf. e.g. Thurneysen, *Grammar* 365.

[30] Once granted that the Old Irish A II 3rd singular conjunct -i (as in ·*léici*) is derived from a thematic stem, we may trace it from *-ii̯et rather than from a more archaic configuration *-ii̯e; the etymological presence/absence of *-t would then account for the following contrast:

3rd singular conjunct *-ii̯et > *-īt > -i: e.g. *léici*
2nd singular imperative *-ii̯e > *-ī > -ø: e.g. *léic*.

Alternatively, we may posit that 3rd singular -i is a phonological reflex of *-ii̯e, and that the 2nd singular imperative -ø is the result of morphological truncation. For more on the latter phenomenon, cf. the discussion of the Gothic 2nd singular imperative, § 7 *infra*. For further discussion of *léici/léic*, cf. n. 32.

As for the B II 3rd singular conjunct -ø (as in ·*gaib*), an original *-i̯e is probable: that is, the 3rd singular conjunct of several inherited B II verbs may well be derived from an older *-i̯e rather than from *-i̯et. I will cite *infra* (§ 5.4) apparent instances of both; in the meantime, however, the form *-i̯et will be suitable as a cover-symbol, since its phonological reflex would not be different from that of *-i̯e in the extant phase of Old Irish.

[31] Cf. § 5.8; the task will be to show that *-it is not inherited from IE.

could have been preserved in Goidelic was, I propose, the divergent phonological treatment of *-i̯i̯- and *-i̯- before *-e-, vs. that of *-i̯i̯- and *-i̯- before *-o- or *-ā-:

$$
\begin{array}{ll}
\text{*-i̯i̯e-} > \dots > -i & \text{vs. } \text{*-i̯i̯o-} > \dots > -e \\
\text{*-i̯e-} > \dots > -\text{\o}^{32} & \text{*-i̯o-} > \dots > -e \\
& \text{*-i̯i̯ā-} > \dots > -e \\
& \text{*-i̯ā-} > \dots > -e.
\end{array}
$$

(3) As in Brittonic, Sievers' Rule as applicable to *-i̯i̯-/-i̯- had apparently broken down also in Goidelic: Old Irish reveals sporadic instances of *i*-verbs with conjunct 3rd singular -ø even after heavy syllable. For example, a form like ·*báid* "immerses, drowns"[33] seems to force the reconstruction *bād-it from the traditional standpoint of Celtic phonology:[34] in any case, *bād-īt is impossible; what at first seems an alternative to *bād-it is the claim that ·*báid* is a morphological innovation, and that the inherited form is rather ·*báidi*, also attested.[35] In terms of the Old Irish verbal system at its extant stages, however, it is unlikely that ·*báid* could have mechanically displaced ·*báidi;* the residual and unproductive B II conjugation is hardly fit to impose its synchronically unpredictable patterns on any constituent of the regular A II conjugation. Even if the given constituent

[32] For further elaboration, cf. § 5.9 *infra*. If we interpret the distinction between 3rd singular conjunct *léici* and 2nd singular imperative *léic* as phonologically motivated (cf. n. 30), then a word-final *-t must be affixed to *-i̯i̯e- (and perhaps at least secondarily to *-i̯e-); but if we interpret this distinction as morphologically motivated (cf. again n. 30), no such corollary is needed. The latter of the two interpretations, however, removes the necessity of positing the transitional *-īt in the sequence {*-i̯i̯et > *-īt > -*i*} (and therefore possibly also the *-it in {*-i̯et > *-it > -ø}); for that reason, *-īt and *-it will henceforth be designated with a preceding question-mark. But cf. n. 77.

[33] Cf. Pedersen, *Vergleichende Grammatik* II (n. 24 above) 458 f, s.v.

[34] As for the standpoint of IE phonology, the root is apparently *gʷādh-: cf. J. Pokorny, *Indogermanisches etymologisches Wörterbuch* (Bern 1959) s.v.

[35] E.g. *do·bádi* "extinguishes, destroys": cf. Lewis/Pedersen, *Celtic Grammar* (n. 10) 340; Pedersen, *Vergleichende Grammatik* II (n. 24) 458, does indeed suggest that ·*báid* is an innovation, in view of the fact that *báid-* is otherwise a "regelmässiger -ī-Stamm."

is a synchronically unmotivated form, as is the case with the deverbative A II verb *báid-*, it still belongs to a productive paradigm—the weak conjugation (here A II), which regularly shows *s*-preterite and *f*-future as its main distinctive features.[36] Thus too in the instance of an *i*-verb like *tib-* "laugh" (cf. 1st singular *ní·thibiu*), the very fact that *s*-preterite and *f*-future forms are attested in its paradigm[37] is enough to warrant its classification as "*ī*-stem" (= A II)[38] rather than "*ĭ*-stem"—this even though the conjunct 3rd singular (present) is attested as *·tib* besides *·tibi*.[39] In sum, since we cannot justify the presence of *·tib* (vs. *·tibi*) or of *·báid* (vs. *·báidi*) from the standpoint of the synchronic Old Irish verbal system, we may uphold the traditional reconstruction (from the phonological standpoint) of *-it (vs. *-īt) for the ending of the conjunct 3rd singular of these forms. But if we dispense with the reconstruction *-it/-īt in favour of *-i̯et/-ii̯et, under the already-announced assumption that the former are at best a transitional phase of the latter, we are then encouraged to discern here the apparent reflex of an IE-inherited opposition between unproductive -V̆C̣iV- vs. productive -V̆C‖ii̯V-. With the breakdown of synchronic motivation in a form like *bād‖ii̯et, the morpheme-boundary is eroded and marked syllabic *-i- (= *-ii̯-) thereupon reverts to unmarked non-syllabic *-i̯-, whence *bādi̯et. The fact that the syllable preceding *-ii̯et was heavy did not impede a regression to *-i̯et: hence the conclusion that Sievers' Rule had already become inoperative in Goidelic. During the period of morphological

---

[36] Cf. Thurneysen, *Grammar* (n. 21) 336.

[37] The relevant material can be found in Pedersen, *Vergleichende Grammatik* II 648.

[38] *Ibid*. Cf. likewise R. Thurneysen, *Old Irish Reader* trans. D. A. Binchy and O. Bergin (Dublin 1949) 106 s.v. *tibid*.

[39] Cf. Pedersen, *Vergleichende Grammatik* II 648, also Thurneysen, *Grammar* 535.

attrition in *i*-stem deverbative verbs, the proposed phonological developments resulting in {*-i̯et > -ø} and {*-ii̯et > -*i*} (with the possible mid-stages *-it and *-īt) freeze the ultimate distribution, so that those *i*-stem deverbative verbs which had still been synchronically motivated at the time of these phonological transformations could survive with 3rd singular conjunct -*i* (e.g. ·*léici*),[40] while those which were then already unmotivated reveal -ø in the same grammatical slot (e.g. ·*gaib*).

(4) The earlier those verbs with stem *-ii̯e-/-ii̯o- become synchronically unmotivated (whence *-i̯e-/-i̯o-), the likelier it is that Old Irish will preserve them—if they are to be preserved at all—in the strong conjugation rather than in the weak. There are even instances where the strong conjugation of B II (stems in *-i̯e-/-i̯o-) shifts to that of B I (stems in *-e-/-o-).[41] By contrast, the most recent group of verbs losing synchronic motivation just before the irreversible phonological split resulting in {*-i̯et > -ø} and {*-ii̯et > -*i*} could survive already endowed with the characteristics of a weak conjugation (*s*-preterite, *f*-future, etc.) except for this one crucial idiosyncrasy in terms of Old Irish: 3rd singular conjunct -ø (<?*-it) < *-i̯et rather than the expected -*i* (<?*-īt) < *-ii̯et. I propose that ·*báid* and ·*tib* are such forms. And the structural circumstance that *báid*- and *tib*- are otherwise representatives of a synchronically predictable and regular paradigm, the A II conjugation, can generate the new 3rd singular constituents ·*báidi* and ·*tibi* by means of a simple leveling process; in other words,

---

[40] The exemplar usually cited for A II, *léici*, shows a base with heavy syllable; this factor, however, is no prerequisite: for instances of A II 3rd singular conjunct with light syllable in the base, cf. e.g. (*di*)·*cathi* "spends," (*do*)·*mathi* "threatens," etc.

[41] Cf. Thurneysen, *Grammar* § 549, § 593. For the oldest layer of Old Irish B II verbs, we may reconstruct the 3rd singular conjunct as *-i̯e rather than *-i̯et: e.g. ·*nig* "washes" < *nigi < *nig^wi̯e; cf. nn. 28, 30 *supra*.

the likely explanation is that the latter two are innovations from ·*báid* and ·*tib* rather than the reverse.

(5) The verbal developments in Romance afford a striking parallel to the Irish trends just outlined, in that the residual Latin *ĭ*-stems of the 3rd conjugation (cf. Irish B II) become transformed into either (a) *ī*-stems of the 4th conjugation (cf. Irish A II) or (b) simple thematic stems of the 3rd conjugation (cf. Irish B I). For example, reflexes in Romance show that (a) *rapere* (of *rapiō*, etc.) can be replaced by **rapīre* (cf. French *ravir*) while (b) *faciunt* (of *faciō*, etc.) can give way to *facunt* (cf. French *font*); and the latter form is already attested in Latin.[42] Trend (b) involved simply the leveling out of an -*i*- from the 1st singular and 3rd plural in the present tense, and it is confined to those verbs with conjugational idiosyncrasies which defied synchronic predictability: "Ce doivent être ceux dont l'infinitif, le parfait et le participe étaient d'un emploi très courant et opposaient par là-même une plus grande résistance à l'analogie du présent. Ils ont, du reste, gardé une forme de parfait archaïque : *cēpī*, *fēcī*, *iēcī* et ils ont donné des formes nominales courantes tirées du participe : *trāiectus*, etc."[43] By contrast, trend (a) is prompted by the paradigmatic regularity and productivity of the 4th conjugation: the points of formal identity between the residual *i*-stem 3rd conjugation and the productive *i*-stem 4th level out the synchronic irregularities of the former and warrant the ultimate prevalence of the latter. The two trends, then, can be summed up thus: "le latin tendait à éliminer la 3e conjugaison en -*iō*, en la transformant en 4e conjugaison, ou bien, lorsque cela n'était pas possible, en éliminant l'-*i*-."[44] To ascribe these

---

[42] Cf. A. Graur, "La quatrième conjugaison latine," *Bulletin de la Société de Linguistique de Paris* 40 (1939) 127–150, esp. 138–141.

[43] Graur, "La quatrième conjugaison" 140.

[44] *Ibid.*, 141.

processes to Latin generally instead of Romance specifically is quite proper, in a teleological sense: what is more, in the case of trend (a), it may even be justifiable to designate it an Italic phenomenon.[45] Nor need we look so far ahead in time for replacements such as that of e.g. *rapere* by a **rapīre* reconstructed in terms of Romance: in this instance, it is simply that trend (a) took so long in coming to fruition that the new form is too late to be extant in what we know as Latin. But in many other instances, the trend has left its effects attested not only in classical but even in preclassical Latin; for example, besides the irregular pattern *fodiō/ fodere* which is still standard in the classical period, there are already sporadic instances of *fodiō/fodīre* in archaic Latin (hence e.g. Catonian *fodīrī* vs. Ennian *fodentes*), but the latter regular pattern finally wins out only in the postclassical period of imperial Latin (cf. the writings of Columella, Ulpianus, Ammianus Marcellinus, etc.); in sum, the *fodīre* of Romance (cf. French *fouir*) can be motivated in terms of extant stages in Latin linguistic history.

Not all instances, however, of attested coexistence between *-ere* and *-īre* on the same base imply that the latter is necessarily a replacement of the former. For example, let us consider the contrast in the classical period between standard simplex *pariō/parere* and its etymological compounds *comperiō/ comperīre, reperiō/reperīre*; here the ancestral form of the simplex had undergone morphological attrition, reflected in its survival as *ĭ*-stem rather than *ī*-stem.[46] Yet in the corresponding two compounds, the antiquity of which is assured by their preservation of the semantic function originally

---

[45] On the prevalence of *ī*-stem over *ĭ*-stem primary verbs in Oscan and Umbrian, cf. C. D. Buck, *A Grammar of Oscan and Umbrian*[2] (Boston 1928) 164 ff, 361.

[46] E.g. 2nd singular **par‖ijesi* becomes [a]*parjesi > [b]*parisi > [c]*paris;* cf. note 48 *infra.*

inherent and then eroded in the simplex (where "pro-curer" ⇒ "enfanter"),[47] there is retention of synchronic motivation up to the period of a phonological shift { *-iįe- > *-ī-}.[48] As a result, they are preserved as constituents of the 4th conjugation. Thus *comperiō/comperīre* and *reperiō/reperīre* reveal not innovation but retention, and we must distin-guish these instances of the 4th conjugation from the classi-cally substandard simplex *pariō/parīre*[49]—which is really an innovation, ultimately displacing the classically standard residual simplex *pariō/parere*. Here again, then, is a Latin development strikingly similar to Goidelic: parallel with Latin instances of simplex ĭ-stem vs. compound ī-stem (as with *pariō/parere* vs. *comperiō/comperīre, iaciō/iacere* vs. *amiciō/amicīre*[50]), so also in Old Irish, a verb like *scuich-* is "ĭ-stem" in the simplex but "ī-stem" in its compound attestations.[51]

(6) An important obstacle to the present argument that deverbative A II and B II verbs in Old Irish reflect an original opposition between -V̆C‖iįe- and -V̆Cįe- respectively is the contention of e.g. Meillet[52] that the thematic grade *-e- of verbs in *-įe-/-įo- was not inherited by Celtic, the inference being that IE originally had an *i*-conjugation which was half-thematized as in e.g. Celtic (hence *-i-/-įo-) and which

---

[47] For an interesting discussion, cf. A. Ernout/A. Meillet, *Dictionnaire étymolo-gique de la langue latine*[4] (Paris 1949) s.v. *pariō*: listed are archaic attestations where the meaning of the simplex is still "procurer" rather than the later specialization, "enfanter"; also established is the synchronic as well as etymolo-gical relationship of *pariō/parere* with *parō/parāre*. Cf. also s.vv. *pau-per* and *opi-parus*.

[48] E.g. 2nd singular
[a]*kompar‖iįesi > [b]*komparīsi > [c]*comperīs; cf. the corresponding *a b c* in note 46 *supra*.
(The chronological order for the raising *-ar-* > *-er-* is not specified here.)

[49] For which cf. Graur, "La quatrième conjugaison" 139.

[50] Cf. Ernout/Meillet, *Dictionnaire étymologique* s.v.

[51] Cf. Thurneysen, *Grammar* 336 and Pedersen, *Vergleichende Grammatik* II 617, 840.

[52] *Dialectes* 112.

was later completely thematized as in e.g. Greek (hence *-ie-/-io-). The most salient disadvantage to such a theory, even aside from IE structural considerations, is that it requires the positing of an athematic *-ī- besides *-i- in Celtic, whence 3rd singular -*i* (A II) vs. -ø (B II) respectively; and it seems an impossible task to formulate both phonological and morphological motivations leading to the ultimate distribution of supposedly original *-ī- and *-i-. But perhaps the most decisive argument against the theory of inherited semithematic conjugation in Celtic *i*-verbs is the evidence to be extracted from the Old Irish treatment of IE iteratives with suffixal formant *-eie-/-eio-, the type *loukéieti (as in Sanskrit *rocáyati* "illuminates").[53] In Celtic as also in such other IE dialects as Germanic and Indo-Iranian, there is an early shift in this verbal category from iterative to causative function.[54] The structural framework leading to such parallel development is the hierarchy of oppositions commonly inherited. An iterative derived verb (A) is primarily in opposition to the active diathesis of its motivating verb (B) and only secondarily in opposition to the mediopassive diathesis (C); but once the iterative function of form (A) is lost, whether by atrophy or by displacement, this same form (A) becomes iso-functional with the originally motivating form (B), and as the marked member of the two, it shifts from secondary into primary opposition to the mediopassive form (C). Hence e.g. Vedic mediopassive *várdhate* "grows" (C) is primarily opposed to *vardháyati* "makes grow" (A), only secondarily (and indirectly) to *várdhati* "makes grow" (B). As a general rule even, we may expect the forms synchronically motivating causatives to be mediopassive or at least intransitive,[55] as with *léuketoi* →

---

[53] For an important survey, cf. Kuryłowicz, *Apophonie* 86–94.

[54] Cf. Kuryłowicz, *Apophonie* 86–94 and Watkins, *Celtic Verb* I 120 f.

[55] Cf. Kuryłowicz, *Apophonie* 93.

*loukéįeti = Vedic *rócate* "shines" → *rocáyati* "illuminates."
Hence also in e.g. Gothic we find such intransitive/causative
pairs (C/A) as the following: *brinnan* "burn" (intransitive)
vs. *brannjan* "burn" (transitive), *bi-leiban* "remain" vs.
bi-laibjan "leave," *sigqan* "sink, descend" vs. *sagqjan* "make
sink," *sitan* "sit" vs. *satjan* "seat," etc.[56] Causatives of the
type *loukéįeti and with the same relationship (C/A) are
likewise attested in Old Irish; e.g.:[57]

*splend- as in Latin *splendēre* vs. *splond-éįe- as in Old Irish
sluind- "designate."[58]
said- "sit" vs. *sáid-* "set, lay" as if from IE *sōd-éįe- (cf. *saditi*
in Old Slavonic).
said- "sit" vs. *suid-* "set, lay" as if from IE *sod-éįe- (cf. *satjan* in
Gothic).
laig- "lie" vs. *luig-* "set, lay" as if from IE *logh-éįe- (cf. *lagjan*
in Gothic and *ložiti* in Old Slavonic).

Actually, the intransitive form which had originally motivated *luig-* could have been with root *leg-,[59] not with
laig-; likewise, an intransitive *sed-* and not *said-* must have
motivated *suid-*. In this case, the *e*-grade is still preserved
in the future *seiss*. Once radical *e*-grade is ousted from the
present intransitive, the inherited motivation

{...e... + intransitive desinence →

......o... + transitive desinence}

must shift apophonically; hence e.g. new *said-* → new
sáid-.[60] In sum, the very nature of the innovations in

---

[56] Cf. Kuryłowicz, *Apophonie* 92.

[57] For a detailed collection of evidence on the type *loukéįeti, cf. M.-L.
Sjoestedt, "Les itératifs-causatifs dans les langues celtiques," *Mélanges linguistiques offerts à M. J. Vendryes* (Paris 1925) 323–340.

[58] For the etymology (involving Celtic *spl- > *stl-), cf. H. Pedersen,
Vergleichende Grammatik der keltischen Sprachen I (Göttingen 1909) 83 f and II
(n. 24) 340; also Thurneysen, *Grammar* 139.

[59] For another possibility besides *leg-, cf. the discussion of *loing-*, n. 63 *infra*.

[60] For the relative lateness of *said-* as intransitive stem, cf. Sjoestedt, "Itératifs-
causatifs" 336.

apophonic pattern suggests that the productivity of causatives may have extended well into the dialectal phase of Celtic.

(7) Besides the stage when intransitive and mediopassive verbs motivate causative derivatives in a given IE language, we can expect an earlier stage when verbs of any diathesis, active included, motivate iterative derivatives. Thus e.g. in Vedic, there are still attestations of the formal type *loukéjeti with iterative meaning (cf. *mādáyati* "becomes intoxicated"),[61] although such instances are strictly residual and the productive function of the type *loukéjeti is exclusively causative. In Old Irish too, there is lexical evidence for the existence of such an earlier iterative stage besides the later causative stage; e.g.:

boing- "break" (from *bhong-e-) vs. *buig-* (from *bhog-éje-).
brenn- "effervesce" (from *bhrend-e-) vs. *bruinn-* (from *bhrond-éje-).
dloing- "split" (from *dlongh-e-) vs. *dluig-* (from *dlogh-éje-).
geir- "heat" (from *gʷher-e-) vs. *guir-* (from *gʷhor-éje-).

Despite the immense lapse of time since iteratives had last constituted a productive category, there is still occasional preservation of distinctions in nuance of meaning between an iterative and its etymologically motivating verbal form: hence apparently the following juxtaposition of *dluig-/dloing-* "split" (intransitive) in the *Book of Leinster* (8 b 43): *go ro dluigset ⅂ go ro dloingset a sceith a m-bile go a m-bróntib* "si bien que leurs boucliers s'ouvrirent et se fendirent depuis leur bord jusqu'à leur milieu."[62] It is even possible to deduce

[61] Cf. T. Burrow, *The Sanskrit Language* (London 1955) 356 f.
[62] Sjoestedt, "Itératifs-causatifs" 331. As another example, cf. the semantic distinction between intensive (= iterative) *guir-* "brûler" (cf. Welsh *gori* "couver") vs. the attenuative (= non-iterative) *fo·geir-* "chauffer," as documented by Sjoestedt, "Itératifs-causatifs" 332: *ma gorith loch . . . fo·geir anggelan in uile corp* "si elle enflamme une petite place . . . la maladie échauffe ensuite tout le corps."

apparent trends of formal distribution in the period when iteratives were productive; from e.g. such pairs as *boing-/buig-* "break," *bronn-/brúi-* "damage," *dloing-/dluig-* "split," etc., M.-L. Sjoestedt has concluded that in Celtic, nasal-infix verbs stand in the same sort of relation to the iterative type *loukéi̯eti as e.g. *-cumbere* to *-cubāre* in Latin.[63] In still other instances, the surviving relationship between originally motivating verb and its iterative is suppletive: thus e.g. the iterative stem *bruinn-* has displaced *brenn-* from the primary function of present-marker, but *brenn-* nevertheless persisted as stem-formant in other tenses and moods.[64] The iterative stem *bruinn-* is to be analyzed as a strong verb not only on the basis of its paradigm-correlates outside the present tense: in the *Milan Glosses* (81 c 14) we read *du·brúinn dinaib slebib forsnatalmana cobsaidi inchre fechtnach sin* "then flows from the mountains over the flat lands this rich silt."[65] From this attestation of the 3rd singular conjunct follows the definitive conclusion that the iterative stem *bruinn-* "effervesce" belongs to the B II conjugation; all the more interesting, then, is that *bruinn-* survives also in the more recent function of causative, this time meaning "smelt" and belonging to the A II conjugation.[66]

(8) That *bhrond-éi̯e- in the more recently productive function of causative should be preserved in a productive weak conjugation is indeed predictable; likewise, that in the earlier function of iterative such a stem becomes relegated to the unproductive strong conjugation. Of even deeper

---

[63] "Itératifs-causatifs" 331. Formally parallel to the types *buig-* and *boing-* are *luig-* and *loing-*; the verb *loing-* is attested in both transitive and intransitive usage (basically "lay" vs. "lie"; cf. Pedersen, *Vergleichende Grammatik* II 570), and it is the latter diathesis which could ultimately generate a causative *luig-*.

[64] Cf. Thurneysen, *Grammar* 355, 424 and Watkins, *Celtic Verb* I 120.

[65] Gloss for the Latin *in quas felix limus influxerit*. For the phonological factors involved in (*·bruinn >*) *·brúinn*, cf. Thurneysen, *Grammar* 32, 355.

[66] Cf. Thurneysen, *Grammar* 355.

significance, however, is that the IE type *loukéi̯eti has
ultimately undergone a formal split into the A II and B II
conjugations of Old Irish, and that this split had been
regulated by whether at a given prehistoric point, the reflex
of the IE formant *-ei̯e-/-ei̯o- was still motivated or already
unmotivated on a given base: whence accordingly the 3rd
singular conjunct types ·suidi "sets"[67] vs. ·brúinn "effervesces"
respectively.

From such pairs, we note that as also with the
IE formant *-(i)i̯e-/-(i)i̯o-, the lightness or heaviness of the
preceding syllable seems to exert no effect on the Old Irish
reflexes of *-ei̯e-/-ei̯o-: only the morphological factor is
operative.[68] But this circumstance is itself phonologically
relevant, for it warrants the conclusion that *-ei̯e-/-ei̯o- is
reflected as *-ii̯e-/-ii̯o- in Goidelic,[69] and that this configuration in turn is subject to becoming *-i̯e-/-i̯o- by morphological

[67] E.g. a-t·suidi "fixes": St. Gall Glosses 66 a 20. For the archaic 3rd plural
causative sudiot "they establish," with disyllabic -ïot metrically ascertained, cf.
Watkins, "Metrics" (n. 16) 225 n. 1.

[68] For other examples, cf. the 3rd singular conjunct form ·lugi "lays" (as in
do-d·lugi) vs. ·sóid (as in con·sóid); for the vocalism in sóid- (vs. sáid-), cf. Sjoestedt,
"Itératifs-causatifs" 334, 336. Contrary to Pedersen's view (Vergl. Gram. II
605 f) that con·sóid- is to be separated etymologically from sáid- "set," its very
meaning "bring (someone) into combat" is a semantic extension from "set
together," as argued and documented by Sjoestedt, "Itératifs-causatifs" 336.
This semantic extension, however, must have coincided with loss of causative
function—hence (1) the breakdown in synchronic motivation by intransitive
said-, (2) the resulting opportunity for a vocalic shift from sáid- to sóid- (in composition with preverb con-, vs. unchanged sáid- in composition with preverb
in-), and (3) the 3rd singular conjunct -ø instead of -i, revealing that con·sóid-
had already been ousted from the productive category of i-stem verbs at a
time when the opposition between synchronically motivated *-‖i̯e-/-‖i̯o- vs.
unmotivated *-i̯e-/-i̯o- was still operative. On the second of the three factors
listed here, it is noteworthy to add that wherever composition with preverb
con- is attested with the meaning "set together" rather than "bring into combat," there the root-vocalism reveals ·sáid-, not ·sóid-; the former could be
synchronically regenerated at a relatively late period.

[69] In fact, {*-ei̯- > *-ii̯-} in prevocalic position is probably a development
common to Celtic as a whole: cf. Thurneysen, Grammar § 78.2, § 197, § 304,
§ 549, etc. Cf. also J. Pokorny, "Zum indogermanischen Kausativum," [A.
Kuhn's] Zeitschrift für vergleichende Sprachforschung 60 (1933) 253: "[urkeltisches]
-ei̯e- noch vor der Synkope uririsch zu -ī- geworden ist."

attrition,[70] just like genuine *-i̯e-/-i̯o-. Hence e.g. the
following reconstructions:

·brúinn-ø (<?*-it) < *-i̯et (attrition from *-‖ii̯et)

vs.

·suid-i (<?*-īt) < *-ii̯et (= *-‖ii̯et).

It now becomes apparent why the Old Irish reflexes of the
IE type *loukéi̯eti furnish an important argument against
Meillet's positing an IE-inherited semithematic conjugation
in Celtic *i*-verbs (*-i-/-i̯o- rather than *-i̯e-/-i̯o-). Since the
clearly thematic-stem *-ei̯et(i) of the IE type *loukéi̯eti could
ultimately undergo a split into Old Irish -ø vs. -*i*, there are
no internal grounds for positing an IE-inherited *-it (in
broader terms, *-i-/-i̯o-) from the evidence of Celtic.

(9) The reconstruction of e.g. 3rd singular conjunct
·*daim* from *dami̯et (with IE-inherited *-i̯et rather than
*-it) still leaves a phonological problem to be resolved;[71]
we can see the issue at hand from the following statement by
Thurneysen:

> After *i* (whether consonantal i̯ or syllabic *i* i̯, all of which fell
> together in Irish, §197), the vowels of all final syllables, including
> such as were lost in every other position, were retained as follows:
> *i* and *u* (irrespective of origin) unchanged,
> *a* (also *a* < *o* §§ 90, 4; 93 b) as *e*,
> ĕ as *i*.[72]

I put forth the arguments which follow with the prospect of
developing an alternative to this formulation. The main objection to the latter is prompted by morphological factors:
on the assumption that the Old Irish B II conjugation reflects
an original stem in *-i̯e-/-i̯o- rather than *-i-/-i̯o-, I have

[70] For this term, cf. again § 3 *supra*.
[71] Cf. § 5.2 *supra*.
[72] Thurneysen, *Grammar* 60.

already posited the following developments for the 3rd singular conjunct -*i* and -*ø* of ·*léici* and ·*gaib*:

$$*\text{-i̯et} \ (> \ ?*\text{-īt}) \ > \ \text{-}i$$
$$*\text{-i̯et} \ (> \ ?*\text{-it}) \ > \ \text{-ø.}[73]$$

But there then remains the problem of explaining the -*i* of *aili*, masculine and neuter genitive singular (from *alī̯ī), or of *duini*, masculine vocative singular (from *donī̯e). It is these types which had been the models for Thurneysen's phonological formulations {*-i̯ī > -*i*} and {*-i̯ĕ > -*i*}; yet the factors involved in the formal evolution of *aili* and *duini* are better explained as primarily morphological and only secondarily phonological. If we observe the intra-paradigmatic hierarchy in the declension of simple thematic-stem nominals from the IE standpoint, the relationship between vocative singular (*-e), genitive singular (*-ī), and nominative singular (*-os) is as follows:

$$*\text{-os} \rightarrow \begin{cases} *\text{-e} \\ *\text{-ī.}[74] \end{cases}$$

Likewise with thematic *i*-stem nominals:

$$*\text{-i̯os} \rightarrow \begin{cases} *\text{-i̯e} \\ *\text{-i̯ī.} \end{cases}$$

Thus in Goidelic, the expected phonological developments {*-i̯e(> ?*-i) > -ø} and {*-i̯ī(> ?*-ī) > -ø} are subject to morphological interference by the formant which determines *-i̯e and *-i̯ī, namely nominative singular *-i̯os. The precise

[73] Cf. § 5.2 and § 5.3; also nn. 30 and 32.

[74] The nominative singular is the functionally unmarked and fundamental member of declension. Thus it is the nominative singular which predicates the other members of the paradigm; cf. the designation of nominal inflection as πτώσεις or πλάγιαι from the nominative, in Greek grammatical tradition (also Latin *cāsūs oblīquī*); to be consulted: E. Schwyzer/A. Debrunner, *Griechische Grammatik* II (München 1950) 53 f. For a general discussion, cf. R. Jakobson, "Beitrag zur allgemeinen Kasuslehre," *Travaux du Cercle Linguistique de Prague* 6 (1936) 240–288; reprinted in *Readings in Linguistics* II, ed. E. P. Hamp, F. W. Householder, R. Austerlitz (Chicago 1966) 51–89.

nature of this morphological interference is inextricably linked with the phonological development of *-i̯- and *-i̯i̯- before back vowels (= -O-) in Goidelic:

$$*\text{-i̯i̯O-} > *\text{-iO-}$$
$$*\text{-i̯O-} > *\text{-iO-}.$$

Where -O- = *-ă̆-, there is this further development:

$$*\text{-i̯ă̆-} > *\text{-eă̆-}.[75]$$

At this point, then, we are ready to dispense with the formulation of Thurneysen, in that there is no need to assume that absolute-final vowels were retained after original *-i̯- or *-i̯i̯-. Hence the Goidelic declensional development (singular) of IE-inherited nominals in *-C(i)i̯os can be outlined as follows:

	1	2	3	4	5
N	-C(i)i̯os	-Cioh	-Ceah		-C'e
G	-C(i)i̯i	-Cii			-C'i
D	-C(i)i̯ū	-Ciū		-Ciᵘū	-C'u
V	-C(i)i̯e	-Cie			-C'i

Stage 4 represents *u*-epenthesis, while stage 5 (the attested period of Old Irish) shows the loss of vowels in absolute word-final position. The paradigmatic pressure exerted by the nominative singular prevented the genitive and vocative singular from undergoing split phonological developments into what would ultimately become -C'i (from -Ci̯e and -Ci̯ī) vs. -C'ø (from -Ci̯e and -Ci̯ī). It remains to be asked, then, why e.g. the 1st plural, originally *-i̯omo, or the 3rd plural, originally *-i̯ont, did not exert similar paradigmatic pressure on the 3rd singular *-i̯e(t) as in *dami̯e(t). The answer is found in the universal syntactic

---

[75] This rule is an extension of the one formulated by Thurneysen, *Grammar* § 73. The theory of {*-i̯- > *-i-} in prevocalic position (followed by {*-i- > *-e-} before *-ă̆-) I derive from lectures by C. Watkins on Celtic (spring 1966).

circumstance that the 3rd singular constitutes the fundamental member of the paradigm, both functionally and
structurally; thus it tends to influence the forms of other
persons, rather than the reverse.[76] We can therefore conclude that there is no morphological pressure sufficient to
prevent the phonological shift *-i̯et(> ?*-it) > -ø, as in
*dami̯et(> ?*damit) > ·daim; likewise *-ii̯et(> ?*-īt) >
-i, as in *dālii̯et(> ?*dālīt) > ·dáli.[77]

(10) In sum, the IE-inherited opposition between -C‖i̯i̯V-
and -Ci̯V- has survived in Goidelic verbs because of the
phonological fact that V = e in the fundamental member of
the present conjugation, the 3rd singular; by contrast,
traces of the same opposition have been obliterated in
Goidelic nominals because of the likewise phonological fact
that V = o or V = ā in the fundamental member of the
declension, the nominative singular:

-ii̯et (> ?-īt) > -i   3rd singular conjunct ("weak")
-i̯et (> ?-it) > -ø   3rd singular conjunct ("strong")

$\left.\begin{array}{l} \text{*-ii̯os} > \text{*-ios} > \text{-}e \\ \text{*-i̯os} > \text{*-ios} > \text{-}e \end{array}\right\}$ nominative singular masculine

$\left.\begin{array}{l} \text{*-ii̯ā} > \text{*-iā} > \text{-}e \\ \text{*-i̯ā} > \text{*-iā} > \text{-}e \end{array}\right\}$ nominative singular feminine

*-iī > -i   genitive singular masculine
*-ie > -i   vocative singular masculine.

---

[76] Cf. E. Benveniste, "Structure des relations de personne dans le verbe,"
Bulletin de la Société de Linguistique de Paris 43 (1946) 1–12; cf. also the significant
elaborations and applications of the theory by Watkins, *Celtic Verb* I 90 ff.

[77] Cf. again § 5.2 *supra*. A further adjustment on this proposition might
make it more satisfactory:

$$
\begin{array}{lllll}
& \text{*-ii̯e(t)} & > & \text{*-ie} & > & \text{-}i \\
& \text{*-i̯e(t)} & > & \text{*-i} & > & \text{-ø} \\
\text{vocative} & \text{*-(i)i̯e} & \text{to} & \text{*-ie} & > & \text{-}i.
\end{array}
$$

In other words, the transitional stages from *-ii̯e(t) to -i and from *-i̯e(t) to
-ø may not be parallel: we could posit that *-ii̯e- did not become *-ī-, but that
*-i̯e- became *-i-. Meanwhile, the vocative *-ie is a secondary morphological
creation, and not a direct phonological inheritance from *-(i)i̯e.

§6. From the synchronic standpoint of attested classical Latin, the reflex of IE postconsonantal/prevocalic *-i̯- is -i-, as in trisyllabic *alius, medius* from *alios, *medhi̯os.[78] This circumstance may encourage the initial impression that this one phonological development would have wiped out all traces of any original opposition between -C‖i̯V- and -Ci̯V-. But as in Goidelic, the change {-Ci̯V- > -CiV-} has been obviated when e.g. V = *e*. A definition of the conditions will follow presently; more immediately important, however, is that even in instances where e.g. V = ŏ in an original configuration -Ci̯V-, certain prehistoric phonological developments nonetheless result in the irrevocable formal differentiation of this residual -Ci̯V- from -C‖i̯V-. Thus e.g. when C = *d, g, s* in Italic, -VCi̯o- survives as -Vi̯i̯u- in Latin:

peius /pei̯i̯us/ < *pedi̯os; cf. *pessimus*
maius /mai̯i̯us/ < *magi̯os; cf. *magis*
eius /ei̯i̯us/ < *esi̯os; cf. Sanskrit *asyá*, Middle Welsh *eidd-aw*
  (< *esi̯o).[79]

Such survivals with the configuration -ViV-, in contrast to the numerous synchronic patterns with -Vd‖iV-, -Vg‖iV-,

[78] Cf. Leumann, *LG* 110.
[79] Cf. Leumann, *LG* 155 f, 289 f, 296; also *LG* 49, for a collection of arguments proving /-V̆i̯iV-/ (hence not /-V̆i̯V-/):
  (1) the evidence of Romance: e.g. Italian *peggiore* from *pĕiiōrem*
  (2) attested spellings like EIIVS, EIVS, EIIVS, EIIVS
  (3) *testimonia* like that of Quintilianus (1.4.11) on Cicero's spelling *aiio*, etc.
  (4) Plautine *cuiius, aiiebas*, etc. in the *Ambrosianus*
  (5) formal statements in the Latin grammatical tradition, as e.g. that of Priscianus (*GLK* II 14.5–14):
    ... antiqui solebant geminare eandem *i* litteram et *maiius, peiius, eiius* scribere, quod non aliter pronuntiari posset quam cum superiore syllaba prior *i*, cum sequente altera proferretur, ut *pei-ius, ei-ius, mai-ius.* nam quamuis sit consonans, in eadem syllaba geminata iungi non posset. ergo non aliter quam *tellus, mannus* proferri debuit. unde Pompeiii quoque genetiuum per tria *i* scribebant, quorum duo superiora loco consonantium accipiebant, ut si dicas Pompelli. nam tribus *i* iunctis qualis possit syllaba pronuntiari? quod Caesari doctissimo artis grammaticae placitum a Victore quoque in Arte Grammatica de syllabis comprobatur.

1. §6

-Vr‖iV-,[80] show conclusively that non-syllabic *-i̯- had existed (in -C̯iV-) at an ancestral phase of what is ultimately Latin. Only after e.g. *pedi̯os has become *pei̯i̯os does e.g. *ali̯os become *alios.

Even more conclusive is the evidence from such contrasts as between 3rd conjugation *capiō/capis*, *pariō/paris*, *speciō/specis*, *fugiō/fugis* and 4th conjugation *ueniō/uenīs*, *feriō/ferīs*, *sitiō/sitīs*, *rugiō/rugīs*.[81] Such distributions clearly suggest that *-i̯eC and *-ii̯eC had already become *-iC and *-īC respectively by the time that the phonological shift {-C̯iV- > -CiV-} took place. Hence an original opposition between productive -C‖ii̯V- and unproductive -C̯iV- is preserved where V = *e* etymologically—an ultimate development comparable with that in Goidelic.[82]

[80] E.g. *acu-ped‖ius* (← *ped-*, as in *pēs*, *pedis*), *stud‖ium* (← *stud-*, as in *studēre*), *pug‖iō* (← *pug-*, as in *pungere*, *pupugī*), *frag‖ium* (← *frag-*, as in *frangere*, *fractus*), *arbor‖ius* (← *arbor-*, as in *arbōs*, *arboris*), etc.

[81] The 2nd singular is representative of the conjugational distinctions, unlike the 3rd singular, where *-it* > *-it* by the classical period. For a summary of the distributions *-is/-īs*, cf. Leumann, *LG* 320 ff, and especially Graur, "La quatrième conjugaison" (n. 42); also § 5.5 *supra*. It is needless to assume that the ancestral configuration of *-is* in e.g. *capis* had lacked the thematic vowel *-e-*; cf. the Celtic evidence in § 5.8. Certainly the type *capiō/capis* cannot be adduced to confirm the theory that *ferō/fers* or *edō/ēs* inherited from IE a supposedly semithematic conjugation. For the likelihood that the latter two residual paradigms have left traces of a phonological process of *e*-syncope too long inoperative to have survived elsewhere in the once-productive simplex thematic conjugation of Latin, cf. Leumann, *LG* 311 f.

[82] The evolution of the type *maiestās* involves morphological interference with the phonological process {*-i̯e- > *-i-} herewith posited: from the apophonic hierarchy of formants {*-es-tāt- ← *-os} as in *tempestās ← tempus*, we may expect the generation of *maiestās* from *maius*. Likewise by morphological motivation: e.g. *circum-iectus ← circum-iēcī*, vs. the unencumbered phonological development of *am-ictus* (← *amicuī* or *amixī*); the verb *amiciō amicīre amicuī/amixī amictus* is a compound which has become detached from the synchronic motivation of simplex *iaciō iacere iēcī iactus* (cf. § 5.5 *supra* for a parallel: *comperiō comperīre comperī compertus* vs. *pariō parere peperī partus*). However, the partial convergence of forms between present-tense *amiciō/amicīs* and *circumiciō/circumicis* has preserved at least a potential opportunity for synchronic perception of etymological factors linking the former of these compounds with the simplex *iaciō/iacis;* hence the following intuitive statement by Varro, *De lingua latina* V 131: *amictui dictum quod amiectum, i.e. circumiectum*. Having resurrected, so to

31

In a few instances, not only this phonological factor of V = *e* but also that of C = *d, g, s* have been reflected in the same residual pattern -C̦iV- (as distinct from -C‖i̦iV-): this is apparently the case in the reflex of 2nd singular *ag̦esi, *ais*, with the attested scansion ⏑⏑ (hence /ăĭs/) vs. the reflex of the 1st singular *ag̦ō, *aiō*, with the regular scansion - - (hence /ai̦i̦ō/).[83] The nominal derivatives of *aiō* illustrate another circumstance crucial for an understanding of the Latin evidence for an original contrast between -C̦iV- and -C̦i̦iV-: besides the *nomen agentis* *ag̦ios reflected by the archaic tautological syntagmata *Aius Locūtius* and *Aius Loquēns*, the names of a divinity,[84] there is also an inanimate *nomen actionis* *ad-āgi̦iom reflected by *adāgium*. The length in -*āg*- we can ascertain from the failure of the language to develop *adigium, and from the Latin morphophonemic relationship {-V- : -V̄-} of the type *tangō : contāgium, frangō : suffrāgium*, etc. (also *aiō : adāgium*).[85]

> *ag̦io- > *ai̦io- > *Aius*
> *-āgi̦io- > *-āgio- > -*āgium* in *adāgium*.

---

speak, the once-synchronic relationship of *amiciō/amicīs* with *iaciō/iacis*, Varro's *Sprachgefühl* proceeds forthwith to generate the hypothetical *amiectum*, which we see in the quoted gloss as if it were some incidental replacement of the genuine *amictum;* hence

> *circum-iciō : circum-iectus = am-iciō : am-iectus.*

[83] For a brief discussion of the metrical evidence, cf. F. Sommer, *Handbuch der lateinischen Laut- und Formenlehre*[2] (Heidelberg 1914) 155, 545 f; cf. also n. 79 *supra*. As for the metrically-attested variant *āĭs* (e.g. Plautus, *Menaechmi* 820) vs. *āīs* (e.g. Plautus, *Rudens* 1072), it is the former which shows innovation from the latter, in that *āĭs* could be synchronically generated to replace *ais* at any given stage of Latin, but the reverse possibility does not hold (cf. also n. 86 *infra*); for a parallel, cf. the discussion of e.g. *fodīs (fodīre)* vs. *fodis(fodere)* in § 5.5: so also with *āĭs* vs. *ais*, it is the productive 4th conjugation which is destined to win out over the residual 3rd, the sanctions of classical Latin notwithstanding.

[84] Cf. Varro (as cited by Gellius 16.17.2): *Aius deus apellatus araque ei statuta est, quae est ⟨in⟩ infima noua uia, quod in eo loco diuinitus uox edita est.* Cf. also Ernout/Meillet, *Dictionnaire étymologique* (n. 47) s.v. *aiō*.

[85] For a discussion of these types, including *aiō:adāgium*, cf. Watkins, *Celtic Verb* I 19–21.

The contrast here between light and heavy syllable in the base has resulted in divergent suffixal development—a circumstance which suggests that unlike Old Irish, Latin has preserved traces of Sievers' Rule: -V̄Ci̯V- vs. -V̆Ci̯V-.

It is the verbal evidence, however, which is decisive in showing that Sievers' Rule had not broken down before the phonological shift {-Ci̯V- > -Ci̯V-}; the crucial synchronic factor is that there exist no *i*-stem verbs with heavy-syllable base in the Latin 3rd conjugation (hence no type *audis*, only *audīs*), and from this we can conclude that Sievers' Rule had prevented attrition from -V̄C‖i̯i̯V- to -V̄Ci̯V-. Thus -V̄Ci̯V- remained even after the loss of morpheme-boundary; the only attrition possible was from -V̆C‖i̯i̯V- to -V̆Ci̯V-, whence the already-mentioned types *capiō/capis*, *pariō/paris*, *speciō/specis*, *fugiō/fugis*.[86]

Besides such primary deverbative *i*-stem verbs as *ueniō/ uenīs*, *feriō/ferīs*, *rugiō/rugīs*, which reflect (perhaps only indirectly) an original -V̆C‖i̯i̯V- in contrast to -V̆Ci̯V-, there are also secondary denominative *i*-stem verbs where the reflex of *-i̯e-/-i̯o- still constitutes a productive formant in classical Latin. Significantly, all such denominatives belong to the 4th conjugation: e.g. *ērudiō/ērudīs*, *stabiliō/stabilīs*, *impediō/impedīs*, *equiō/equīs*, etc.;[87] also denominative, of course, are e.g. the desideratives in *-turīre*, founded on the supine: *nupturiō/nupturīs*, *canturiō/canturīs*, *micturiō/micturīs*, *parturiō/parturīs*, etc. We have already noted the parallel

---

[86] Graur, "La quatrieme conjugaison" (n. 42), has refuted the theory that e.g. *kapīs*, *fakīs* had been inherited, later producing *capis*, *facis* by iambic shortening; perhaps the most serious objection to invoking the latter phenomenon is that we are dealing here not with a generally Italic but rather a specifically Latin phonological mechanism. Thus any notion that iambic shortening is the key factor in generating e.g. *facis* fails to account for parallel instances of *-ĭ- in Oscan and Umbrian: cf. e.g. Oscan *factud* "facitō," where the syncope warrants the reconstruction *fakĭtōd rather than *fakītōd.

[87] Cf. R. Thurneysen, *Über Herkunft und Bildung der lateinischen Verba auf* -io (Leipzig 1879) 3–17.

development in Old Irish, where the denominative *i*-stem verbs, likewise still productive in the attested language, consistently belong to the conjugational class A II, not to B II.[88] In sum, the opposition between -Ci̯V- and -Ci̯V- had been motivated both phonologically (heavy vs. light syllable preceding -C-) and morphologically (presence vs. absence of morpheme-boundary following -C-) in a prehistoric phase of Latin; in the classical phase, such opposition had become leveled into a uniform -CiV-; towards the period of Vulgar Latin and onwards into Romance, this uniform -CiV- (as also -CeV-) became -Ci̯V-.[89]

§7. In Germanic as in Celtic, the phonological shift of prevocalic *-ei̯- to *-ii̯-[90] makes the IE verbal type *loukéi̯eti a category indispensable for any attempt to evaluate how the IE-inherited phonological opposition {-V̄Ci̯V- : -V̆Ci̯V-} and the morphological opposition {-C‖ii̯V- : -Ci̯V-} may have survived, specifically in Gothic. Like Old Irish, Gothic too shows a split in the ultimate development of the type *loukéi̯eti; only here the split was motivated by phonological pressures alone: e.g. heavy base-syllable *ĝouséi̯eti (cf. Sanskrit *joṣáyati*) > Gothic *kauseiþ*[91] "examines" vs. light base-syllable *loghéi̯eti (cf. Old Slavonic *ložiti*) > Gothic *lagjiþ* "lays." Now the last productive function of the type *loukéi̯eti in Germanic had been as causative—a function still preserved lexically by e.g. the just-mentioned *lagjan* "lay" vs. the surviving *e*-grade *ligan* "lie."[92] The attested patterns of the type

---

[88] Cf. § 5.1, § 5.5.

[89] For the latter process, cf. e.g. Sommer, *Handbuch* (n. 83) 133, 156.

[90] Cf. e.g. E. Prokosch, *A Comparative Germanic Grammar* (Philadelphia 1939) 92.

[91] Of course, Gothic *-ei-* = /-ī-/ *hic et ubique*.

[92] Cf. § 5.6 for a discussion of the Gothic etymological relationships *brinnan* "burn" (intransitive) → *brannjan* "burn" (transitive), *bi-leiban* "remain" → *bi-laibjan* "leave," *sigqan* "sink" → *sagqjan* "make sink," *sitan* "sit" → *satjan* "seat," etc.

lagjan are therefore crucial: that the 3rd singular of such a verb should survive as *lagjiþ* rather than as *lageiþ implies morphological attrition from -C‖iịeti to -Cịeti before the phonological development from *-iịe- to *-ī-.[93] But the attested contrast {*kauseiþ* : *lagjiþ*} is equally crucial: it in turn implies that at such a period of morphological attrition from -C‖iịeti to -Cịeti, the phonological opposition {-V̄CiịV- : -V̄CịV-} was still operative and continued to be operative until original *-iịe- finally became *-ī-: hence the /-īþ/ after heavy syllable in *kauseiþ*. In this respect, then, the Gothic development resembles not Old Irish but Latin, where *i*-stem verbs with preceding heavy syllable in the base could survive only in the 4th conjugation to the exclusion of the 3rd, even if such verbs no longer belonged to a productive category.[94]

Parallel to the attested situation in both Old Irish and Latin, denominative *i*-verbs apparently still constitute a productive category in Gothic: e.g. *maurþr* "murder" → *maurþrjan* "to murder" as in *maurþrjandam*.[95] In this category, then, we would expect to find instances of 3rd singular /-īþ/ rather than /-jiþ/, reflecting original -C‖iịeti as contrasted with -Cịeti. Hence such denominative 3rd singular forms as *riqizeiþ* "becomes dark" ← *riqis/riqiz* "darkness" and *mikileid* "extols" ← *mikils* "big." There is no compelling internal evidence to justify the positing of a special extension, as it were, of Sievers' Rule, wherein Germanic (or at least Gothic) -CịV- becomes -CiịV- after not only preceding heavy syllables but also preceding disyllables; this traditional explanation[96] merely accounts for attested forms,

---

[93] Whether IE *-e- had already been raised to Germanic *-i- is of no immediate consequence here.

[94] Cf. § 6.

[95] For a representative list, cf. E. Kieckers, *Handbuch der vergleichenden gotischen Grammatik* (München 1928) 288 ff.

[96] Cf. e.g. Prokosch, *Germanic Grammar* (n. 90) 92.

as in the present discussion it would apply to *riqizeiþ* and *mikileid*.

From contrasts between 3rd singular *-jiþ* and *-eiþ*, we expect that the 2nd singular imperative of the latter should be *-i*, by shortening in absolute word-final position of an original *-ī < IE *-ii̯e or *-ei̯e. Yet instead, Gothic shows not /-i/ but /-ī/ in this inflectional slot: hence e.g. *sōkei*. A morphological factor has interfered here with the expected phonological development: what is inherited in *-ei* represents not so much the IE form *-ii̯e or *-ei̯e but rather, the relationship of the latter to the functionally and formally basic member of the paradigm, 3rd singular *-ii̯et(i) or *-ei̯et(i).[97] From the formal point of view, such a relationship between 2nd singular imperative *-ii̯e/*-ei̯e and 3rd singular indicative *-ii̯et(i)/*-ei̯et(i) was synchronically subtractive: the 2nd singular imperative is the 3rd singular indicative minus the accessory *-t(i) in the latter. Hence the Gothic inheritance of {*-ii̯e-ti/*-ei̯e-ti → *-ii̯e-ø/*-ei̯e-ø} as {*-ei-þ → -ei-ø}. But there still remains the task of explaining the spread of imperative formant *-ei* from bases with heavy last syllable to bases with light last syllable, as in *nasei*, *bugei*, *hugei*, *tawei*. In such instances the *-ei* is generated in terms of the whole conjugation rather than a basic constituent of the conjugation; for such interparadigmatic transposition, two synchronic factors are especially relevant:

(1) the stem (i.e., the segment after base and before desinence) of Gothic weak verbs reflecting IE *-ei̯e-/-ei̯o-;

singular			vs.		cf.	
	1st	*-ja-ø*		*-ja-ø*		*-ō-ø*
	2nd	*-ji-s*		*-ei-s*		*-ō-s*
	3rd	*-ji-þ*		*-ei-þ*		*-ō-þ*
plural	1st	*-ja-m*		*-ja-m*		*-ō-m*
	2nd	*-ji-þ*		*-ei-þ*		*-ō-þ*
	3rd	*-ja-nd*		*-ja-nd*		*-ō-nd*

[97] For theoretical background, cf. n. 76. There are extensive applications of the theory in C. Watkins' forthcoming book, cited in n. 28.

(2) the already-discussed circumstance that verbs with stem *-ja-/-ei-* are still apparently productive as denominatives, whereas verbs with stem *-ja-/-ji-* are strictly residual. It follows, then, that the stem-interrelation {*-ja-* → *-ei-*} is operative, but not {*-ja-* → *-ji-*}; rather, *-ji-* is a synchronically unmotivated survival. Thus a verb with unproductive stem *-ja-/-ji-* could generate a new 2nd singular imperative *-ei* on the basis of partial identity with the productive stem *-ja-/-ei-*; in other words, *-ja-* (of the stem *-ja-/-ji-*) → *-ei*, parallel to *-ja-* (of the stem *-ja-/-ei-*) → *-ei*. Such extension of a productive paradigm at the expense of an unproductive one partially identical to it has already been posited with reference to Latin, where the *i*-verbs of the unproductive 3rd conjugation tend to become leveled out on the model of the productive 4th conjugation.[98]

There are also extrinsic factors which have a bearing on whether the inherited morphological opposition {-C‖i̯V- : -C̦iV-} is to survive in Gothic; an illustrative instance is the ultimate reflex of IE nominal stem *-(i)i̯o- in the neuter. The phonological development in the nominative/accusative singular was this: IE *-(i)i̯om > Germanic *-(i)i̯ą > *-i, as in Gothic *-i*.[99] That is, *-ą is dropped in absolute word-final position. Thus *-i, with no vowel after it, is no longer capable of responding phonologically to whether the preceding syllable is heavy or light. In effect, then, the phonological opposition {-V̄Cii̯V- : -V̆C̦iV-} broke down in the nominative/accusative singular of neuter nominals reflecting the IE stem *-(i)i̯o-. Now the Germanic genitive singular of the latter stem would have been *-(i)i̯esa for both masculine and neuter. But since the neuter genitive singular was primarily motivated by the unmarked nominative/accusative singular, the cancellation of the phonological opposition

---

[98] Cf. § 5.5, § 6.
[99] Cf. Prokosch, *Germanic Grammar* (n. 90) 134 f.

37

{-V̄Cii̯V- : -V̄Ci̯V-} in the latter case after {*-ii̯ą > *-i} could entail a similar development in the former case: hence the opposition {-V̄Cii̯es : -V̄Ci̯es} in the neuter genitive singular can be neutralized in favor of -V̆Ci̯es,[100] as a result of declensional leveling. Thus it is that in the Gothic genitive singular of neuter stems derived from IE *-(i)i̯o-, -jis is attested after heavy syllables as well as light: e.g. *arbjis, kunþjis, gawairþjis, andbahtjis, waldufnjis*, etc., besides regular *gawairþeis, andbahteis, waldufneis*, etc.[101] In the corresponding masculine reflex of IE stems in *-(i)i̯o-, the ultimate divergence of -jis/-eis after heavy syllable did not take place, presumably because at the time when the nominative/accusative singular in the neuter was already *-i, the nominative of the corresponding masculine was still *-(i)i̯as;[102] hence masculine -V̄Cii̯as/-V̄Ci̯as vs. neuter -V̆Ci; then nominative *-ii̯as, *-i̯as > *-īs, *-i̯is; also genitive *-ii̯es, *-i̯es > *-īs, *-i̯is. Thus the ultimate development in Gothic is that the nominative singular masculine becomes formally identical with the genitive singular; e.g. N *harjis* G *harjis* "host, multitude" vs. N *hairdeis* G *hairdeis* "herdsman."[103]

[100] Cf. again n. 93.

[101] For these forms and others, cf. Kieckers, *Handbuch* (n. 95) 110 f.

[102] Whether the *-a- was already raised e.g. to *-e- is of no immediate consequence here.

[103] For an apparently productive formant -eis (reflecting IE *-‖ii̯os) after a light syllable, cf. nominative singular *ragineis* "counsellor." I again refrain from proposing that the disyllabic base here was a phonological factor in determining -eis instead of -jis, just as with the verbs *riqizeiþ* and *mikileid*. It goes without saying that the proposals I do submit here constitute merely an outline of how Sievers' Rule is reflected in Gothic. There has been much written on the problem, and I am grateful to H. A. Roe for acquainting me with the full extent of the bibliography. One of the most interesting among recent words has been an attempt by W. Winter ("Juncture in Proto-Germanic: Some Deliberations," *Language* 31 [1955] 530–532) to explain the Gothic type *ragineis* in terms of mora-structure in the base—a synchronic factor for which he finds a typological parallel in his native Low German dialect, spoken at Haselau (twenty miles northwest of Hamburg). While this theory is attractive, I still maintain that a diachronic explanation, in terms of IE heritage, is preferable. Also useful as

In sum, IE *-ii̯e- and *-i̯e- become Gothic /-ī-/ and /-ji-/ respectively. Corresponding to the latter is West Germanic and Nordic /-i-/,[104] comparable to the Latin /-i-/ resulting from IE *-i̯e-.[105] Thus e.g. in West Germanic, no gemination of the preceding consonant is caused by an etymological *-i̯e- as opposed e.g. to *-i̯ō-; hence Old Saxon 1st/2nd singular *leggiu, legis* vs. Gothic *lagja, lagjis*.

§8. By now we have found arguments against the necessity of positing, as did Meillet,[106] an inherited conjugation in *-i-/-i̯o- for Celtic, Italic, and Germanic.[107] In each instance, I have proposed an original *-i̯e-/-i̯o- instead. The same might now be attempted for Albanian, which Meillet had later added to the list of IE dialects showing a supposed *-i-/ -i̯o-.[108] While the latter formulation again might not be impossible on the basis of the Albanian internal evidence, neither is it the inevitable solution, as we can see from the discussion of the relevant verbal classes by La Piana.[109] Granted, the conjugational types in *-ni̯ō and *-ti̯ō do preserve an alternation that may phonologically be reconstructed as reflecting *-i-/-i̯o-:

{1} *-ni̯ō, {2} *-nis, {3} *-nit > {1} -ń, {2} -n, {3} -n
{1} *-ti̯ō, {2} *-tis, {3} *-tit > {1} -s, {2} -t, {3} -t.

---

background for the present discussion have been J. W. Marchand's "The Converse of Sievers' Law and the Germanic First-Class Weak Verbs," *Language* 32 (1956) 285–287, and a reply by W. P. Lehmann, *Language* 37 (1961) 71–73, among other works. The conclusions reached here resemble those of Marchand, at least with respect to a general attitude on morphological factors.

[104] Cf. Prokosch, *Germanic Grammar* (n. 90) 214.

[105] Cf. § 6.

[106] *Dialectes* 109–113.

[107] Cf. § 5, § 6, § 7 respectively.

[108] *Dialectes*, "Avant-propos de la réimpression" 14; further elaborated in "La flexion du suffixe *-ye/o- en albanais," *Mémoires de la Société de Linguistique de Paris* 19 (1916) 119–121.

[109] M. La Piana, *Studi linguistici albanesi* (Palermo 1949) 74–87; this work was brought to my attention by R. Wright.

Also, the *i*-vocalism of {2} and {3} exerts an *Umlaut* on the vowel of the preceding syllable; hence:

$$*...a...iC\# > *...e...iC\# > \text{ attested } ...e...\#$$

as seen in e.g.

{1} *flas* vs. {2} *flet*, {3} *flet*.

But even the phonological evidence for a stage showing stem *-i-/-i̯o- cannot be held decisive for proving that this is IE-inherited, since there is also in Albanian a conjugational class which must be reconstructed with stem *-i-/-o-, e.g. the Albanian cognate of Greek γιγνώσκω:[110]

	Siculo-Albanian	Tosk	Geg	
{1}	ngóx	njoh	njof	< *...-ō
{2}	ngéx	njeh	njef	< *...-is
{3}	ngéx	njeh	njef	< *...-it.

Likewise the following two verbs in Geg:

{1}	dal	zââ	< *...-ō
{2}	del	zêê	< *...-is
{3}	del	zêê	< *...-it.

In the conjugation of all three cited words the *Umlaut* {*-a/o- > -e-} presupposes *-is, *-it for {2} and {3}, while evidence is seemingly lacking for *-i̯ō instead of *-ō in {1}. Yet surely the supposition of an IE-inherited conjugation in *-i-/-o- is precluded, so that we are forced to ask whether an Albanian conjugation in *-i-/-o- does not in reality show the phonological reflex of the IE thematic conjugation in *-e-/-o-. Then it could even be posited that e.g. prehistoric Albanian *-is/*-it has two phonologically converging IE sources: *-es/*-et and *-i̯es/*-i̯et. Or perhaps we should

reconstruct *-(i̯)esi/*-(i̯)eti > *-isi/*-iti. The central point
insisted upon here, however, is not the precise reconstruction
but rather a theory that IE *-i̯e- and *-e- had undergone a
phonological merger in Albanian. With this much posited,
it is possible to formulate one earlier phase in the chain of
phonological developments leading to the 3rd singular of
the important verbal type *ban*, as already attested in the
writings of Buzuku (date: 1555); formulated by La Piana,[111]
the successive stages involve

*banít > *bandít > *bándit > *ban*.

To be added now is *bani̯ét > *banít, followed by La
Piana's proposed changes. As for the verbal type without
Umlaut, as in {1} *hap*, {2} *hap*, {3} *hap* (instead of *hap*, *hep*,
**hep*), it probably reflects not the IE-inherited thematic
conjugation in *-e-/-o-, but rather, some derivative conjugation (e.g. with stem *-āi̯e-/-āi̯o-).

§9. The Indo-Iranian evidence for the phonological
opposition {-V̄Cii̯V- : -V̆Ci̯V-} and the morphological
opposition {-C‖ii̯V- : -Ci̯V-} has already been outlined by
Kuryłowicz,[112] whose conclusions I propose here to examine
and to expand.

(1) The productive category which we will choose as
illustration is the Indo-Iranian nominal formant *-(i)ya-,
inherited from IE *-(i)i̯e-/-(i)i̯o-. In both Avestan and Vedic
there is evidence for the archaic existence of -V̄Ciya- besides
-V̆Cya-, through metrically-preserved syllabification: hence
e.g. Avestan *išiya-* vs. *išya-* "desirable," *vairiya-* vs. *vairya-*
"worthy, choice," etc.[113] and Vedic *ápiya-* vs. *ápya-* "watery,"

[111] *Studi* 78.
[112] "Keilschrift" (n. 1) 563–569.
[113] For a list, cf. Kuryłowicz, "Keilschrift" (n. 1) 567. For an early discussion of -*iya-* after light syllable, cf. H. Hübschmann, "Iranische Studien,"
[*A. Kuhn's*] *Zeitschrift für vergleichende Sprachforschung* 24 (1879) § 38 ("Excurs:
i-y, u-v") 362–367.

mádiya- vs. *mádya-* "intoxicated," etc.[114] Sometimes the variation between *-iya-* and *-ya-* on the same base is even attested in the same line; e.g.,

Rig-Veda 7.1.11c *prajávatīṣu dúriyāsu dúrya.*

That a variant in *-ya-* juxtaposed with one in *-iya-* should occur here and elsewhere too[115] in verse-final position is in itself a sign of archaism,[116] and we may surmise an early morphological attrition[117] from e.g. *dúr‖iya-* to *dúrya-*. It is from such attrition that there arises the poetic option of either retaining syllabic *-iy-* in a given word, as sanctioned by inherited usage, or allowing non-syllabic *-y-*, on the precedent of apparently current usage. This option, however, is strictly circumscribed: several nominals with *-iya-* have no alternate with *-ya-* in the *Rig-Veda* (e.g. *kṣámiya-*, *gáṇiya-*, *dámiya-*, etc.),[118] leading to the conclusion that morphological attrition had not yet commenced for such nominals at the period of Rig-Vedic composition—or at least not early enough to set precedent for usage of *-ya-*. What is more, forms with *-iya-* after light syllable persist into the period of Middle Indic, as attested e.g. in the orthography of the Aśoka-edicts and of Pāli;[119] for the latter, we can even formulate specific morphological constraints: postconsonantal/prevocalic *-iy-* survives in the declension of *i*-stems (e.g. genitive

---

[114] For a list, cf. E. V. Arnold, *Vedic Metre* (Cambridge 1905) § 136; cf. also Arnold, *Historical Vedic Grammar* (New Haven 1897; reprinted from the *Journal of the American Oriental Society* 18 [1897]) § 94. On the transcription *-iya-* vs. *-ia-*, cf. J. Wackernagel, *Altindische Grammatik* I (Göttingen 1896) 200, 203.

[115] Cf. Arnold, *Vedic Metre* § 136.

[116] For a discussion of metrical factors contributing to the general tendency of preserving archaisms in verse-final position, cf. Watkins, "Metrics" (n. 16) *passim*.

[117] For the concept, cf. again § 3 *supra*.

[118] Cf. Arnold, *Vedic Metre* § 136: likewise in Avestan: cf. Kuryłowicz, "Keilschrift" (n. 1) 567.

[119] Cf. Wackernagel, *Altindische Grammatik* I (n. 114) 201. The orthographic representation *-iya-* is of course already current in archaic texts, even aside from metrical considerations.

singular *-iy‖ā*, nominative plural *-iy‖o;* cf. Vedic *-iy‖ās*, *-iy‖as*) and in nominals with formant *-iya-* (hence *-‖iya-*).[120] Likewise in Iranian: for example, the Old Persian material reveals that there are still extant nominals with formant *-iya-* after light syllable. Here the evidence for *-iya-* is not from metrics, nor directly from orthography, but rather from the phonologically divergent development of *p*, *t*, *č* before original *-iya-* and before *-ya-*, i.e. *-piya-*, *-tiya-*, *-čiya-* vs. *-fiya-*, *-θiya-*, *-šiya-* respectively;[121] as for the uniform

---

[120] Cf. Wackernagel, *Altindische Grammatik* I 201; note too Edgerton's acknowledgement that what he terms Sievers' Law is "in ... later Indic ... virtually restricted to certain morphological categories": "IE Semivowels" (n. 1) 90. Cf. also L. Renou, *Grammaire sanscrite*[2] (Paris 1961) § 196, last paragraph.

[121] Cf. Kuryłowicz, "Keilschrift" (n. 1) 567 ff: e.g. adjectival *Harauvatiy‖a-* "Arachosian" (← *Harauvati-* "Arachosia"); cf. Vedic *sárasvatī* "rich in waters") vs. *xšāyaθiya-* "king" (< *kšāyatya-*; cf. the Sanskrit verb *kṣáyati* "possesses"). The retention of *-θy-* in the latter is actually a Median idiosyncrasy; in Old Persian proper, the inherited opposition between *-θy-* and *-šy-* collapses in favor of the latter; hence e.g. Old Persian *hašiya-* "true" (< *satya-*) vs. *xšāyaθiya-* (< *kšāyatya-*), "a word of the Median officialdom" (New Persian *šāh*): R. G. Kent, *Old Persian*[2] (New Haven 1953) § 80. Cf. also W. Brandenstein/M. Mayrhofer, *Handbuch des Altpersischen* (Wiesbaden 1964) § 30. Perhaps *kšāyatya-* is the nominalization (with *vṛddhi*) of an archaic syntagma *kšayati-ya*, "he who has power"; cf. Old Persian *xšay-* "rule," Avestan *xšāy-* "have power," Sanskrit *kṣay-* "possess." For a parallel syntagma in Celtic, cf. Old Irish 3rd plural relative *bertae* "they who bear" < *bheronti-jo*; likewise Gaulish *dugiiontiio* "they who serve," discussed by C. Watkins, "Preliminaries to a Historical and Comparative Analysis of the Syntax of the Old Irish Verb," *Celtica* 6 (1962) 24. Such a syntactical order is well-attested in Indo-Iranian: cf. *Rig-Veda* 1.70.5: *dāśad yó asmāi* "he who awaits him," as discussed again by Watkins, *op cit.* 29. I propose to elaborate on this explanation of *xšāyaθya-* elsewhere. For the present, I will simply add here some possible parallels suggested to me by C. Watkins:
Lūcetius, the name of one of the followers of Turnus: Vergil, *Aeneid* IX 590. Servius *ad loc.*: ... *lingua Osca Lucetius est Iuppiter dictus a luce.* Cf. also Gaulish *Leucetios*, epithet of the god of war. For references and further instances (including a possible occurrence in the *Carmen Saliare*), cf. J. Whatmough, *The Prae-Italic Dialects of Italy* II (Cambridge/Massachusetts 1933) 197.
Δουκέτιος, the name of a king of the Sicels: Diodorus Siculus 11.78.7. For references and further instances, cf. again Whatmough, *PID* II 452.
Hence *leuketi-jo "he who shines" and *deuketi-jo "he who leads," both nominalized. There is a parallel syntagma in Hittite: e.g. in *Laws* I 25, *paprizzi*

43

spelling with -*iy*-, it implies an ultimate collapse of the morphological opposition {-C‖iya- : -Cya-} by phonological leveling, apparently in favour of -Cya-.[122]

(2) Already in Avestan and Vedic, however, there are also nominals with light-syllable base followed regularly by -*ya*- rather than -*iya*-; e.g. the cognates *haiθya*- "true"[123] and *satyá*- (same meaning)[124] respectively, to be reconstructed as *sn̥ti̯o-. This is precisely the syllabic pattern we expect from a word with a prehistorically eroded morpheme-boundary. The original motivation of an adjectival *i̯o*-stem by a participial *nt*-stem as in {*sn̥t-‖i̯i̯ó- ← *sent-/sont-[125]} is no longer productive in extant Indic and Iranian, whence e.g. the excessive rareness of *satyá*- in Vedic.[126] Then too, if a whole grammatical category with formant -‖iyV- had already become unproductive by the period of early Vedic, we may expect lexical survivals from such a category to be attested as a rule with the pattern -yV- rather than with -iyV- in the *Rig-Veda*. Thus for example deverbative verbs with formant -(*i*)*ya*- (i.e., the fourth, *div*-class), unlike the deverbative nominals with formant -(*i*)*ya*- (i.e., unlike gerundives),[127] show as regular pattern -*ya*- rather than -*iya*- after light syllable; this verbal trend in distribution (as opposed to the nominal trend) we can connect directly

---

kuiš "he who defiles" (a well, in this case); also, in an Akkadian-Hittite vocabulary (*Keilschrifttexte aus Boghazköi* I 42 31), the Akkadian participle *ḫābilu* "gewalttätig" is glossed as *dammešḫiškizzi kuiš*, literally "welcher schädigt."

[122] Cf. Kuryłowicz, "Keilschrift" (n. 1) 567 ff.

[123] Cf. Kuryłowicz, "Keilschrift" (n. 1) 567; likewise Old Persian *hašiya*- < *satya-, not *satiya-: cf. n. 121.

[124] Cf. H. Grassmann, *Wörterbuch zum Rig-Veda* (Leipzig 1873) s.v.

[125] As in Latin *ab-sent-is*, Greek ὄντ-ος.

[126] Besides several scores of instances showing *satyá*-, Grassmann can find only one metrical attestation of *satiyá*- in the *Rig-Veda*: cf. *Wörterbuch* s.v. *satyá*-.

[127] For a list of gerundives with regular formant -*iya*- after light syllable, cf. Arnold, *Vedic Metre* (n. 114) 84.

with the fact that the *div*-class is an unproductive category in attested Indic.[128] But there still remains the problem of explaining the trend found in the three productive verbal classes originating from the residual *div*-class; i.e., the future with *-sya-*, the passive with *-yá-* (both productive inflectional categories), and lastly, the denominative with *-yá-* (a productive derivational category).[129] Each of these verbal classes regularly reveals (after light syllable) the pattern *-ya-* rather than *-iya-* in Rig-Vedic meter,[130] and this circumstance presents a distinct aporia in view of the productive nominal class with formant *-iya-* frequently warranted by the same metrical evidence. I propose that the reason for this divergence is concealed in the morphemes accessory to the *-ya-* of these productive verbal classes: in the future, the postconsonantal formant *-s-ya-* becomes replaced by *-iṣ-ya-*,[131] while in the passive and denominative, there is obligatory accentuation of *-yá-*. In other words, the accessory morphemes (1) *-i-* and (2) marked stem-accentuation (*-yá-*) set off productive *sya-* and *ya-*verbs respectively from the unproductive counterparts with (1) no *-i-* and (2) unmarked base-accentuation (*-ya-*). From this standpoint,

---

[128] Cf. W. D. Whitney, *A Sanskrit Grammar*[3] (Leipzig 1896) § 761, who counts over 130 extant *div*-class stems: this low figure, compared with e.g. the 150-odd extant constituents of the residual and archaic sixth, *tud*-class (i.e., the type *tudáti*), is in itself a telling sign of the diachronic span involved in positing a once-productive derivative category of deverbatives with formant *-(i)ya-*. For some rare instances of *-iya-* after light syllable, a vestige of long-lost productivity in this category, cf. Arnold, *Vedic Metre* 100.

[129] Cf. chap. iii § 5.

[130] Cf. Wackernagel, *Altindische Grammatik* I (n. 114) 202. What is more, passive *-iyá-* (vs. *-yá-*) is not at all to be found in the *Rig-Veda*, while future *-siya-* is attested but once, by Whitney's count: *Sanskrit Grammar* § 771 g, § 932 b.

[131] For the extension of complex *-iṣ-* from *seṭ*-roots as replacement of simplex *-s-* and for the morphophonemic conditioning, cf. Kuryłowicz, *Apophonie* 252–257. In the *Rig-Veda*, there are only seven occurrences of future-formant *-sya-* not preceded by *-i-*: cf. F. Edgerton, "Sievers's Law and IE Weak-Grade Vocalism," *Language* 10 (1934) 254.

then, the -*i*- and the stem-accentuation are iso-functional with the prevocalic generation of syllabic complex -*iy*- in opposition to non-syllabic simplex -*y*-: all three are accessory morphemes and all three polarize productive categories from unproductive counterparts; hence -*iṣya*- vs. -*sya*-, -*yá*- vs. -*ya*-, -*iya*- vs. -*ya*-.[132] In the case of the productive verbal categories discussed so far, the first two polarizing mechanisms have been generalized at the expense of the third. Nevertheless, such displacement of the opposition {-C‖iyV- : -CyV-} is not a universal trend in Indic verbals as opposed to nominals: in e.g. the optative, only -*iy*- (vs. -*y*-) is the accessory morpheme, whence the numerous Rig-Vedic attestations of -*iyā*- vs. -*yā*- as optative-formant even after light syllable.[133]

(3) In the oldest extant phases of Indic and Iranian, there are also clear reflexes of the phonological opposition {-V̄Cii̯V- : -V̄Ci̯V-}. In the *Rig-Veda*, for example, even constituents of the residual *div*-class of verbs occasionally show -*iya*- after long syllable: hence the imperfect of *asya*- "throw" is attested metrically as *āsiya*- besides *āsya*-.[134] The latter form, however, betrays the ultimate breakdown of Sievers' Rule (specifically, the opposition {-V̄Cii̯V- : -V̄Ci̯V-}) already in the Vedic period; in unproductive categories such as the *div*-class, the metrical preservation of -*iya*- after heavy syllable is merely an exceptional archaism rather than an operative mechanism: hence regular -*ya*- in such constituents of the *div*-class as *śrāmya*-, *sīvya*-, *medya*-, etc.[135] But in grammatical categories where the morphological opposition {-C‖iyV- : -CyV-} has survived, the chances

---

[132] Here again, then, is an illustration of Kuryłowicz's axiom I, already quoted in note 5 and already applied to the contrast {-C‖ii̯V- : -Ci̯V-} in § 2.

[133] For a list, cf. Arnold, *Vedic Metre* (n. 114) 96.

[134] Cf. Edgerton, "Sievers's Law" (n. 131) 255.

[135] Listed by Edgerton, "Sievers's Law" 255.

for the parallel survival of the phonological opposition {-V̄CiyV- : -V̄CyV-} in Vedic diction are appreciably enhanced. For example, in the productive category of nominals with formant -iya-, there are two factors which promote the prevalence of -iya- after heavy syllable in the *Rig-Veda*: (1) the actual preservation of Sievers' Rule by words embedded in archaic formulae, and (2) additionally, the prevention of a shift from -V̄C‖iya- to -V̄Cya- in a given word (despite loss of morpheme-boundary and suspension of Sievers' Rule), because of the precedent set by its attestation elsewhere as -V̄Ciya- in the tradition. These two factors combine to leave in the *Rig-Veda* nine instances of nominal -iya-/-iyā- for every one of -ya-/-yā- after heavy syllable.[136] Even in the case of the two most frequent nominals with -ya- after heavy syllable, namely *dáivya-* "divine" and *sū́rya-* "sun," they are outnumbered by *dáiviya-* and *sū́riya-* 64 to 14 and 230 to 122 respectively.[137] Nonetheless, the anomalous ratio here implies that morphological attrition from the productive nominal category in -iya- took place especially early for *sū́riya-* (thanks to the early desuetude of its founding form *súvar*), in comparison with other instances of -ya- after heavy syllable. In other words, I propose that resistance to the usage of *sū́rya-* (vs. *sū́riya-*) in Vedic composition is relatively weaker because the loss of morpheme-boundary here is relatively older. As for *dáivya-*, it is inherited as a formulaic correlate of *divyá-* in Vedic composition (cf. e.g. the mutual collocations with *jána-*), and the light-syllable base of the latter could have imposed an adherence to -y- (vs. -iy-) in the former. The central point, however, is that the phonological opposition {-V̄CiyV- : -V̄CyV-} had been suspended at an early period of Indic. Likewise in

---

[136] Arnold's statistics: *Vedic Metre* 85.
[137] Edgerton's statistics: "IE Semivowels" (n. 1) 121 n. 71.

Iranian, there are attestations of the pattern -V̄CyV-
already in Avestan: e.g. *vāstrya-* vs. *vāstriya-* "agricultural,"
zəvištya- vs. *zəvištiya-* "quickest, most impetuous," etc.[138]

---

[138] For a list and accompanying statistics, cf. Kuryłowicz, "Keilschrift"
(n. 1) 556 f. As for Old Persian *martiya-* "man," it could have been synchronically motivated by *marta- "mortal" (< *morto-): cf. Vedic *mártiya-* ← *márta-*
"mortal." In other words, Old Persian *martiya-* need not be considered a form
directly inherited from Indo-Iranian, provided that *marta- = /marta-/
"mortal" was inherited. The latter form is not to be confused with the attested
Old Persian *marta-* = /mr̥ta-/ "dead" < *mr̥tó-; cf. Vedic *mr̥tá-*, Avestan
mərəta-. Actually, both */marta-/ and /mr̥ta-/ are reflected in New Persian:
märd "man" vs. *murd* "dead" respectively; cf. Chr. Bartholomae, *Altiranisches
Wörterbuch* (Strassburg 1904) s.vv. *marəta-* and *mərəta-*. Also, Avestan *mašya-*
"mortal" may be derived from *mr̥tya-, which raises the question whether
Old Persian *martiya-* might be interpreted as /mr̥tya-/: cf. A. Debrunner, *Die
Nominalsuffixe* (Vol. II 2 of J. Wackernagel's *Altindische Grammatik*; Göttingen
1954) 789. In sum, it would be inadequate to posit any preservation of Sievers'
Rule from the evidence of the Old Persian contrast between *martiya-* and *uvā-
maršiyu-* (= adjectival "by a natural death": used of Kambyses; cf. Herodotos
III 64–66); the reconstructed contrast between *martiya- and *-mrtyu- (cf.
Vedic *mr̥tyú-*, Avestan *mərəθyu-* "death") can be explained on morphological
grounds: the former configuration had been synchronically motivated while the
latter was already a residual inheritance. For a cogent discussion of *uvāmaršiyu-*
and its connection with e.g. the Latin phrase *suā mort.*, cf. W. Schulze, "Der
Tod des Kambyses," *Sitzungsberichte der königlich preussischen Akademie der
Wissenschaften* (1912) 685–703, reprinted in his *Kleine Schriften* (Göttingen 1933)
131–148.

To_____

Date_____ Time_____

WHILE YOU WERE OUT

M_____

of_____

Phone_____
    Area Code   Number   Extension

TELEPHONED		PLEASE CALL	
CALLED TO SEE YOU		WILL CALL AGAIN	
WANTS TO SEE YOU		URGENT	
	RETURNED YOUR CALL		

Message_____

_____

_____

_____

                         _____
                              Operator

CHAPTER II

REFLEXES OF NOMINAL
*-(i)i̯o-, *-(i)i̯ā- IN LITHUANIAN

Der enge Zusammenhang, der zwischen *iā-* und *ē-*Flexion
besteht (*dìdė—didžiõs* usw.), der unverkennbare Parallelismus,
der in der Motion zwischen *-ias/-ia* einerseits, *-is(-ys)/-ė* andrer-
seits herrscht, zwingen zu der Fragestellung, ob nicht diese
Verteilung sich aus einer ursprünglichen Einheit ableiten lässt,
dergestalt, dass man, wie früher allgemein, auf unkontrahierte
und kontrahierte *io-* und *iā-*Stämme zurückgeht. Tatsächlich
stellt sich heraus, dass die Bedingungen, unter denen *-ias, -ia*
auftritt, im Maskulinum wie im Femininum die gleichen sind.
                                               —F. Sommer (1914).[1]

§1. As in the statement just cited, the specific examples
upon which the exposition here is to rely will be taken from
Lithuanian, but the general conclusion is meant to hold for
Latvian and Old Prussian as well.[2] Before any attempt to

---

[1] F. Sommer, *Die indogermanischen iā- und io-Stämme im Baltischen* (Abhandlungen der philologisch-historischen Klasse der königlich sächsischen Gesellschaft der Wissenschaften 30.4 [Leipzig 1914]) 368.

[2] Among the most important works with discussions of this problem are:
J. Kuryłowicz, "Les thèmes en *-ē-* du baltique," *Bulletin de la Société de Linguistique de Paris* 61 (1966) 13–20; H. Pedersen, *La cinquième déclinaison latine* (Det
Kongelige Danske Videnskabernes Selskab. Historisk-Filologiske Meddelelser
11.5 [København 1926]); W. R. Schmalstieg, "Baltic *ei* and Depalatalization,"
Lingua 9 (1960) 258–266; W. P. Schmid, *Studien zum baltischen und indogermani-
schen Verbum* (Wiesbaden 1963); F. Sommer, *Stämme*, see n.1; Chr. S. Stang,
Vergleichende Grammatik der baltischen Sprachen (Oslo/Bergen/Tromsö: Univers-
itetsforlaget, 1966).
  The Lithuanian reference-works used throughout this chapter are: E.
Fraenkel, *Litauisches etymologisches Wörterbuch* I/II (Heidelberg: Winter, 1962/
1965); A. Leskien, *Litauisches Lesebuch* (Heidelberg 1919); J. Otrębski, *Grama-
tyka języka litewskiego* I (Warszawa 1958), II (1965), III (1956); A. Senn,
Handbuch der litauischen Sprache I: *Grammatik* (Heidelberg 1966); P. Skardžius,
Lietuvių kalbos žodžių daryba (Vilnius 1943); Z. Zinkevičius, *Lietuvių dialektologija:
lyginamoji tarmių fonetika ir morfologija* (Vilnius 1966).

describe the Baltic phonological conditions which could have prompted the ultimate development of e.g. standard Lithuanian -*is*(-*ȳs*)/-*ė* and -*ias*/-*ia* as reflexes of postconsonantal *-ii̯os/-ii̯ā and *-i̯os/-i̯ā respectively, we must first examine the relevant morphological factors. The initial premise is that in Baltic, opposition between productive -C‖ii̯V- and unproductive -Ci̯V- persisted regardless of whether the preceding syllable was heavy or light.[3] Accordingly, the IE-inherited nominal class in postconsonantal *-(i)i̯o-, *-(i)i̯ā- becomes Baltic *-ii̯a-, *-ii̯ā- (productive) vs. *-i̯a-, *-i̯ā- (unproductive). Lithuanian in turn reflects this opposition in a transformed state, since e.g. *-ii̯as/-ii̯ā are contracted into -*is*(-*ȳs*)/-*ė*, as distinct from uncontracted -*ias*/-*ia*. Here we see the ultimate products again given specifically in Lithuanian, though the actual phenomenon of what I presently call contraction is apparently Baltic. For example, the contrasting -*ia*/-*ė* of Lithuanian is directly comparable not only with Latvian -'*a*/-*e* but also with the Old Prussian -*i*/-*e* in the orthographic system of the *Elbing Glossary*.[4]

§2. Besides IE *-o-/-ā-, a formally more complex relationship of nominal formants is, to repeat, *-ii̯o-/-ii̯ā-, copiously attested in the various IE languages. From a selective survey of these attestations in chapter I,[5] I have posited that loss of productivity in the affixation of *-ii̯o- and *-ii̯ā- to any

---

[3] I.e., the phonological opposition {-V̄Cii̯V- : -VCi̯V-} had collapsed.

[4] Cf. Schmid, *Verbum* 17 f.

[5] Conspicuously absent from the discussion has been the relavant Old Church Slavonic evidence, where e.g. we see a variation between -*jь* and -*ьjь* as reflex of IE *-(i)i̯os. The precise grammatical nature of this variation is hard to define: cf. the examples and comments offered by A. Meillet, *Études sur l'étymologie et le vocabulaire du vieux slave* II (Paris 1905; re-edited by A. Vaillant, 1961) 375 ff. Part of the difficulty has been the lack of an authoritative collection of attestations, a situation now being remedied by D. Cooper's forthcoming "Possessive Adjectives in -*jь*, -*ьjь* in Old Church Slavonic" (the title is tentative); in this valuable work, Cooper has been able to formulate a clear morphophonemic rule for the distribution, using as illustration many forms previously uncited in other published discussions.

base results in the loss of vocalic *-i-, whence *-i̯o- and *-i̯ā- respectively. What makes Baltic in general and Lithuanian in particular an important control of this theory is

(1) the sharp formal distinction between reflexes of *-ii̯os/-ii̯ā as -is(-ȳs)/-ė and of *-i̯os/-i̯ā as -ias/-ia

(2) the productive motivation of -ė by -is(-ȳs).

§3. Phonological difficulties aside, deriving -ė from *-ii̯ā is at least intuitively feasible from such parallelisms as in {orė̃ "plowing" and kūlė̃ "threshing" vs. sėjà "sowing"},[6] and it has long been recognized that -ė in such instances seems to be the postconsonantal variant of original postvocalic *-i̯ā (as in sėjà), whence the direct or indirect etymology {-ė from *-ii̯ā}.[7] If indeed we may consider -Cė to be the reflex of *-Cii̯ā, it follows that -C'a (spelled -Cia) is derivable from *-Ci̯ā.

§4. Proposing the etymology {-is(-ȳs) < *-ii̯os} involves fewer phonological difficulties than the conjectured {-ė < *-ii̯ā},[8] but even here it is clearly the morphological distribution which carries conviction. For example, there is an interesting parallel to other IE languages in the attestation of Lithuanian -is(-ȳs) as productive compound-formant. The contingent facts are these: for simplex substantive with o-stem, there is a corresponding compound adjective with i-stem, as in Greek ἧλος → ἔφ-ηλις, Latin

---

[6] The intonational pattern (4) of all three indicates deverbative foundation by árti "plow," kùlti "beat, thresh," and sė́ti "sow" respectively. For the pattern, cf. Kuryłowicz, *Accentuation* 247 ff. The variants ōrė̃ (2) "plowing" and kū̃lė (2) "threshing" are innovations from orė̃ (4) and kūlė̃ (4): cf. Stang. *Vergleichende Grammatik* (n. 2) 147. The fact that kūlė̃ can also bear the concrete meaning "club" (⇐ "beater") suggests the ouster of this form from the primary function of abstract-marker—a further indication of archaism relative to kū̃lė (abstract only); cf. § 9 and § 11 *infra* for a discussion of the trend {abstract ⇒ concrete} and its implications. For a general discussion of kūlė̃/kū̃lė, cf. Fraenkel, *LEW* (n. 2) s.v. *kálti*.

[7] Cf. Sommer, *Stämme* (n. 1) 11; also Schmalstieg, "Baltic *ei*" (n. 2) 263.

[8] For a proposed solution covering both -is(-ȳs) and -ė, cf. § 29–§ 32 *infra*.

clīuos → *prō-clīuis*, Sanskrit *árdhah* → *práti-ardhih*, etc.[9] This apparently IE-inherited relationship is also amply attested in e.g. Lithuanian, but in a transformed state on account of a wholesale ouster of *i*-stem adjectives by *iio*-stems,[10] whence the function of *iio*-stems as the productive compound variant of simplex *o*-stems, e.g. *vaĩkas* "child" → *be-vaĩkis* "childless," etc. Given that an athematic *i*-stem declension has been replaced by a thematized *i*-stem declension in such categories as the compounds now in question, what here becomes a crucial factor is that the latter are consistently reflected with the declension *-is(-ȳs)/-io/...*, not *-ias/-io/...*; in other words, the second of these two declensional types cannot function as productive compound-formant. In fact, Lithuanian *-ias/ -io/...* does not function as productive formant of any other nominal category either, except in instances where it has become frozen onto a positionally preceding suffix-marker so that the ensemble is productive but not its constituent elements,[11] as in the superlative suffix *-iáus-ias/-iáus-io/...*; on the other hand, the formant *-is(-ȳs)/-io/...* is productive even in positions where it is attached directly to the nominal base, as in the already-mentioned instance of such compound types as *be-vaĩkis* (vs. *vaĩkas*); likewise *antrãdien-is* "Tuesday" (a neologism, from *añtras* "second" + *dienà* "day"), *dúonkubil-is* "kneading-trough" (from *dúona* "bread" + *kùbilas* "vat"), etc.[12] Not only that; *-is(-ȳs)/-io/...* is also a productive formant attached directly to verbal bases as well, in compounds of the type *véidrod-is* "mirror" (from *véidas* "face" + *ród-yti* "show"), *kaminbrauk-ȳs* "chimney

---

[9] For details about such compounds from the IE standpoint in general and from the Greek standpoint in particular, cf. Schwyzer, *GG* I 450 f.

[10] Cf. § 14.

[11] For a typological discussion of productive compound morphemes made up of unproductive constituents, cf. Kuryłowicz, *Inflectional Categories* 52 f.

[12] For a descriptive survey, cf. Senn's "Nominalkomposition," *Grammatik* (n. 2) 340–351.

sweep" (from *kãminas* "chimney" + *braũk-ti* "scour"), *žiemkent-ȳs* "male pig kept past wintertime" (= "winter-surviver"; from *žiemà* "winter" + *kę̃s-ti* "suffer through, endure"), *bobved-ȳs* "one who marries an old woman" (from *bóba* + *vès-ti* "marry"), etc. In sum, just as -*Cia* is the unproductive equivalent of -*Cė*, so also -*Cias* of -*Cis*(-*Cȳs*).

§5. Once the phonological contraction {*/-ii̯a-/ > */-ī-/} took place,[13] a nominative singular originally in post-consonantal *-ii̯as (< *-ii̯os) could irrevocably become what is now -*is*(-*ȳs*) in Lithuanian,[14] while postconsonantal *-i̯as (< *-i̯os) survives as -*ias*, i.e., simple thematic -*as* + palatalization of the preceding consonant. If a form consisting of base + productive suffix *-ii̯as had already become unmotivated at the time of contraction, the morpheme-boundary before the *-ii̯as was *ipso facto* obliterated and the formant *-ii̯as could lose the formal mark of its productivity, syllabic *-i-; whence *-i̯as > Lithuanian -*ias*. Thus an adjective like *slãpč-ias* ("clandestine") with its dialectal by-form *slãpt-as* (same meaning)[15] indicates that the inherited iso-function of *-ii̯a- and *-a- as adjectival formants had in this case already broken down functionally before the contraction {*/-ii̯a-/ > */-ī-/}; hence *slapt-‖ii̯as ⇒ *slapti̯as > *slãpčias*. However, in e.g. the specialized function of marking *nomen agentis*, the correlation {*-a- : *-ii̯a-} has remained productive beyond this same stage of contraction, whence the survival of such lexical pairs as *gaidȳs* "rooster" (⇐ "singer") vs. *gaidas* (archaic) "singer."[16] The factor of historical iso-function between latter-day Lithuanian nominals in -*as* and -*is*(-*ȳs*) is especially apparent in the many composite suffixal pairs, such as -*klas* vs. -*klis*.

[13] For which cf. § 29.
[14] For the phonological conditioning of the contrast -*is* vs. -*ȳs*, cf. again § 29.
[15] For a discussion of such pairs, cf. Skardžius, *Daryba* (n. 2) 63.
[16] Cf. further in § 9.

II. §5

And from the historical rather than synchronic standpoint, this same factor even resulted in the partial reconstitution of the declension -is(-ȳs) etc. with original formant *-iįa- on the model of the declension -as etc. with original formant *-a-: e.g. dative plural -(C)iams modeled on -(C)ams.[17] As for the residual declension -ias etc. with original unproductive formant *-įa-, phonological developments have made it an unstable and disruptive paradigm in latter-day Lithuanian, as we see in e.g. singular nominative/genitive/ vocative svēč'as/svēč'o/svet'ė (spelled svečias/svečio/svetė) "guest" vs. var̃gas/var̃go/var̃g'e and gaid'ȳs/gaidž'o/gaid'ȳ. But points of formal convergence with the regular declensions can become extended to level out the synchronic irregularities, whence e.g. var̃go : var̃g'e = svēč'o : new svēč'e, dialectally attested;[18] or again, gaĩdž'o : gaid'ȳ = svēč'o : new svet'ȳ, spelled svetȳ, the regular vocative singular of svečias in standard Lithuanian; the locative singular svetyjė in the standard language (vs. e.g. residual medė, locative singular of mēdžias) is likewise imposed by the type gaidyjė. Aside from such partial encroachment of a regular paradigm upon an irregular one, a further possible stage is complete leveling, whence the dialectal types svetȳs (vs. svečias) and élnis (vs. élnias) "stag." At times it is the standard language which shows the completely leveled variant, while the residual declension still survives in dialects: e.g. jáutis vs. jáučias "ox," mēdis vs. mēdžias "tree, wood."[19] A comparison of Latvian alnis "elk" with Lithuanian élnis/élnias or of mežs "woods" with mēdžias/mēdis suggests the kindred progress of a declensional leveling mechanism in Latvian as well. No wonder, then, that reflexes of nominals with formant *-įa- (vs. *-iįa-)

[17] Cf. n. 160 infra.
[18] Cf. n. 146.
[19] For the geographical range of jáučias and mēdžias, cf. Zinkevičius, Lietuvių dialektologija (n. 2) § 294. For a list of such doublets as jáutis vs. jáučias, cf. Otrębski, Gramatyka (n. 2) II 64 f.

54

are sporadic; the very unproductivity of this formant formally predestines the sort of declension which can become leveled out with the regular declension evolved by the productive formant *-iِa-.

Nor can we rule out a possibility which the attestation of e.g. dialectal *jáučias* vs. standard *jáutis* implies—that the contraction {*/-iِa-/ > */-ī-/} might have taken place not only after the period of Common Baltic, but also in an already dialectal stage of prehistoric Lithuanian. The same contraction is clearly attested for Latvian as well,[20] a circumstance which might lead some to trace this phenomenon all the way back to Common Baltic. Such an outlook is unnecessary, however, even aside from the *termini post et ante quem* which will be adduced to show the relative lateness of {*/-iِa-/ > */-ī-/};[21] if we keep in mind that Lithuanian, Latvian, and Old Prussian are (from the standpoint of linguistic theory) self-contained systems closely akin to one another, then common innovation, occurring separately in each dialect (or even sub-dialect), cannot merely be viewed as a vague sort of parallel coincidence. In other words, we can invoke the axiom that kindred structures tend to generate kindred innovations independently.[22] In prehistoric Lithuanian, then, *ِautǁiِas could have occurred in some dialects, *ِautِas in others: whence */ِautīs/ vs. */ِautِas/ after contraction, and ultimately *jáutis* vs. *jáučias*. An objection to this theory seems feasible: one could claim that *jáučias/jáučio/*... resulted from a leveling of *jáutis/jáučio/*..., on the model of thematic nominals declined -*as/-o/*..., without etymological *-(i)ِ-. What makes this possibility unlikely is the already-established fact that

---

[20] Cf. n. 161; also Stang, *Vergleichende Grammatik* (n. 2) 188–192.
[21] Cf. § 29 and § 30.
[22] For an interesting typological discussion, cf. in general C. Watkins, "Italo-Celtic Revisited," *IE Dialects* 29–50.

the declensional type -is(-ỹs)/-io/... is a synchronically productive formant, whereas -ias/-io/... is not. Thus to argue that *jáučias* is an innovation from *jáutis* implies the improbable metastasis of the base *jaut-* from a productive and regular declensional model into an irregular and no longer motivated paradigm. True, there is some leveling on the model of -as/-o/... even in the declensional type -is(-ys)/ -io/..., but this occurs within the structural framework of the latter *system*; it is one thing to detect various levelings in the oblique cases of a productive declensional system and quite another to posit an isolated replacement of e.g. a productive nominative formant -is by an unproductive -ias (-as + palatalization of the base-final consonant), resulting in an unmotivated form *jáučias*.

§6. If a form consisting of base + productive suffix *-iịā had become unmotivated, the consequent loss of morpheme-boundary implied the simultaneous loss of the formal mark of productivity, syllabic *-i-: whence *-ịā, > Lithuanian -ia. Meanwhile, *-iịā becomes subject to a contraction parallel to {*/-iịa-/ > */-ī-/}, namely {*/-iịā/ > */-ē-/}; whence Lithuanian -ė: even the absence of shortening in the latter (vs. *-ịā > -ia) implies contraction.[23]

Parallel to the iso-functional pair {*-a- : *-iịa-} was the feminine {*-ā- : *-iịā-}; in e.g. the specialized function of marking *nomen actionis*, the latter correlation apparently remained productive beyond the period of contraction, whence the survival of such lexical pairs as *dainà* vs. *dainė̃* "song" (⇐ "singing").[24] This inherited iso-function {*-ā- : *-iịā-} becomes especially apparent in productive composite formants such as the suffixal pair -ysta vs. -ystė: what is more, in Daukša's *Postille* (published 1599), e.g. the forms *karalysta*

---

[23] Cf. § 29.
[24] Cf. further in § 9. For a collection of pairs in -a/-ė, cf. Otrębski, *Gramatyka* (n. 2) II 48; also Zinkevičius, *Lietuvių dialektologija* (n. 2) 229.

and *karalystė* "kingdom" still coexist in free variation.[25] Within the framework of their correlation as formants, even the declension of *ė*-stems is historically modeled on that of *a*-stems.[26] Those substantives which ceased being motivated before the period of contraction (*/-iĩā-/ > */-ē-/) survive in latter-day Lithuanian with the residual declension *-ia* etc. (vs. the productive *-ė* etc.). Thus according to the present theory, a substantive like *kančià* "torment," a *nomen actionis* from the diachronic standpoint, must have been already unmotivated at the time of contraction.[27] Left to be explained, then, are doublets like dialectal *prieminià* vs. standard *priemenė̃* "Vorhaus, -zimmer," or again standard *negalià* vs. dialectal *negãlė* "infirmity."[28] Granted, just as in the case of *-ias* vs. *-is(-ỹs)*, we cannot rule out, here either, the possibility that some instances of attested dialectal variation between *-ia* and *-ė* might actually stem from a prehistoric geographical disparity in the non-perception or perception of the morpheme-boundary within given words (*-i̯ā vs. *-‖ii̯ā) at the very time that contraction occurred, with its irrevocably divergent phonological results. But here again it is relevant to stress that only a small number of substantives survives with the declension *-ia* etc.; as also in the instance of *-ias* etc., this very fact of scarcity suggests that most words with this residual *ia*-declension have undergone metastasis into the *ė*-declension. Thus the occurrence of *-ia* vs. *-ė* on the same base in two different dialects may often mean only that the given word escaped declensional leveling in one

[25] Cf. Otrębski, *Gramatyka* (n. 2) II 260.
[26] For a survey, cf. Stang, *Vergleichende Grammatik* (n. 2) 201–206.
[27] Cf. further in § 10.
[28] For a list, cf. Otrębski, *Gramatyka* (n. 2) II 72; also Zinkevičius, *Lietuvių dialektologija* (n. 2) 223–226, esp. § 324. For reasons which will become obvious in § 27 *infra*, the testimony of *Žemaičiai*-dialects on words in *-ė* (vs. standard *-ia*) is not used here.

dialect (hence -*ia*) but not in the other (hence -*ė*). The formal convergences which lead to the leveling from -*ia* etc. to -*ė* etc. vary from dialect to dialect, according to the phonological idiosyncrasies of the various regions.[29] But since the standard language itself shows instances of -*ė* vs. dialectal -*ia* on the same base, it in itself suffices here for an examination of formal channels whereby an inherited substantive in -*ia* can be reconstituted as one in -*ė*. There is indeed formal convergence for -*Cia* vs. -*Cė* (= [-C'æ] vs. [-C'ee]) in e.g. the dative singular, -*Ciai* vs. -*Cei* (= [-C'æi] for both); likewise in the singular accusative, instrumental, vocative and the plural genitive, accusative. The *terminus post quem*, of course, for any such leveling on the basis of declensional convergences is the stage when consonants became palatalized before front vowels.

Granted that this sort of paradigmatic convergence and leveling may be cited to account generally for words with the dialectal variation -*Cia* vs. -*Cė*, such an explanation nevertheless must be modified specifically on account of -*čia* vs. -*tė* and -*džia* vs. -*dė*: here the only available source of convergence is the genitive plural (-*čių* and -*džių*). While even this is enough to allow an entire paradigmatic rearrangement (from -*Cia* etc. to -*Cė* etc.), there might also be another factor operative in producing the first member in such standard/dialectal pairs as *kaltė/kalčià* "crime" and *kandė/kándžia* "moth"; as for *kertė/kerčià* "corner," both actually coexist in the standard literary language.[30] Assuming that the variants in -*ia* here are synchronically unmotivated, being survivals of categories long unproductive, we must ask what

---

[29] Among the factors: (1) barytone (vs. oxytone) pattern, and whether or not this allows shortening of long vowels in word-final syllable; (2) the reflex of Baltic *ā*. The first of these two involved a serious structural disruption of the *ė*-declension, in e.g. the idiom of Palomenė. For a discussion, cf. Zinkevičius, *Lietuvių dialektologija* (n. 2) 223–226, esp. § 326.

[30] Cf. Otrębski, *Gramatyka* (n. 2) II 72.

morphological force could possibly have helped remotivate them into the regular formations in -*ė*. It is therefore no coincidence, I propose, that for each of the variations just listed, there is attested a by-form with athematic *i*-stem: *kaltìs* "crime," *kandìs* "moth," *kertìs* "flaw"; nor does this pattern hold only for words with base-final *t* or *d*: e.g. besides *musė̃/musià* "fly," there is also a *musìs*.[31] From such distribution it appears as if *i*-stems and *ė*-stems were still coexisting after the period of contraction (*/-ii̯ā-/ > */-ē-/). Put another way, an original foundation {*-i- → *-ii̯ā-} survived as {*-i- → -ė-}. According to this theory, the latter structural mechanism could have helped generate e.g. a new *nomen actionis* *kertė "cutting" from an older *nomen actionis* *kertis "cutting,"[32] before the semantic development of these two[33] into what has come to be the contextual bifurcation of "corner"[34] for the former and "flaw"[35] for the latter. Of course the actual generation of *kertė by *kertis would have had to be through the intermediacy of what is now *kerčià*, the genitive plural of which (*kerčių̃*) affords a convergence of all three (*kertė̃, kerčià, kertìs*).[36]

---

[31] Cf. Fraenkel, *LEW* (n. 2) 474. For further examples of coexisting *i*-stem and *ė*-stem in both Lithuanian and Latvian, cf. Skardžius, *Daryba* (n. 2) 54.

[32] The founding verb is *kìrs-ti* (3rd singular present *kért-a*). From here on, any founding verb of deverbative substantives will regularly be cited in its infinitive form—for convenience of identification only; actual foundations, however, are to be derived from the present-tense stem (e.g. *kért-a* in this case).

[33] For a discussion of the trend {abstract ⇒ concrete}, cf. § 9–§ 11 *infra*.

[34] Said of an old maid with whitlow: *iñ kér̃tę inkìr̃sti sù nagaìs negál* "sie kann mit ihren Nägeln nicht in die Ecke hineinschlagen" (from the collection of A. Juškevič); this interesting collocation of *kertė̃* and *kìr̃sti* (with its implication of *figura etymologica*) is noted by Fraenkel, *LEW* (n. 2) 245.

[35] Said, with approbation, about a girl: *mergà bè jokiõs kertiė̃s* "ein Mädchen ohne irgendeine Scharte" (again, from the collection of A. Juškevič); like *kertìs*, German *Scharte* is likewise to be linked with the IE root *(s)ker- "cut": Fraenkel, *LEW* (n. 2) 245.

[36] For a survey of declensional convergences between *i*-stem and *ė*-stem in the dialects, cf. Zinkevičius, *Lietuvių dialektologija* (n. 2) 242–247: especially valuable is the listing of local words with *i*-stem corresponding to standard words with *ė*-stem (e.g. *bitìs* "bee" vs. standard *bìtė*), even in areas where *ė*-declension as a

§7. We have by now observed that the clear formal distinction between Lithuanian -*ias*, -*ia* on one side and -*is* (-*ỹs*), -*ė* on the other is matched by a correlative functional distinction: namely, the latter pair is the reflex of the IE productive formants *-i̯o-/-i̯ā-, while the former reflects the unproductive counterparts *-i̯o-/-i̯ā-, with loss of syllabic *-i-. Among the productive functions of -*is*(-*ỹs*) is that of compound-formant, as seen in the types *be-vaĩkis*, *žiem-kentỹs*, etc., and the point presently to be made can be adequately illustrated with this category. But first, a crucial circumstance affecting our analysis: such compound nominals in -*is*(-*ỹs*) must be divided into two basic functional categories, involving (1) retention of adjectival usage and (2) specialization of substantival usage; hence *be-vaĩkis* and *žiem-kentỹs* respectively. With this functional split taken into account, we note that the corresponding feminine of all such compounds in -*is*(-*ỹs*) is regularly -*ė*, whence e.g. *be-vaĩkė* and *žiem-kentė̃;* yet it now becomes apparent that not all of these substantives need have a corresponding feminine as in the instance of *žiemkentė̃* "female pig kept past wintertime" (vs. the male *žiemkentỹs*): for example, the type *véidrodis* "mirror" is exclusively masculine. In sum, substantives in -*ė* like *žiemkentė̃* represent the optional survival of a feminine correlate to the masculine in -*is*(-*ỹs*). Likewise a simplex substantive such as *senė̃* "old woman" constitutes the feminine of the now-substantive masculine *senìs* "old man" (vs. *sẽnas* "old"), and even instances like *vìlkė* "she-wolf" may presuppose the former existence of a masculine *vilkis (← *vil̃kas* "wolf").[37] What is more, in

---

rule levels out the *i*-declension; but in such instances, we cannot always rule out the possibility of hypercorrection.

[37] This is the view of Kuryłowicz, "Thèmes en -*ē*" (n. 2) 16 f; actually the form *vilkis which he posits is even attested, in e.g. the compound *šuva-vilkis* "wolf-like hound" (cf. Otrębski, *Gramatyka* [n. 2] II 9).

adjectives the motivation of feminine -é by masculine -is(-ỹs)
is still synchronically productive in Lithuanian, and this
relationship itself is an important reflex of the adjectival
relationship {feminine *-ii̯ā- ← masculine *-ii̯o-}, an extension of the simplex {feminine *-ā- ← masculine *-o-}.

§8. With the productive correlation between -is(-ỹs) and
-é clearly recognized, it nevertheless does not follow that
all Lithuanian substantives in -é had at least once been
motivated by a corresponding masculine now in -is(-ỹs).
An admirable starting-point for this argument is the evidence
of Greek, with its attested archaisms in the relationship of
*-ā- to *-o-. As a specific example, I cite the old deverbative
adjective of ἀείδω "sing," namely ἀοιδός "tuneful, singing"
⇒ "singer, bard." The original adjectival usage is still
found in e.g. the *Helen* of Euripides (1109: ἀοιδοτάταν
ὄρνιθα), whereas ἀοιδός is already attested as substantival
in the Epic (e.g. γ 270). The feminine substantival form
ἀοιδή (> Attic ᾠδή), however, means not "songstress"
but "song" (e.g. B 599). The actual word for "songstress"
is ἀοιδός, as in the Hesiodic *ainos* about the hawk and the
nightingale, in lines 202–212 of the *Erga*. When the hawk
(ἴρηξ, line 203: masculine substantive) seizes the nightingale
(ἀηδών, *ibidem*: feminine substantive) in his sharp talons,
she cries pitifully while the hawk says (*Erga* 208): τῇ δ' εἶς
ᾗ σ' ἂν ἐγώ περ ἄγω καὶ ἀοιδὸν ἐοῦσαν—"you will go wherever
I take you, songstress that you are."[38] The participle ἐοῦσαν
is decisive here, and there are several other clear attestations
of feminine ἀοιδός elsewhere too in Greek literature. From
such distributions as in ἀοιδός/ἀοιδή, then, we can conclude
that *-ā- had been an abstract substantival marker even
before it became the feminine adjectival correlate of masculine *-o-. More precisely, the formant *-o- had been an

---

[38] The designation of ἀηδών as ἀοιδός is also of etymological interest; cf.
Frisk, *GEW* s.v.

animate adjectival marker (without specifying masculine or
feminine gender) at a time when *-ā- was already an abstract
substantival marker. Later on, a new feminine correlate
*-ā- does develop for what becomes specifically masculine
adjectival *-o-,[39] but an original adjective like ἀοιδός which
had early become substantive can by this time fail to develop
a feminine correlate in *-ā- meaning "songstress," simply
because of the already-existing abstract substantive ἀοιδή
"song."[40] Of course, the archaic neutralization of masculine/
feminine distinction in the adjectival formant *-o- is still
productive and obligatory in classical Greek compounds,
such as masculine/feminine ἄ-σημος "sine nota";[41] what is
more, even non-compound adjectives in -ος can optionally
describe feminine nouns during the same period, especially
adjectives in -ιος (e.g. πάτριος, πάτριον).[42] At a certain

[39] The relatively late redistribution resulting in adjectival {masculine *-o-:
feminine *-ā-} was modeled on the substantival/pronominal gender-system,
for which cf. chap. iv n. 63.

[40] Kuryłowicz, *Inflectional Categories* 215 f.

[41] In fact, this morphological constraint has survived in such latter-day
Greek dialects as that of Calabria, in southern Italy. The simplex adjectival
formants at issue are -o in the masculine (from -ος), -i in the feminine (from
-η); so much for simplex adjectives: as for compounds, the West Greek equivalent of ἄσημος (namely ἄσᾱμος, as in *DGE* 526.42, from Orchomenos), when it
qualifies the now ā-stem feminine substantive derived from ancient αἴξ,
becomes (*mia èga*) *ásamo* "an unmarked she-goat" in latter-day Calabrian Greek
rather than *ásami*, as attested in e.g. latter-day Cretan. Likewise *mia jinèka
áplito* "an unwashed woman" (cf. classical ἄπλυτος), *mia elèa ákarpo* "a barren
olive-tree," etc. In the neighboring dialect of Apulia (as also in most other
Greek dialects, including standard Dhimotikí), this constraint on the distribution of feminine -i (from -η) in compounds has broken down: e.g. Apulian (*mia
jinèka*) *ábliti*, vs. Calabrian *áplito*. For these and other examples, cf. G. Rohlfs,
Historische Grammatik der unteritalienischen Gräzität (München 1950) 107 f.

[42] For documentation, cf. Schwyzer, *GG* I 458 n. 1 and W. Kastner, *Die
griechischen Adjektive zweier Endungen auf -ΟΣ* (Heidelberg 1967). The motivation
of feminine -ιᾱ by a masculine -ιος was hindered by the already-existing productivity of -ιᾱ as abstract-suffix: Kastner 61 f (cf. also n. 78 *infra*). Aside from
the specific analysis of -ιος/-ιᾱ, Kastner's general discussion of o-stem adjectives + feminine substantives in Greek is especially useful in pointing out and
documenting such preservative factors as the metrical exigencies of the Epic
and the inheritance of certain adjective-substantive combinations. In the latter

prehistoric stage, then, the type ἀοιδός did not motivate ἀοιδή, but rather, both were motivated by the verb ἀείδω; and the former deverbative was originally adjectival, later to become *nomen agentis*, while the latter was *nomen actionis*. Besides this distribution of *-o- and *-ā-, the same sort of relationship is also attested in Greek for the formants *-ii̯o- and *-ii̯ā-, albeit in a state of near-total atrophy. A rare example is the form πεν-ία "poverty," at one time seemingly motivated directly by the verb attested as πέν-ομαι "be poor";[43] then too, such deverbatives with formant *-ii̯o- as βρύχιος, πάγιος, σφάγιος, etc. show by their residual attestations and adjectival usage that this particular grammatical category became defunct in Greek even before it could develop a substantival function.[44]

§9.

ἀείδω → { nomen agentis ἀοιδός
nomen actionis ἀοιδή

sérg-ēti "bewachen, guard" → { nomen agentis *sárgas* "Wächter, custodian"
nomen actionis *sárga* "Bewachung, custody"[45]

---

case, the effect achieved by the conscious and selective perpetuation of *o*-stem adjective + feminine substantive is of course the solemnity of archaism— whence the preponderance of such collocations in e.g. the sacral, legal, and administrative spheres; Kastner's Index B (pp. 121–131), a list of feminine substantives attested with *o*-stem qualifiers, is invaluable for perspective; likewise the *Anhang* (*Die wichtigsten Wortfelder*: pp. 131 f), with its separate rubrics for religion (sacrifice, hearth, festivals, oath, oracles, etc.), government and law, heredity, epichoric features, etc.
There are still instances of simplex adjectives in *-o* (from *-os*) qualifying feminine substantives in Calabrian Greek: e.g. *mia èga stèrifo* "a barren she-goat" (cf. classical στέριφος "barren"), *mia jinèka ètimo* "a pregnant woman" (cf. classical ἕτοιμος "ready"), *mia elèa prásino* "a green olive-tree" (cf. classical πράσινος "leek-colored"), etc.; cf. Rohlfs, *Historische Grammatik* (n. 41) 107 f.
43 P. Chantraine, *La formation des noms en grec ancien* (Paris 1933) 81.
44 For a survey of this rare type, cf. Chantraine, *Formation* 35.
45 For a list including several such pairs, cf. A. Leskien, *Die Bildung der Nomina im Litauischen* (Abhandlungen der philologisch-historischen Classe

Such parallelisms between Greek and Lithuanian show that Baltic too had inherited the same type of deverbative relationship as in Greek ἀοιδός/ἀοιδή. Likewise in Baltic, there had been besides *-o- an iso-functional deverbative nominal formant in *-i̯o-, attested in such *nomina agentis* as *gaidỹs* "rooster" (⇐ "singer"; ← *gied-óti* "sing"),[46] *sėdỹs* "child who cannot walk" (⇐ "sitter"; ← *sėd-ěti* "sit"), etc.[47] Furthermore, the Baltic formant *-i̯ā- had occurred besides *-ā- as productive marker of deverbative abstract substantives, surviving as e.g. Lithuanian *rankė* "collection" (← *riñk-ti* "collect"), *šėrė̃* "cattle-feeding" (← *šér-ti* "feed cattle"), etc.[48] This is not to say, granted, that substantives in simplex *-ė* are still a productive category in Lithuanian: only that they had been productive at a prehistoric stage of the Baltic languages when the proposed phonological contraction {*/-i̯ā-/ > */-ē-/} took place. Moreover, even the deverbative substantives with original formant in simplex *-ā- are likewise no longer productive in Lithuanian, and a clear indication of breakdown in both these grammatical categories is the specialization from abstract to concrete

---

[sic] der königlich sächsischen Gesellschaft der Wissenschaften 12.3 [Leipzig 1891]) 167–175 and 207–213 (for ...*a*...*as* and ...*a*...*a* respectively). The word *sárga* is attested as the compound *at-sargà* in the standard language.

[46] The corresponding *nomen agentis* with simplex formant *-o- (instead of complex *-i̯o-) is also attested: archaic *gaidas* "singer"; cf. Otrębski, *Gramatyka* (n. 2) II 32. Despite the corresponding *nomen actionis gaidà* "melody" which has survived along with the once-adjectival *gaidas*, the latter as substantive generated a formally ambiguous corresponding feminine *nomen agentis*, archaic *gaida* (Otrębski, *Gramatyka* II 37). By contrast, the survival of *nomen actionis* ἀοιδή in Greek helped preserve ἀοιδός as not only masculine but also feminine *nomen agentis*.

[47] This type is surveyed by Otrębski, *Gramatyka* II 68. There are Slavic parallels, as with *storg-jъ ← *sterg-ti, whence e.g. Polish *stróż* "guard, protector" and *strzec* "guard, protect" respectively; cf. A. Meillet (/A. Vaillant), *Le slave commun*[2] (Paris 1934) § 402. For a Latin parallel, cf. *socius* < (*sokʷi̯os ⇐) *sokʷ-ii̯os ← verbal *sekʷ-, as in *sequor*. For examples from Welsh, cf. chap. 1 § 4.

[48] Surveyed by Otrębski, *Gramatyka* II 47 f; cf. also Leskien, *Bildung* (n. 45) 265–281, esp. 271 f.

designation among many of their substantives, with each lexical entry undergoing its own separate semantic evolution. Hence the development of such specific meanings as in the following, accompanied by atrophy of synchronic grammatical links with the originally founding verbs: *dagà* (also archaic *dagė*) "summer's heat, harvesting time" ← *dèg-ti* "burn (intransitive)," *laidà* "sunset" ← *léis-ti* "release," *lendẽ* "Kriechloch, beehive-entrance" ← *lĩs-ti (leñda)* "creep," *velkẽ* "bar, bolt" ← *vilk-ti (velka)* "pull," etc.[49] In Greek too, the type ἀοιδή is clearly unproductive in the classical period, with some forms in this category retaining the old abstract function (e.g. σπουδή "haste" ← σπεύδω "hasten"), and others innovating a concrete specialization (e.g. δορά "hide" ← δέρω "flay").[50] The main issue now, however, is not that such forms as *rankė* and *lendẽ* are synchronically unproductive: instead, that during the latest phase when this category was productive, its substantives in *-ii̯ā-* had been formally constituted from verbs, not from some masculine correlate in *-ii̯a- (< IE *-ii̯o-). In other words, just as the type ἀοιδή had been formally constituted from ἀείδω rather than from ἀοιδός, so also *rankė* and *lendẽ* had been founded directly on the present-tense stems of *riñk-ti* and *lĩs-ti* respectively.[51] In sum, there is a basic etymological difference between the Lithuanian substantival types *sēnė* (← *sēnis*) and *rankė* (← *riñk-ti*).

§10. I conclude that in prehistoric Lithuanian the abstract formant in *-ii̯ā-* was already functionally moribund, whence such variations as *-ii̯ā* (still motivated) vs. *-i̯ā* (unmotivated).[52] The oncoming phonological process {*/-ii̯ā-/ > */-ē-/} thereupon separates these variants from a

---

[49] Surveyed by Otrębski, *Gramatyka* II 40 f, 68.
[50] Cf. Schwyzer, *GG* I 460. The two well-known Latin examples are *toga* (etymologically founded by *tegō*) and *rota* (← *retō; cf. Old Irish *rethid* "runs").
[51] Cf. § 6.
[52] Cf. § 6.

formal standpoint, whence -*é* vs. -*ia*. The latter declensional type is still attested in e.g. *kančià* "torment" ← *kę̃s-ti* (*keñčia*) "suffer," dialectal *pó-laidžia* "thaw, melting" ← *léis-ti* (*léidžia*) "release," etc.[53] There is, however, an important etymological complication in this residual category, as Kuryłowicz has pointed out:[54] in the types *kančià* and *pó-laidžia*, the synchronically-perceived boundary separating base and ending falls between -*a* and the palatalized consonants -*či*- and -*dži*- (= -*č'*- and -*dž'*-). Since in these particular instances the palatalized consonant is also present within the paradigm of the founding verb-form (*keñčia*, *léidžia*), we might therefore be inclined to argue that the original morpheme-boundary (between verb-bases *kent-, *leid- on one side and *-i- on the other) had broken down by the time that the deverbative substantive was founded: hence supposedly

$$\text{*kent'- } \rightarrow \text{ *kant'-ā } > \textit{kančià}$$
$$\text{*leid'- } \rightarrow \text{ *laid'-ā } > \textit{-laidžia}$$

rather than

$$\text{*kent- } \rightarrow \text{ *kant\|iiā } \Rightarrow \text{ *kantiā } > \text{ *kant'ā } > \textit{kančià}$$
$$\text{*leid- } \rightarrow \text{ *laid\|iiā } \Rightarrow \text{ *laidiā } > \text{ *laid'ā } > \textit{-laidžia.}$$

The former solution implies that simplex *-ā- was still a productive formant of deverbative abstract substantives at a stage which is so late that the verbal bases were already perceived as *kent'- and *leid'- rather than *kent- and *leid-; the accessory assumption, of course, is that *-Ci- was already -C'-, whence the actual opportunity for breakdown of the morpheme-boundary between verbal base and *-i-. On the surface, this first alternative seems to be a more economical solution than the second, until we observe that besides the types *kančià* and *pó-laidžia*, there are also numerous instances of such types as *pa-kantà* "endurance" and

[53] Surveyed by Otrębski, *Gramatyka* (n. 2) II 70 f.
[54] "Thèmes en -*ē*" (n. 2) 17.

laidà "sunset";[55] likewise *dangà* "covering, clothing, snow-cover" ← *deñg-ti* (*deñgia*) "cover," *lankà* "valley, meadow in a valley" ← *leñk-ti* (*leñkia*) "bend," etc.[56] Conversely, there are substantives in -*Cia* with corresponding verbs lacking the original stem-formant *-i̯-: e.g. *kándžia* "moth" ← *ką̃s-ti* (*kánda*) "bite," *ė́džios* "fodder-rack" ← *ė̃s-ti* "auffressen, eat up," *sė́džia* "Fangnetz, snare"[57] ← *sė̃s-ti* (*sė́da*) "aufsitzen, mount," etc.[58] Such a distribution of Lithuanian deverbative substantives in -(*C*)*a* and -(*C*)*ia*, irrespective of the presence or absence of original *-i̯- as formant in the motivating verbal base, helps justify the reconstruction of -(*C*)*ia* as *-(C)i̯ā, the residue of earlier *-(C)‖i̯ā. The loss of syllabic *-i- from the latter we can ascribe to the suspension of derivational motivation by the respective verbal base, so that originally deverbative substantives in -(*C*)*ia* may be divided etymologically (even if not synchronically) as -(*C*)-*ia*. This much argued, we have yet to point out the most salient shortcoming of the first alternative solution: it fails to explain not only the coexistence of e.g. the deverbative substantives in -(*C*)*a* and -(*C*)*ia*, but also the original generation of -(*C*)*ė*. A study of just the root-apophony exerted by the deverbatives in -(*C*)*a*, -(*C*)*ia*, and -(*C*)*ė* is enough to show clearly that besides structural parallelism between the substantives -(*C*)*a* and -(*C*)*ia*, there is an equally strong link between those in -(*C*)*a* and -(*C*)*ė*. Hence e.g. *dagà/dagė* (vs. *laidà/-laidžia*), etc.[59] There are even instances of parallelism in

[55] Cf. § 9.
[56] Surveyed by Otrębski, *Gramatyka* II 39.
[57] The probable semantic evolution: "Fangnetz" ⇐ "Setzer" ⇐ "Sitz," as in Latvian *sêža* "Sitz." Cf. Sommer, *Stämme* (n. 1) 120; also § 11 *infra*.
[58] Surveyed by Otrębski, *Gramatyka* (n. 2) II 70 f.
[59] Cf. also § 6. For other instances, cf. Stang, *Vergleichende Grammatik* (n. 2) 149. As with substantives in -(*C*)*ia*, those in -(*C*)*ė* are derived from verbs either with or without original stem-formant *-i̯-: e.g. *kū̃lė* ← *kùlti* (*kùlia*) vs. *dagė* ← *dègti* (*dèga*). Cf. Greek *stel-i̯ō → *stol-ā, *ager-i̯ō → *agor-ā, whence στέλλω vs. στολή, ἀγείρω vs. ἀγορά, etc.: here too, then, the *-i̯- of the present-formant exerted no influence on the formation of the deverbative substantive.

secondary root-apophony: just as *į-vóda* "conduit" is motivated by *į-vadži-óti*[60] (rather than directly by *į-vės-ti* "lead in") and *į-vor-a* "depth of penetration" by *į-var-ýti* "drive in," so also *naktì-gonė* "pasturing at night" is motivated by *gan-ýti* (rather than directly by *giñ-ti* "drive cattle to pasture") and *iš-monė* "invention" by *iš-man-ýti* (rather than directly by *iš-miñ-ti* "discover").[61] In sum, *-ā- and *-ijā- were iso-functional formants of abstract deverbative substantives; if the latter became unmotivated in a given word before the contraction {*/-ijā-/ > */-ē-/}, the loss of syllabic *-i- (concomitant with loss of motivation) led to the latter-day Lithuanian -(C)ia; if on the other hand *-ijā- had still been motivated in a given word at the time of this contraction, it then survives as Lithuanian -(C)ė.

§11. Since deverbative abstract substantives in *-a -ia -ė* (without accessory suffixes) have all become unproductive categories, having been replaced by formations with *-imas/-ymas*,[62] they are consequently subject to specialization into concrete designations, whence the already-mentioned types *dangà* "snow-cover," *ėdžios* "fodder-rack," *lendė* "beehive-entrance," etc.[63] But this particular semantic development is not the only available trend in contextual restriction. An abstract substantive defining a given action can come to represent, by metonymic extension, an agent whose primary characteristic happens to be this very action. A quaint typological example emerges from *De rerum natura* IV 1160 ff, where Lucretius has composed a catalogue of complimentary names which love-sick males bestow on females—euphemisms disguising the ladies' individual flaws: one of these lovelies happens to be *labeosa* (1169), thus prompting the

---

[60] Dialectal *-vad-ýti*.

[61] Cf. Kuryłowicz, *Apophonie* 295. For an analysis of the intonation on deverbative substantives in -(C)ė, cf. *idem, Accentuation* 251.

[62] Cf. Senn, *Grammatik* (n. 2) 321.

[63] Cf. § 10.

epithet *philema* (ibidem) = φίλημα "kissy" (⇐ "kiss"). The latter usage is attested not only as epithet but also as name, and likewise its diminutive Φιλημάτιον—which in one case belongs, deservedly perhaps, to a *hetaira*.[64] As for Lithuanian, several deverbative substantives in -*a* have undergone such a specialization from *nomen actionis* to *nomen agentis*: e.g. *dìlba* "someone who lowers his eyes, Müssiggänger" (← *délb-ti* "lower eyes"), *niurà* "grumbler, Brummbär, Murrkopf" (← *niùr-ti* "become sullen, mürrisch werden"), etc.[65] Sometimes the original function of *nomen actionis* still coexists with the new restricted function, as in the following minimal pair of syntagmata involving *gyrà* (← *gìr-ti* "praise"):

taĩ tokià gyrà "this is such boasting!"
taĩ tõks gyrà "he is such a braggart!"[66]

Likewise with deverbative substantives in -*ia*: there has been a parallel semantic specialization affecting several members of this category, leading to the restricted function of *nomen agentis*. Among these are the already-discussed *kándžia* "moth" (⇐ "biter"; ← *kás-ti* "bite")[67] and *sėdžia* "snare"

---

[64] For documentation, cf. F. Bechtel, *Die Attischen Frauennamen* (Göttingen 1902) 137; cf. in general chap. xvi, "Frauennamen aus Abstracten," 129–140. For a brief typological discussion, cf. J. Wackernagel, *Vorlesungen über Syntax* II² (Basel 1928) 16 f.

[65] Surveyed by Otrębski, *Gramatyka* (n. 2) II 42 f. For the possibility of intonational specialization accompanying the functional, cf. Kuryłowicz, *Accentuation* 248 f.

[66] Cf. Kuryłowicz, *Inflectional Categories* 214.

[67] There are also sporadic instances of a parallel semantic specialization even in substantives with -*ė*: cf. e.g. besides *kándžia* (East Lithuanian *kúndžia*) the likewise attested forms *kándė/kandė̃* "moth" (Kuryłowicz, *Accentuation* 251); also the Latvian cognate, *kuôde* (same meaning). As for *kañdis* "bite, sting," we cannot assume that it is a masculine correlate of *kandė̃*: rather, it belongs to an independent category which is at least partially a continuation of old neuters in *-ijom (cf. Kuryłowicz, *Apophonie* 296 n. 10); for a survey of the type *kañdis*, cf. Otrębski, *Gramatyka* (n. 2) II 67 f. Actually, the specific formation *kánde/kandė̃* involves a conflation of two founding forms: (1) verbal *kásti* and (2) *i*-stem *kandìs* (genitive *kandiẽs*) "moth"; formally parallel to *kándė/*

(⇐ "Setzer"; ← *sės-ti* "aufsitzen").[68] Other examples are *ėdžia* "Fresser" (← *ės-ti* "auffressen"), *skùndžia* "Kläger" (← *skų́s-ti* "klagen"), *krìčios* "Hosen" (⇐ "Scheisser"), etc.[69] The Latvian equivalent to the third Lithuanian form is *kreša* "Vielfrass" (⇐ "Scheisser"; ← *krēs-t* "scheissen"); other Latvian examples are *luôža* "Herumschleicher, Schnüffler" (← *luôdâ-t* "kriechen"), *glemša* "Träumer, Schwätzer" (← *glems-t* "schwatzen"), etc.;[70] cf. also *sēņu lauža, lapu guļa* "Jemand, der zu oft Pilze bricht, und im Laub liegt."[71] Finally, there is an additional complication with the Lithuanian forms *lìžia* and *mìžia*, in that these had once been apparently feminine correlates of masculine *lìž(i)us* and *mìž(i)us*:

lìžia "Brotschieber" ⇐ "Schaufel, Löffel" ⇐ "Lecker," vs.
lìžius "Zeigefinger" = "Lecker" (← *liêž-ti* "lecken")[72]
mìžia "Pisserin, vagina" vs.
mìžius "Bettpisser, penis" (← *mỹž-ti*; cf. Latin *mingere*, etc.).[73]

§12. The formant *-ā- (or its extension, *-ii̯ā-), surveyed until now in its function of marking deverbative abstract substantives, also inherited the function of marking abstract substantives derived from adjectives.[74] Again, the Greek parallel provides a convenient introduction. We have already

---

kándžia vs. *kandìs* is *kertė̃/kerčià* vs. *kertìs*, discussed in § 6 *supra*. But deverbation from *ką́sti* can involve other formants besides *-ii̯ā-*: cf. the simplex deverbative formant *-ā- in e.g. *pasal-kandà* "a dog who bites insidiously" (vs. *-ii̯ā- ⇒ *-i̯ā-, in *kándžia*).

[68] Cf. § 10 and n. 57.

[69] Cf. Sommer, *Stämme* (n. 1) 140.

[70] Cf. Leskien, *Bildung* (n. 45) 313 f.

[71] Cited by J. Endzelin, *Lettische Grammatik* (Heidelberg: Winter, 1923) 200.

[72] For a semantic parallel, cf. Greek λιχανός "forefinger" (← λείχω "lick"); besides *lìžia*, cf. also *lìžà* and *lìžė̃*: discussed by Sommer, *Stämme* (n. 1) 141.

[73] Cf. Sommer, *Stämme* (n. 1) 140 f and Leskien, *Bildung* (n. 45) 322 f; for *-ia* as feminine correlate of masculine *-us*, cf. § 15.

[74] For a theory actually deriving the former type in *-ā- from the latter, cf. Kuryłowicz, *Apophonie* 84 f: symbolically put in terms of classical Attic, a derivational chain {verbal τεμ- → adjectival τομός → substantival τομή} becomes simplified into {verbal τεμ- → substantival τομή}.

seen that adjectives in -os/-ov originally had no feminine correlate, simply because -os itself originally qualified animate categories vs. inanimate correlates in -ov, rather than masculine entities vs. feminine correlates in -η (< -ā).[75] At such a given stage of Common Greek, adjectives in *-os/-on had motivated abstract substantives in *-ā; e.g. *thermós/thermón "hot" → *thermá "heat." But with the onset of a new tripartite gender-system in simplex adjectives (whence masculine *thermós vs. feminine *thermá, and masculine/feminine *thermós/thermá vs. inanimate *thermón),[76] the old abstract type *thermá could be either (1) ousted altogether by the new feminine type *thermá or else (2) formally differentiated from it if both were to survive functionally. Greek shows traces of the latter alternative development, whence the intonational displacement seen in attested θέρμη "heat" vs. θερμή "hot" (feminine); likewise ἔχθρᾱ "hostility" vs. ἐχθρᾱ́ "hostile"; λεύκη and λέπρᾱ (skin-diseases) vs. λευκή "white" and λεπρᾱ́ "scaly, scabby"; κάκη "baseness" vs. κακή "base"; etc.[77] Of course the type κάκη is no longer productive in classical Greek, as is evident not only from the meager attestations but also from the semantic specializations in some of the constituent forms (e.g. ὃς ἂν ... λέπρην ἢ λεύκην ἔχῃ: Herodotos I 138). The productive type replacing κάκη is κακίᾱ "baseness, the opposite of ἀρετή," synchronically motivated by κακός (/κακή/κακόν); likewise σοφίᾱ (vs. σοφός), καρτερίᾱ (vs. κατρερός), μαλακίᾱ (vs. μαλακός), πονηρίᾱ (vs. πονηρός), etc.[78] The same relationship is amply attested also in e.g. classical

---

[75] Cf. § 8.

[76] Cf. n. 39; as for the Latin cognate, it is *formus/forma/formum* "hot."

[77] Cf. Kuryłowicz, *Accentuation* 115; also *idem, Inflectional Categories* 212.

[78] Cf. Schwyzer, *GG* I 468 f; also Chantraine, *Formation* (n. 43) 78 f, who points out the synchronic independence (from -ιος) of -ία as substantival formant. Besides adjectives, substantives could likewise motivate abstract substantives in -ία. The channel for such a transfer was probably decomposition: e.g. positive καρπία ← substantive καρπός on the basis of negative ἀκαρπία

71

Latin: *āstūtia* (vs. *āstūtus*), *fācundia* (vs. *fācundus*), *modestia* (vs. *modestus*), *superbia* (vs. *superbus*), etc.[79] As for Baltic, the type κάκη is residually attested: hence Lithuanian *dorà* "morality" ← *dõras* "moral," *geltà* "yellowness, yellow yarn, jaundice" ← *geltas* "yellow," *raudà* "redness, red yarn, erubescence" ← *raũdas* "red," etc.[80] Yet, just as the type κάκη was replaced by κακίᾱ, so also *raudà* by *raũdė* "red color (on e.g. a variegated yarn)"; other Lithuanian examples of this category are *kaltė* "crime" ← *kaltas* "guilty"; *láisvė* "freedom, license" ← *laĩsvas* "free"; *plìkė* "baldness, bare and deserted place" ← *plìkas* "bare, deserted"; *šveñtė* "holiday" ← *šveñtas* "holy"; *vertė* "value" ← *veřtas* "worth-(y)"; etc.[81] This denominative type has become unproductive, however, and an indirect indication of its breakdown is the semantic specialization in several constituents of the category (e.g. *šveñtė* "holiday" ⇐ "holiness"); there is also a direct and conclusive indication, i.e. the replacement of simplex *-ė* by complex *-ýbė* as marker of abstract substantives derived from adjectives: hence e.g. new *kaltýbė* vs. old *kaltė*.[82] We have already seen a parallel development,

---

← adjective ἄκαρπος/ἄκαρπον. In fact, there are several abstract substantives in -ίᾱ which are attested only as compounds: e.g. ἀδικίᾱ, ἀναρχίᾱ, γεωργίᾱ, ἐπιδημίᾱ, etc. This type of constraint is noticeably frequent in the Homeric corpus: cf. Chantraine, *Formation* 79 f. Compound-formations might also be the original impetus for the extension of abstract-formants *-ā- and *-iᾱ- onto athematic stems: e.g. πέδ-η "fetter," while seemingly motivated by the substantival athematic-stem πεδ-/ποδ- (as in Doric πώς and Ionic πούς "foot"), actually could have been constituted by the adjectival thematic-stem compound -πεδος, as in ἑκατόμ-πεδος (vs. the coexisting adjectival ἑκατόμ-πους). In other words, I propose that the compound -πέδη was older than simplex -πέδη; the former is also still attested, albeit with its own semantic restriction, in e.g. ἱστο-πέδη "mast-base." Likewise πάτρᾱ could have been constituted by the adjectival thematic-stem -πατρος, as in ὄ-πατρος.

[79] Cf. Leumann, *LG* 208 f.

[80] Surveyed by Otrębski, *Gramatyka* (n. 2) II 38.

[81] Surveyed by Otrębski, *Gramatyka* II 46.

[82] Cf. again Otrębski, *Gramatyka* II 46; for a descriptive survey, cf. Senn, (n. 2) 327 f.

where simplex -*ė* has been replaced by e.g. -*imas/-ymas* as productive marker of abstract substantives derived from verbs.[83] But there is another parallel development even more crucial: previously I have posited that the deverbative formant which is now -*ė* had been already moribund at the period of the prehistoric contraction {*/-iịā-/ > */-ē-/},[84] so that there arise variations predetermined by whether *-(i)ịā- had or had not been perceived as a productive formant on a given base, whence -*ė* and -*ia* respectively; presently I can posit that the corresponding denominative formant which is now -*ė* had been likewise moribund at the same period of contraction: here too there are variations under the same conditions, ultimately leading to pairs such as dialectal *kalčià* vs. standard *kaltė̃* "crime," dialectal *verčià* vs. standard *vertė̃* "value," etc.[85]

§13. We have by now observed that (1) the Lithuanian declensional types -*is*(-*ỹs*), -*ė* are reflexes of the IE formants *-iịo-, *-iịā- respectively and (2) the still-productive adjectival motivation {-*ė* ← -*is*(-*ỹs*)} is in turn a reflex of {*-iịā- ← *-iịo-}. But we have yet to examine certain complications apparent in those instances of -*is*(-*ỹs*)/-*ė* where the pristine adjectival function of these formants is still preserved. A suitable example is the comparative-formant -*ėsnis/-ėsnė*. The problem at hand is that in contrast to e.g. an undetermined *jaun-ėsnis/jaun-ėsnė* "younger," the determined counterpart is *jaun-esnỹsis/jaun-esnióji* "the younger." Why, then, is the productive formant here -*esnióji* in standard

---

[83] Cf. n. 50. The formal divergence between deverbative -*imas/-ymas* and denominative -*ýbė* helps determine whether a given abstract substantive in -*ė* had been motivated by verb or adjective respectively. Actually, ambiguous instances are few, but one of these happens to be *kaltė̃*: cf. the verb *kal̃s-ti* "become guilty" (Leskien, *Bildung* [n. 45] 272) besides the adjective *kal̃tas* "guilty." The fact that it is *kaltýbė* which had replaced *kaltė̃* indicates an original denominative motivation for the latter.

[84] Cf. § 10.

[85] Surveyed by Otrębski, *Gramatyka* (n. 2) II 72; cf. also § 6 again.

contemporary Lithuanian, and not *-esnė̃ji? What has to be explained is the split of -ė́- for simplex (undetermined) vs. -io- for complex (determined).[86]

§14. The key to the whole question is that the type -ėsnis was originally not an i̯o-stem, but rather, a simple i-stem: we find proof for this etymology from the attestations of nominative/accusative singular neuter -esn(i) in Old Lithuanian texts.[87] But instances of the latter form are merely archaic reflexes: the actual state of affairs in contemporary Lithuanian and Latvian is that all etymological i-stems have been replaced with iᵢo-stems in adjectival categories; in substantival categories, on the other hand, i-stems have survived. That the formal displacement of i-stems by iᵢo-stems had thus been restricted to adjectives serves as a signal clue in detecting the channel for this process. In Baltic, as also in other IE dialects, the pronominal and the substantival declension are maximally distinct, while the adjectival declension shares features with both: thus it formally falls between, so to speak, the paradigms of the substantives and pronouns. Consequently, we can expect instances of cross-leveling between adjective and pronoun to the exclusion of substantive, or between adjective and substantive to the exclusion of pronoun. The former of these two possibilities is manifested here: there is cross-leveling between adjectives with i-stem and pronouns with an archaic conflation of i-stem and iᵢo-stem—as seen in the Lithuanian type jìs/jõ/jám/jį̃/juõ/jamè/etc.[88] While

---

[86] The segmentation of -Cio- (= -C'o-) here as -C-io- is only etymological, not synchronic; cf. § 10.

[87] Cf. Stang, (n. 2) 189, 259 ff. Cf. also P. Arumaa, "Sur les adjectifs en -i dans les langues baltiques," *Mélanges linguistiques offerts à M. Holger Pedersen* (Aarsskrift for Aarhus Universitet 9.1 [København 1937]) 431–442.

[88] For an important discussion of jìs/jõ/ ... (masculine) and jì/jõs/ ... (feminine), as well as of the etymologically corresponding enclitics marking determined adjectives (-is/-io/ ... and -ji/-ios/ ...), cf. Stang, *Vergleichende Grammatik* 233 f. Baltic shows traces of declensional quantitative apophony:

74

these Baltic pronominal *i-/ii̯o*-stems served as bridge for the formal transition of adjectival *i*-stems to adjectival *ii̯o*-stems (whence e.g. *-èsnis/-èsnio/*...), the substantival *i*-stems could remain unaffected.[89] Another factor contributing to the interaction of *i-/ii̯o*-stem pronouns and *i*-stem adjectives is that the most basic representative of the former category, the pronoun **i-/ii̯-o-* (feminine **ii̯-ā-*), had been generalized enclitically in Baltic as marker of the determined adjective: thus the obligatory juxtaposition (in the determined adjectival category) of an original *i*-stem or *ii̯o*-stem with the etymological equivalent of *jìs/jõ/*... (as in the type *jaun-esn-ỹs-is/jaun-èsn-io-jo/*...) enhances the cross-leveling in these determined forms, and thence in the undetermined forms as well (as in the type *jaun-èsn-is/jaun-èsn-io/*...).

§15. The task now is to show the connection between the *i*-stem etymology in the masculine type *-èsnis/-esnỹsis* and the simplex/complex split of *-é-/-io-* in its correlate, the feminine type *-èsné/-esnióji*. What at first seems an irrelevant factor turns out to be a crucial element in the proposed solution: to wit, the feminine gender in Baltic *u*-stem adjectives. Here we find a formant **-ī-/-i̯ā-*, added directly to the base, not to the stem with **-u-*; hence the following typical pattern:

	masculine stem **-u-*	feminine stem **-ī-/-i̯ā-*	inanimate stem **-u-*
nominative	*plat-ùs* "broad"	*plat-ì*	*plat-ù*
genitive	*plat-aũs*	*plač-iõs*	
etc.			

ø-grade **i-s* in the masculine nominative singular (cf. *is* in Latin, Gothic) vs. e.g. **i̯-ō* > Lithuanian *juõ*, instrumental singular; the *j-* from such oblique cases then pervades the nominative, whence Lithuanian *jìs*. Likewise, feminine nominative singular *jì* can be reconstructed as **ī* (< **iə₂*), vs. e.g. **i̯-eə₂-s* > **i̯-ās* > Lithuanian *jõs*, genitive singular feminine. For dialectal attestations of *is* and *i* (also of *jis* and *i*, *is* and *jý*, etc.) corresponding to standard *jìs* and *jì*, cf. Zinkevičius, *Lietuvių dialektologija* (n. 2) § 204.

[89] Cf. again Stang, *Vergleichende Grammatik* 189, 258 ff.

It is important to notice that feminine counterparts of *u*-stems do not show constituent formants in -*ė*-, only in -*io*- (the segmentation here is again etymological, facilitated by Lithuanian orthography); e.g. masculine *nuobodùs* "tedious" → feminine *nuobodì/nuobodžiõs/núobodžiai*/etc. Hence we cannot reconstruct *-i̯ā- here for such oblique cases as the genitive singular, only *-i̯ā-. The obsolescence of adjectival *-i̯ā- had been prompted by the absence of a motivating form *-i̯o- (Baltic *-i̯a-), since the foundation here is {*-u- → *-ī-/-i̯ā-}, not {*-i̯o- → *-i̯ā-}.[90] With this set of circumstances in mind, I now propose that there also had been in Baltic a foundation {*-i- → *-ī-/-i̯ā-}; in other words, that *-ī-/-i̯ā- had been generalized in Baltic as feminine formant of *i*-stem as well as *u*-stem adjectives.

§16.

masculine stem	feminine stem	inanimate stem
*-i-	*-ī-/-i̯ā-	*-i-
*-u-	*-ī-/-i̯ā-	*-u-

In Old Lithuanian texts, there are clear traces of *-ī-/-i̯ā- attested for the feminine gender of originally *i*-stem adjectives, such as the type in -*ėsnis*. For each instance to be cited here, we can also adduce a formal parallel from the feminine gender of *u*-stem adjectives. Probably the soundest procedure is to show the relevant feminine correlates of *u*-stem masculine adjectives first, then the corresponding feminine correlates of masculine *i*-stems. The determined feminine, then, of *kartùs* "bitter" (undetermined feminine *kartì*) is regularly *karčióji* in standard Lithuanian; likewise *saldùs* "sweet" → *saldì* → *saldžióji*. But in Daukša's *Postille* (published 1599), we see *kartýji* (spelled *kartiii*) instead of *karčióji;* also *saldýji* instead of *saldžióji*.[91] Of course the type

[90] Cf. § 7. Once a foundation {*-i̯o- → *-iiā-} broke down, *-i̯ā- could become *-i̯ā- (unmotivated); cf. also § 6.
[91] Cf. Senn, *Grammatik* (n. 2) 167; also Sommer, *Stämme* (n. 1) 306 f.

-*yji*/-*iosios* is more archaic than -*ioji*/-*iosios*: the latter simply reveals paradigmatic leveling, with the ouster of *·ī- in *-ī-i̧ī by the *-i̧ā- of oblique cases as in genitive singular -*iosios* (< *-i̧ās-i̧ās). In sum, *u*-stems show feminine nominative singular -*i̧* (< *-ī) in the undetermined form of the adjective, and -*ýji* later replaced by -*ióji* in the determined. Likewise with the suffixal -*ėsn-is*: in the determined form of the adjective, we see the productive nominative singular feminine formant -*esn-ióji*, but there are still residual attestations of -*esn-ýji*.[92] Even more important, there are clear attestations of an archaic undetermined nominative singular feminine -*esni* besides the current -*ėsnė*: not only does the former coexist with the latter in e.g. Daukša's *Postille*,[93] but it is even found later in such strophic "Lieder" as the *dainos* of Garleva (Godlewa).[94] Then too, in the *pasakos* ("Märchen") of Garleva collected by Brugmann,[95] we can actually formulate a surviving synchronic constraint on the distribution of -*ėsni* vs. -*ėsnė;* to wit, simplex -*i* → comparative -*ėsni*, as in *graži̧* → *gražėsni*; vs. the unmarked formal relationship of simplex -*a* → comparative -*ėsnė*, as in *gerà* → *gerėsnė*.[96] Despite such restricted or residual attestations, a

---

[92] Cf. Sommer, *Stämme* 308.

[93] Cf. Sommer, *Stämme* 311 f.

[94] Cf. Sommer, *Stämme* 301, 308, 311 f. Sommer had selected the relevant forms from the texts of *dainos* assembled by K. Brugmann, "Litauische Lieder, Märchen, Hochzeitbittersprüche aus Godlewa," contained in *Litauische Volkslieder und Märchen aus dem preussischen und dem russischen Litauen*, gesammelt von A. Leskien und K. Brugman [sic] (Strassburg 1882).

[95] *Volkslieder und Märchen* (n. 94).

[96] Cf. Sommer, *Stämme* 311. For the value of *pasakos* in contrast with *dainos*, cf. the elegant summary of Gauthiot, *Le parler de Buividze* (n. 132) 2:

En effet, Brugmann a établi dès 1882 (*Litauische Volkslieder und Märchen* p. 84, 85) que les *pasakos* ont une valeur singulièrement plus grande que les *dainos*, au point de vue de la connaissance des dialectes. Il a fait remarquer que les chants sont en style noble; que le mètre est un puissant instrument soit de conservation, soit d'altération; que les *dainos* enfin sont vagabondes, et que pour passer d'un domaine dialectal dans un autre, elles ne sont pas transposées exactement d'un dialecte en un autre.

usual sign of archaism, Sommer doubted that the type
-*èsn-i/-esn-ýji* could have been older than -*èsn-è/-esn-ióji*,
because of this aporia: if -*è* here were a mere innovation
replacing -*i*, then why was there no such replacement also
with e.g. *u*-stems?[97] In other words, why is *nuobodì*, not
*nuobodè, the feminine counterpart of nominative singular
masculine *nuobodùs?* It is to Sommer's lasting credit that he
saw the crucial answer to his own question: "Diese Schwierigkeit könnte man noch vielleicht dadurch umgehen, dass man
die Regel so fasste: -*è* ist nur da beim Adjektiv an Stelle von
-*ī* getreten, wo im Maskulinum eine Form auf -*is* korres-
pondierte, um ein regelmässiges Verhältnis herzustellen:
also wohl . . . -*ēsné* zu -*ēsnis*, aber Bewahrung des Alten in
saldì zu *saldùs*."[98] That he should then reject his intuitive
solution with the remark "Damit wäre indes die Frage nur
verschoben, nicht beantwortet"[99] must not be faulted,
however. Sommer here was simply being a doctrinal minimal-
ist, who chose to avoid a procedure then prevalent in
linguistic investigation, whereby morphological change
could be perfunctorily explained away by the arbitrary
invocation of a nebulous factor termed analogy. And yet, as
Kuryłowicz has shown in the article "Procès analogiques"
often cited here, if function as well as form is taken into
consideration, it is indeed possible to formulate empirically
certain trends of morphological rearrangement in such
strictly analogical frames of reference as proportions,
quadrants, and the like. In the particular instance at hand,
granted, it would be methodologically questionable to posit
the creation of a new feminine -*è* on the basis of masculine
-*is*(-*ȳs*), if it were simply on the grounds of a formal parallelism with pre-existing -*is*(-*ȳs*)/-*è*. This is the level of the solution

[97] Sommer, *Stämme* 308 f.
[98] Sommer, *Stämme* 309.
[99] *Ibid.*

which Sommer must have had in mind, and which as it stood he was justified in rejecting. But we have already seen[100] that there is not just a formal but also a synchronically functional relationship between -*is*(-*ỹs*) and -*ė*, with the declensional ensemble of the latter motivated by that of the former; furthermore, this motivation is diachronically the reflex of an original correlation {*-iịo- → *-iịā-}. Thus it is possible to dismiss Sommer's objection to the solution which he foresaw, if we reformulate as follows: the absence of a foundation {-*is*(-*ỹs*) → -*ė*} is the reason for the survival of e.g. -*i* in *nuobodì*, while the development of this same foundation in e.g. suffixal -*ėsn-is* (because the *i*-stem here became *iịo*-stem) resulted in the displacement of -*i* by -*ė* in -*ėsn-ė* (vs. residual -*ėsn-i*). But such productive displacement of *-ī-/-ịā*- by *-ē-* (in etymological terms) took place only in the undetermined feminine: the older form was generalized in the restricted function of the marked, determined counterpart.[101] Hence *-ē-* in the simplex vs. *-ī-/-ịā*- in the complex: i.e., -*ė*/-*ės*/... vs. -*yịi*/-*iosios*/..., with the latter ultimately becoming leveled into -*ioji*/-*iosios*/.... In standard contemporary Lithuanian, then, we find the following hierarchy of foundations for the comparative formant:

$$-\textit{ėsn-is} \rightarrow -\textit{ėsn-ė} \rightarrow -\textit{esn-ióji}.$$

The ultimate cause, to repeat, of both these new foundations was the formal metastasis in the ancestral form of masculine -*ėsnis* from *i*-stem to *iịo*-stem.

§17. Similarly with the adjectival type *dìdis* "great": its declension can be explained in the same terms as that of

---

[100] Cf. § 7.

[101] Applicable here is Kuryłowicz's axiom IV: "Quand à la suite d'une transformation morphologique une forme subit la différenciation, la forme nouvelle correspond à sa fonction primaire (de fondation), la forme ancienne est réservée pour la fonction secondaire (fondée)." Cf. Kuryłowicz, "Procès analogiques" 169.

-ėsnis. Like the latter, *dìdis* had originally been an *i*-stem adjective, as seen from such attested forms as locative singular *didimè* in Old Lithuanian texts.[102] With the paradigm of *dìdis* as with that of *-ėsnis*, the following hierarchy of foundations is operative in standard Lithuanian:

$$dìdis \rightarrow dìdė \rightarrow didžióji.$$

Just as we have seen sporadic attestations of *-esni/-esnyji* in Lithuanian,[103] so also we find an archaic formant *-ī-/-i̯ā-* in the residual feminine *didì/didžiõs/...* (simplex) and *didýji/ didžiõsios/...* (complex).[104] The older *didýji* is replaced in standard Lithuanian by *didžióji*, as also *-esnýji* by *-esnióji*. (In the *Naujas Testamentas*, the forms *didýji* and *didžióji* still coexist.[105]) In sum, the feminine correlate *didì/didžiõs/...* of an *i*-stem masculine adjective had been displaced by *dìdė/dìdės/...*, once the old *i*-stem had become a new *i̯o*-stem masculine; the displaced *didì/didžiõs/...* then became generalized in the determined function of the adjective, whence *didýji/didžiõsios/...*, homalized as *didžióji/didžiõsios/...* in standard Lithuanian.

§18. A source of controversy remains: besides the standard declension of the simplex feminine of *dìdis* as *dìdė/dìdės/...*, Sommer had found several surviving instances of an apparent hesitation between *dìdė/dìdės/...* and *dìdė/didžiõs/...*;[106] likewise between *-ėsnė/-ėsnės/...* and *-esnė/-esnios/...*.[107] For example, the genitive singular appears as both *dìdės* and *didžiõs* in the *Naujas Testamentas*.[108] On the basis of such distributions, Sommer decided that the pattern *dìdė/didžiõs/...*

---

[102] Cf. Stang, *Vergleichende Grammatik* (n. 2) 260.

[103] Cf. nn. 92–94.

[104] Attestations of the rare nominatives *didì* and *didýji* have been collected by Sommer, *Stämme* (n. 1) 308.

[105] *Ibid.*

[106] Sommer, *Stämme* 288 ff.

[107] Sommer, *Stämme* 300 ff; also "Nachlese" 399.

[108] Sommer, *Stämme* 288, 292.

was inherited and that the intraparadigmatic distinction between -*é*- and -*io*- should be explained in terms of phonologically divergent developments in absolute vs. merely syllabic *Auslaut*.[109] From the preceding etymological considerations, however, there emerges a satisfactory alternative explanation, based on morphological rather than on phonological grounds. Put briefly, the displacements of e.g. *didì* by *dìdé* and of *didžiõs* by *dìdés* are not on the same structural level. In the unmarked nominative singular, *dìdé* ousts *didì* as the result of a functional and formal motivation by the unmarked masculine counterpart, nominative singular *dìdis;* in such a marked case as the genitive (singular), on the other hand, the motivation of feminine *didžiõs* by masculine *dìdžio* is indirect and secondary to its motivation by the old nominative singular, *didì*.[110] Thus with the displacement of *didì* by *dìdé*, the primary motivation of the feminine genitive singular by the feminine nominative singular ultimately wins out, and results in the displacement of *didžiõs* by *dìdés*. But this, to repeat, is an indirect ouster in comparison with the displacement of *didì* by *dìdé*. From the lexical point of view, then, motivation of one declension (*dìdé/dìdés/*...) by another (*dìdis/dìdžio/*...) is channeled primarily through the functionally unmarked case-category of nominative singular. The motivation of *dìdés* by *dìdé* is a separate development, perhaps chronologically distinguishable from {*dìdis* → *dìdé*}; in that case, we could even posit

[109] Sommer, *Stämme* 290 *et passim*. For a brief discussion and bibliography of the disputes generated by Sommer's theory, cf. Schmalstieg, "Baltic *ei*" (n. 2) 261 ff.

[110] In general terms of declensional slots rather than specific forms here, I assume that the masculine nominative singular is unmarked in both case and gender, while the corresponding feminine is unmarked in case only. For a typological discussion of case-systems, with definitions and illustrations of the feature marked/unmarked as frame of reference, cf. R. Jakobson, "Beitrag zur allgemeinen Kasuslehre," *Travaux du Cercle Linguistique de Prague* 6 (1936) 240–288; reprinted in *Readings in Linguistics* II, ed. E. P. Hamp, F. W. Householder, R. Austerlitz (Chicago 1966) 51–89.

three declensional stages in the simplex feminine of *dìdis*:
(1) *didì*/*didžiõs*/..., (2) *dìdė*/*didžiõs*/..., (3) *dìdė*/*dìdės*/.... But
such an issue is marginal, and the essential fact remains that
in standard Lithuanian, formal parallelism between *dìdės*
and *dìdė* has taken precedence over that between *didžiõs* and
dìdžio (masculine genitive singular).

§19. One further complication has to be considered in the
history of this contextually widespread and semantically
overloaded word *dìdis*. Besides an archaic *i*-stem configuration, there is also attested a *u*-stem counterpart, *didùs* "exalted,
proud."[111] The regular pattern of *u*-stem adjectives implies
the simplex feminine counterpart *didì*/*didžiõs*/..., as seen
in *platùs* "broad" → *platì*/*plačiõs*/...; likewise, parallel to
e.g. (*saldùs* →) *saldì* → *saldžióji* is *didì* → *didžióji*. From the
synchronic standpoint, we can therefore expect formal
convergence in the determined feminine slots of *dìdis* and
didùs:

$$didùs \rightarrow didì \rightarrow didžióji$$
$$dìdis \rightarrow dìdė \rightarrow didžióji.$$

The syncretism in the third column could be canceled if the
feminine of *dìdis* were not to undergo the operative formal
split of -*ė*- for the undetermined and -*io*- for the determined
function of the feminine adjective. In other words, for the
sake of maximal distinction between the two paradigms of
dìdis and *didùs*, the less essential distinction between simplex
-*ė*- and complex -*io*- within the one paradigm of *dìdis* is
liable to suspension,[112] whence the following rearrangement:

$$didùs \rightarrow didì \rightarrow didžióji$$
$$dìdis \rightarrow dìdė \rightarrow didėji.$$

---

[111] Cf. Senn, *Grammatik* (n. 2) 153: also Fraenkel, *LEW* (n. 2) s.v. *dìdis*.
As for the latter-day standard form, it is the compound *iš-didùs*.

[112] Applicable here is Kuryłowicz's axiom V: "Pour rétablir une différence
d'ordre central la langue abandonne une différence d'ordre plus marginal."
Cf. Kuryłowicz, "Procès analogiques" 170.

The form *didĕji* is clearly attested in Daukša's *Postille*: nominative singular *didéii*, genitive singular *didesios*, etc.;[113] likewise in Klein's *Grammatica Lituanica* (published 1653): nominative singular *dideji*.[114] In e.g. the dialect of Tverečius too, we find genitive singular *dz'idĕs'ās* besides *dz'idz'ãs'ās* (= standard *didžiõsios*).[115] Finally, there is also an interesting extension: on the model of determined feminine genitive singular and nominative plural *-iosios*, there had apparently developed from the genitive singular *did-ĕsios* a leveled form *did-ĕsés*, attested as *didḁsseś* in Daukša's *Katechismus* (published 1595)[116] and also sporadically in contemporary dialects, e.g. in the Dozuhnen-*pasakos* edited by C. Cappeller.[117]

§20. From the preceding discussion, there emerges this axiom: if the feminine stem-formant of a Lithuanian adjective is *-é-* in the undetermined and *-io-* in the determined categories, then the corresponding masculine in *-is(-ȳs)* is to be derived from an original *i*-stem, not *i̯o*-stem. As already seen, the type *didĕji* is exempt because of an original conflict between *i*-stem (whence *dìdis*) and *u*-stem (whence

[113] Cf. Sommer, *Stämme* (n. 1) 292 f.
[114] *Apud* A. Bezzenberger, *Beiträge zur Geschichte der litauischen Sprache auf Grund litauischer Texte des XVI. und des XVII. Jahrhunderts* (Göttingen 1877) 7.
[115] Cf. Otrębski, *Gramatyka* (n. 2) III 119.
[116] Cf. Sommer, *Stämme* (n. 1) 357, 360. For other posited instances of similar desinential leveling, cf. *Stämme* 142, 212, 311.
[117] "Zwölf Pasakos aus dem preussischen Südlitauen," *Indogermanische Forschungen* 31 (1912–1913) 447: *iš tos didĕsés ùpés*; cf. also Sommer, *Stämme* 360 f; also e.g. Senn, *Grammatik* (n. 2) 166. There is a variant *-osés* commonly cited in grammars as a dialectal form of the determined genitive singular and nominative plural of *ā*-stem adjectives. For an important discussion of such alleged attestations cf. Sommer, *Stämme* 356–360, where he argues that *-osés* is simply a false standardization of *-oses* = *-os'æs* < *-āsi̯ās*, with shortening of *-ā-* to *-a-* (> *-æ-* after palatalized consonant) in the final syllable. The type *did-ĕsés* is quite distinct, since in e.g. the dialect of Daukša or in the Dozuhnen-material, vowels in final syllable are not shortened, and attestations of *-osios* on other bases coexist with *-ĕsés* on the base *did-*; cf. again Sommer, *Stämme* 360 f.

didùs) in the masculine. With such an exception duly taken into account, we would expect this formulation to be a useful etymological criterion. And yet, a descriptive survey of standard contemporary Lithuanian shows that it is not, for the simple reason that many adjectives have no determined form to match the undetermined. In Senn's grammar, the sum total of adjectives is divided into three classes; class III is comprised of forms in *-is(-ȳs)/-ė* exclusively, while we find *dìdis, -ėsnis*, their respective derivatives, and less than a score of other forms with *-is(-ȳs)/-ė* in the sub-class C of class I.[118] The crucial point is that class III, with its immense lexical repertory, regularly has no determined forms[119]—a constraint which we can connect with the fact that the adjectives of this class are generally free to become functional substantives.[120] Confronted with this formal vacuum in class III, we have no way of testing the criterion just developed, in order to determine whether any constituents of this category were originally *i*-stems, not *i̯o*-stems. But at least for some forms in class III, another criterion is still feasible, because of a curious formal split in the feminine gender. Such is the case with the diminutive suffix in *-áitis/-áitė*. By chance, the factor essential to the new criterion is in this instance the same one which obliterated the previously-formulated criterion: namely, that this suffix had become transformed from marker of adjectives to marker of substantives. In other words, the substantival specialization of what is now *-áitė* had been the impetus for the formal split about to be outlined. The specific productive function of the substantival formant *-áitis/-áitė* as diminutive-marker of a corresponding simplex substantive is still to be detected in e.g. the language of the

---

[118] Cf. Senn, *Grammatik* 142–172.
[119] Cf. Senn, *Grammatik* 162 f; only three exceptions are listed (p. 163).
[120] *Ibid.*

dainos.[121] Among the general and literary attestations of
-áitis/-áitė as diminutive suffix, we find the following:

jaunikáitis ← *jaunìkis* "suitor"
kunigáitis "seminarian" ← *kùnigas* "priest"
lopšeláitis (double diminutive: *-el-* + *-áitis*) ← *lopšỹs* "cradle"
akáitė ← *akìs* "eye"
giráitė ← *gìrė* "forest"
naktáitė ← *naktìs* "night"
sesáitė ← *sesuõ* "sister"
širdužáitė (double diminutive: *-už-* + *-áitė*) ← *širdìs* "heart"
etc.[122]

Besides forms in *-áitė* with diminutive meaning, however,
there also exist substantives with e.g. nominative singular
-aičia, and here the semantic sphere is restricted to the function of marking patronymics:

ércikaičia "Kurprinzessin"
klebonaičia "Pfarrerstochter"
Manichéušaičiomis "Manichäermädchen" (in Daukša's *Postille*)
name *Karaliūnaičia* (← *Karaliūnas*, etymologically "prince")
etc.[123]

For Sommer, this distribution of *-aičia* vs. *-áitė* raises another
aporia: "Warum die unkontrahierte Form [i.e. *-aičia*]
bei den Patronymica, die kontrahierte [i.e. *-áitė*] beim
deminutiven Gebrauch bevorzugt wird, ist nicht mehr zu
ermitteln."[124] But perhaps we can explain this split on the
basis of Kuryłowicz's typological axiom IV:[125] the new form
-áitė has usurped the primary function of diminutive-marker
in the feminine, so that the older form *-aičia* is relegated
to the secondary function of marking the patronymic, a
semantic specialization of the diminutive function. As for

---

[121] Cf. Leskien, *Bildung* (n. 45) 574 f.
[122] *Ibid.*; also Otrębski, *Gramatyka* (n. 2) II 261 f.
[123] Cf. Sommer, *Stämme* (n. 1) 100; also again Otrębski, *Gramatyka* II 261 f.
[124] Sommer, *Stämme* 101.
[125] Cf. n. 101.

the etymology of the older form, I propose that it had been *-aiti/-aičios/..., later leveled to -aičia/-aičios/....[126] In other words, the formal and functional split in the feminine implies that the masculine -áitis had originally been an *i*-stem, and that once this *i*-stem was supplanted by an *iio*-stem, the original feminine *-aiti/-aičios/... was in turn displaced by -áitė/-áitės/..., whence the ultimate availability of a contrast between old and new configurations of the feminine. But whereas the analogous split of e.g. -esn-io- and -esn-ė- is inflectional, it is lexical in the instance of -aič-io- and -ait-ė-.[127] In certain instances, of course, the attestation of -aičia beside -áitė is not functionally motivated but residual, in that some lexical entities with inherited suffixal *-aiti/-aičios could not become specialized as a patronymic, by virtue of the actual semantic content of the stem: thus for example both older and newer feminine counterparts are still attested for masculine dieváitis "Götze," namely dieváičia vs. dieváitė—and yet they are both defined as "Göttin."[128]

§21. For the type -áitis/-áitė, a basic additional shift has yet to be mentioned, from the standpoint of contemporary

---

[126] The IE-inherited type *-ī/-jās/... is regularly leveled to -ia/-ios/... in Lithuanian substantives, from *-i/-ios/...; in standard contemporary Lithuanian, the archaic unleveled type has survived only in patì/pačiõs/... "self (feminine), Ehefrau" and martì/marčiõs/... "daughter-in-law"; cf. Senn (n. 2) 123; cf. also Zinkevičius, Lietuvių dialektologija (n. 2) § 323 for such dialectal forms as viešnì "female guest" (vs. standard viešnià), pačià, marčià.

[127] There is a closely parallel split likewise in the feminine of -ýtis: namely -yč-io- and -yt-ė-. The same explanation holds for this split, but examples of -yč-io- and -yt-ė- are not discussed here on the same level as -aič-io- and -ait-ė- because of a complication with forms in -yč-io-: an additional factor operative here is the possible intrusion of slavisms, if indeed some Lithuanian substantives in -yčia involve borrowings from Slavic correlates in -ica; cf. Otrębski, Gramatyka (n. 2) II 258: e.g. bažnýčia "church" vs. *božьnica; or again, on an apparently suffixal level, akmenyčia (← akmuõ "stone") vs. e.g. Polish kamienica.

[128] F. Kurschat, Wörterbuch der littauischen [sic] Sprache I: Deutsch-littauisches Wörterbuch (Halle 1870–1874) s.v. "Göttin." Cf. also Sommer, Stämme (n. 1) 100.

standard Lithuanian: the type -*áitis*/-*áitė* has ceased to be productive diminutive-marker, and the latter function is now reserved for such types as -*ēlis*/-*ēlė*, etc.[129] With this displacement from the general diminutive function, another cycle has been completed, in that it is now the turn of -*áitis*/-*áitė* to become restricted to the specialized function of patronymic, whereas previously it had been the once-productive diminutive -*áitė* which forced the older -*aičia* into the same patronymic rôle. Examples of -*áitis*/-*áitė* in their latest function of patronymic-marker are readily found in descriptive grammars of contemporary Lithuanian:

kalváitis "smith's son" (also name *Kalváitis*) ← *kálvis* "smith"
karaláitis "king's son" ← *karãlius* "king"
našláitis "Waisenknabe, orphan" ← *našlỹs* "widower"
gimináitis "relative" ← *giminė̃* "family, lineage"
saváitis "relative" ← *sãvas* "one's own [adjectival]"
Kuršáitis (dialectally *Kuršãtis*, germanized *Kurschat*) ← *kuřšis* "Curonian"
etc.[130]

Besides the general correlative function of the patronymic feminine -*áitė* as in e.g. *našláitė* "Waisenmädchen" vs. *našláitis* "Waisenknabe," there is also a productive specialization as suffix for the family-name of girls and unmarried women. Thus for example a girl whose father's name is *Klìmas* can be designated as *Klimáitė*, while her mother's

---

[129] For a list of productive diminutive formants, cf. Senn, *Grammatik* (n. 2) 330 ff. Even -*ēl-ė* is etymologically an *i*-stem, as seen from residual attestations of -*el-io-* (collected by Sommer, *Stämme* 212); but the latter was not preserved in a productive secondary function, as was e.g. -*aič-io-* vs. -*ait-ė-*.

[130] Cf. Otrębski, *Gramatyka* (n. 2) II 261; also Senn, *Grammatik* (n. 2) 329. It is sometimes possible to set specific *termini ante quem* for the obsolescence, in specific areas, of this formant even as productive patronymic; for example, the linguistic evidence of church-records indicates that in the Central Lithuanian of the *Memelgebiet*, -*ātis* (< -*aitis*) had ceased to be a productive marker of patronymics by around 1850: W. Fenzlau, *Die deutschen Formen der litauischen Orts- und Personennamen des Memelgebiets* (Halle an der Saale: Niemeyer, 1936) 113.

name, in the latter's rôle as married woman, would be marked by another suffix, *-ienė*; hence *Klimíenė*. Other examples:

$$Petráuskas \rightarrow \begin{cases} Petrauskíenė \\ Petrauskáitė \end{cases}$$

$$Krêvễ \rightarrow \begin{cases} Krêvíenė \\ Krêváitė \end{cases}$$

etc.[131]

§22. As for the phonological mechanism in the putative Baltic contractions {*/-iį̃a-/ > */-ī̃-/} and {*/-iį̃ā-/ > */-ē̃-/}, I propose that the motivation can be detected from a Baltic trend, {*-ǎ- > *-ǽ-, after *-į̃-}. On the synchronic level, this phenomenon is well attested in Lithuanian—not just in the *Aukštaĩčiai*-dialects generally but also in the standard literary dialect specifically: thus C' + a ⇒ C'æ and Vį̃ + a ⇒ Vį̃æ, as in *svẽčias* [sv'æ̀æ̀č'æs] "guest" and *vẽjas* [v'èeį̃æs] "wind" respectively.[132] Even in such an early Lithuanian text as Daukša's *Postille* (published 1599),

---

[131] For a list of these types and for indications of formal constraints, cf. Senn, *Grammatik* (n. 2) 334. This usage can readily be detected in church-records. For example, in the *Trauregister* of Piktupönen for the year 1833, we read about the wedding of a man "Szuggars mit der Ane Miellulate, des verst. Willus Miellulis von Kreiwoenen Tochter"; but in the same *Register*, there is occasional displacement of *-ātė* (< *-aitė*) by another suffix, *-ikė*: e.g. for the year 1830, we read "Peteratikke, des verst. Ensys Peterat Tochter"; further, while "Gauptate, des Wirt Kristup Gauptys Tochter" is likewise attested for 1830, by 1844 there occurs "Maryke Gauptikke," side-by-side with old formations still showing *-ātė*. Cf. Fenzlau, *Die deutschen Formen* (n. 130) 112 f.

[132] For a description, cf. Senn, *Grammatik* (n. 2) 70; for a general discussion, cf. Leskien, *Litauisches Lesebuch* (n. 2) 146 and Otrębski, *Gramatyka* (n. 2) I 219. It is also apt here to cite a substandard exemplar from the *Aukštaĩčiai*-group: for the dialect of the village Buivydžiai, the standard type *svẽčias* is actually transcribed as *svẽčes* by R. Gauthiot, *Le parler de Buividze: Essai de description d'un dialecte lituanien oriental* (Paris 1903) 105. The value of the latter work in general has been discussed by E. P. Hamp, "Buividze Lithuanian Phonemes," *International Journal of Slavic Linguistics and Poetics* 1/2 (1959) 195–202.

II. §23

there are instances of free variation in the spelling of ⟨a⟩ and ⟨e⟩ after /C'/ or /Vi̯/, as seen e.g. in the representations corresponding to the latter-day standard *svẽčias* and *vẽjas*: hence *swecžei* (nominative plural), *sweczéis* (instrumental plural); *wéias* and *wéies* (both nominative singular), *wéiei* (nominative plural), *wéiamus* and *wéiemus* (both dative plural), etc.[133] Then too, in Klein's *Compendium Lituanico-Germanicum* (published 1654), we read:

Zu mercken ist, wenn in der Littauschen Sprach nach dem *j* folget die Endung auff ein *as*, als *Iśganytojas, kraujas, naujas*, so wird das *a* gar gelinde ausgesprochen fast wie ein *e*. Drumb etliche wol gar ein *e* schreiben dörffen: *Iśganytojes, kraujes, naujes*.[134]

Conversely, Klein's *Grammatica Lituanica* (published 1653) reports that "pro *e* utuntur Wilnenses [i.e., the people of Vilnius] quandoqve *a*, ut . . . *giaras* pro *geras* bonus."[135] The same sort of orthographic ambiguity in representing original */(C)e/ and */(C)i̯a/ is common in Old Prussian texts,[136] and there appear traces of it in the early Latvian evidence.[137]

§23. This general trend {*-ă- > *-ĕ-, after *-i̯-} coincides with the circumstance that there is in Baltic a vacuum in the vocalic spectrum of the slot -Ci̯V-, since -Ci̯ĕ- had become -Cĕ-: hence e.g. the formal contrast between Lithuanian

133 Cf. again Otrębski, *Gramatyka* I 219.
134 *Apud* Bezzenberger, *Beiträge* (n. 114) 55 n. 1.
135 *Apud* Bezzenberger, *Beiträge* 5.
136 Cf. Endzelin, *Lettische Grammatik* (n. 71) 33; also W. R. Schmalstieg, "The Alternation *e/a* in Old Prussian: A Phonemic Interpretation," *Annali dell'Istituto Universitario Orientale di Napoli: Sezione Linguistica* I (1959) 191–195.
137For archaic instances of /Ča/ spelled ⟨Ce⟩ and /ja/ spelled ⟨je⟩, cf. Sommer, *Stämme* (n. 1) 42 and 67; in an East Latvian text of Viļāņi, the spelling ⟨a⟩ after palatalized consonants can even represent *ę* or *ę̄*: cf. J. Endzelin, *Lettisches Lesebuch* (Heidelberg 1922) 141. For a parallel orthographic ambiguity in archaic Lithuanian texts, cf. *giaras* for *gẽras*, as discussed *supra* in § 22 (cited in n. 135).

nominative singular *svẽčias* (< *svetįas) and the dialectal vocative singular *sveté* (< *svetįe).[138] The development {*-Cįĕ- > -Cĕ-} I ascribe to a putative depalatalization of on-glides, whereby Baltic *-įĕ-, a product of both IE *-ĕ- and IE *-įĕ-, becomes plain *-ĕ-.[139]

§24. That a merger into *-įĕ- preceded the development into *-ĕ- might be illustrated with reference to another Baltic phenomenon. The first phase of the latter is a change of *-ev- to *-av- before -O- (= any back vowel), as in the cognate of Greek τεός, Latvian/Lithuanian nominative singular *tavs/tãvas* vs. genitive singular *tevis/tèvęs*.[140] This type of change is also found in Slavic, where e.g. an IE root *reų- (as in Sanskrit *ruváti* "shouts" or in Latin *rūmor*) is reflected in the verbal configuration *rovǫ/reveši/...rjuti* (1st/2nd singular...infinitive), later leveled and split into *rovǫ/roveši/... ruti* and *revǫ/reveši/...rjuti*.[141] Thus {*-evO- > *-avO-} is not only an archaic process in Baltic, but also the reflex of a shared feature in Baltic/Slavic. However, for neither group can we claim that during the period when this phonological rule was operative, there should have already been present an on-glide *-į- before *-ĕ-, since there is no definite reflex of palatalization exerted on a consonant preceding the Baltic/ Slavic *-a-/-o- (< *-e-). But the signal issue is that the process {*-e-v- > *-a/o-v-} later spread from prevocalic to preconsonantal position as well, still early enough to be counted as a shared feature of Baltic and Slavic: hence *-CeuC- is reflected as *-C'auC- in the former and (*-C'ouC- >) *-C'uC- in the latter, as with Lithuanian/Latvian

---

138 Vs. standard *svetỹ*. For nominative *vélnias*, there is possible this series of vocatives: *tù vélne! tù velnè! tù velnỹ! tù vélniau!* "you *devil!*" (cf. Senn, *Grammatik* [n. 2] 112 f).

139 Cf. esp. § 28.

140 These entries are standard, except for the last one, a *Žemaičiai*-form from the Klaipéda-area; cf. Stang, *Vergleichende Grammatik* (n. 2) 32 f.

141 Cf. Meillet/Vaillant, *Le slave commun* (n. 47) § 221.

liáudis/*ļàudis* and Old Slavonic *l'udьje* respectively.[142] The ultimate palatalization of the consonant preceding original *-eu- here suggests that at some period in Baltic/Slavic between (1) the original development of *-e-v- to *-a/o-v- before back vowels and (2) the later extension of this development to preconsonantal position as well, there had evolved a palatal on-glide *-i̯- before *-ĕ- in both Baltic and Slavic. When the later period of depalatalization arrived in e.g. Baltic, so that *-Ci̯ĕ- > -Cĕ-, the original combination *-Ci̯eu- (< *-Ceu-) had by that time already become *-Ci̯au-, whence the type *liáudis* (rather than *laudis).[143]

§25. We find another argument for the anteriority of *-i̯ĕ- (in relation to *-ĕ-) as continuation of both IE *-ĕ- and *-i̯ĕ- in the special evidence of Latvian, where the reflex of an original Baltic *-k-/-g- before front vowel is the same as that of *-k-/-g- before *-i̯-, namely -c-/-dz-; hence e.g. the Latvian vs. Lithuanian correspondences *ticu*, *ticêt* vs. *tikiù*, *tikéti* and *redzu*, *redzêt* vs. *regiù*, *regéti*.[144] From such correspondences it is possible to posit the prehistoric presence of an on-glide *-i̯- before front vowels, which was later deleted— but not before altering the articulation of a preceding velar into a palatal consonant in ancestral Latvian. With depalatalization (so that e.g. *-ti̯ĕ- > *-tĕ-), the new palatals *-k'-/-g'- had already become affricates (so that they could not revert into velars), whence -c-/-dz-. That only the original velars became radically altered after a cycle of palatalization-depalatalization in Latvian can be compared with the

---

[142] Cf. Stang, *Vergleichende Grammatik* (n. 2) 73 f; orthographic ambiguity rules out the testimony of Old Prussian.

[143] *Ibid.* Stang lists Baltic instances where supposedly original *-Ceu- is reflected as -Cau- instead of the expected -C'au-. For some of these, positing an inherited *o*-grade may well be the solution: e.g. the contrast between standard Latvian *šaut* and East Latvian *saut* may well be due to early leveling either by present-base *si̯eu- (< *seu-) or by perfect-base *sau-.

[144] Cf. Stang, *Vergleichende Grammatik* 105.

phonological rearrangement in Indo-Iranian known as the second palatalization.[145]

§26. In e.g. East Latvian, besides diachronic palatalization of consonants before *-i̯-, there is synchronic palatalization before front vowels—as also in Lithuanian. This set of circumstances does not at first seem to square with the proposition here upheld, that Baltic *-Ci̯ĕ- had become -Cĕ-. But the relationship svĕčias/svetė in Lithuanian is decisive: to posit that the attested standard Lithuanian -C'ĕ- (rather than *-Cĕ-) is a continuation of Baltic *-Ci̯ĕ- would only lead to the erroneous notion that the type svĕčе,[146] not svetė, is original. Thus we may assume that the palatalization of consonants before front vowels in e.g. standard Lithuanian is a relatively more recent innovation, and that the archaic state of affairs is in this respect represented by e.g. standard Latvian (vs. East Latvian), where such palatalization

[145] Etymological *k *g *gh before etymological *ĕ *ī̆ *i are reflected as c j h and č ǰ j in Indic and Iranian respectively. I propose that these reflexes reveal the prehistoric generation of a palatal on-glide *I before *ĕ and *ī̆. Later this *I is lost, but it leaves its mark in the conversion of preceding velars into palatals, which in turn are reflected as affricates in e.g. Vedic and Avestan. Positing the development and subsequent obsolescence of an on-glide *I is admittedly not essential for motivating the second palatalization of Indic and Iranian: in fact, it is not even an economical explanation of this one phenomenon. But to suppose the prehistoric existence of a palatal on-glide *I before *ĕ, *ī̆ (and, as a corollary, of a labial on-glide *U before *ŏ, *ŭ) serves to explain more than just the Indic/Iranian second palatalization; herewith are a few of several possible correlations:

(1) the shifts {*ĕ > ă} and {*ŏ > ă} are caused by the depalatalization/delabialization of on-glides in *Iĕ/*Uŏ

(2) depalatalization/delabialization likewise results in the reflex of etymological *ii/*u̯u as i/u in e.g. Indic; for a list of examples, cf. J. Wackernagel, Altindische Grammatik I (Göttingen 1896) § 228

(3) the Vedic sandhi-rules whereby -e + i- ⇒ -a i-, -o + u- ⇒ -a u-, etc.: these patterns may well have been the locus of diffusion for other sandhi-rules involving -e + V-, -o + V-, -ai + V-, -au + V-: cf. Wackernagel, op. cit. § 272aβ, § 274; for a general survey of combinations involving antevocalic -e -o -ai -au, cf. W. S. Allen, Sandhi: The Theoretical, Phonetic, and Historical Bases of Word-Junction in Sanskrit ('s-Gravenhage 1962) 37–45.

[146] In e.g. the dialect of Buivydžiai, the singular nominative/vocative is vĕčes/svĕčе: cf. Gauthiot, Le parler de Buividze (n. 132) 36 f.

before front vowels does not take place synchronically.[147] Granted that {-C-ĕ/ĭ- > -C'-ĕ/ĭ-} is old,[148] it is still to be maintained that {*-Ci̯ĕ- > -Cĕ-} is appreciably older, even prehistoric. Since the former phenomenon is also paralleled in the contiguous Slavic areas, we might ascribe its manifestation in Lithuanian and East Latvian to the spread of an originally extrinsic areal feature.

§27. From here on, the primary factor to consider is not the cause of an original merger {*-Ci̯ĕ-/-Cĕ- > -Cĕ-}, but rather, its consequences. Since a crucial distinction between the Baltic vowels *-ă- and *-ĕ- must have been an opposition of the features back/front, we might expect that loss of the opposition *{-Ci̯ă- : -Ci̯ĕ-} because of *{-Ci̯ĕ- > -Cĕ-} could induce the fronting of *-ă- after *-i̯-. The latter phenomenon, as already mentioned,[149] is operative in Aukštaičiai-dialects. But more crucial now is the relevant evidence of Lithuanian Žemaičiai-dialects: the original combinations *-ti̯ă-/-di̯ă- here develop into -tĕ-/-dĕ- rather than *-č'ĕ-/-dž'ĕ- or *-c'ĕ-/-dz'ĕ-.[150] We might conclude that *-Ci̯ă- becomes *-Ci̯ĕ- in this major dialectal group early enough to cause the new *-Ci̯ĕ- to become subject to the same posited de-palatalization-rule which had produced *-Cĕ- from primary *-Ci̯ĕ-; but the reverse perspective is probably more accurate: the very change {*-Ci̯ĕ- > *-Cĕ-} which had triggered {*-Ci̯ă- > *-Ci̯ĕ-} remained an operative process long enough to produce *-Cĕ- from secondary *-Ci̯ĕ- (< *-Ci̯ă-) in Žemaičiai-dialects.

§28. With the fronting trend {*-i̯ă- > *-i̯ӓ- ... > *-i̯ĕ-}, it is possible to connect a generally more evident Baltic development, well-documented in Old Prussian as well as

---

[147] For a description, cf. Stang, Vergleichende Grammatik (n. 2) 102.
[148] Hence e.g. the archaic spelling giaras for gĕras, as discussed in § 22; cf. also n. 137.
[149] Cf. § 22.
[150] Cf. Stang, Vergleichende Grammatik (n. 2) 88 f, 100 f.

Lithuanian and Latvian: i.e., the trend {*-ĕ- > *-ă̆- ...
> *-ă̆-}. Stang has collected relevant instances,[151] thereby
essentially outlining the *phonologisation/déphonologisation*[152]
of this trend in the synchronic systems of the Baltic dialects
and sub-dialects. Granted, factors other than the one presently to be proposed were also probably operative: hence
e.g. the monophthongization {*-ei- > *-ē-}[153] may well be
connected with instances showing the displacement of
original *-ē- to *-ǣ-. Nonetheless, a general explanation
has been lacking, as seen from such problems as this: "In
allen baltischen Sprachen findet man die Tendenz, anlau-
tendes *e*- durch *a*- zu ersetzen."[154] In this instance the aporia
is how to define the motivation of such variants as Lithuanian
àš/èš "I," both derived from basic *ež- (cognate of Latin
eg-ō). I propose that a key to the overall solution is that the
trend {*e- > *a-} is linked ultimately to the original loss of
palatal on-glide before *-ĕ-.[155] Illustrative are the Lithuanian attestations of the root *i̯ekʷ- (as in Latin *iecur*):
besides *jãknos* (*jéknos* in the standard orthography), there
are also two dialectal variants for this word "liver": *ēknos*
and *āknos*;[156] the corresponding Latvian word is likewise
aknas.[157] We might conjecture an original variation in external *sandhi*, such as (1) *...#i̯ek- vs. (2) *...i̯#ek-. This
posited breakdown of original morpheme-boundary could
be caused by the development of on-glide *-i̯- before all
front vowels. Then, with the later phonological shift {*-i̯ĕ- >

---

[151] *Vergleichende Grammatik* 31 ff, 44 ff.

[152] For these terms, cf. Jakobson, *Selected Writings* I (*Principes de phonologie
historique* [1931]) 202–220.

[153] For which cf. Stang, *Vergleichende Grammatik* (n. 2) 46.

[154] Stang, *Vergleichende Grammatik* 31.

[155] Cf. the similar proposal by Schmalstieg, "The Alternation *e/a*" (n. 136)
194, who cites such Lithuanian/Old Prussian pairs as *ēžeras/assaran* "lake,"
ašvà and *ešvà* "mare"/*aswinan* "mare's milk," etc.; cf. also Stang, *Vergleichende
Grammatik* 31 f. For a list of pairs such as *àš/èš* in Old Lithuanian texts, cf.
Bezzenberger, *Beiträge* (n. 114) 56.

[156] Cf. Otrębski, *Gramatyka* (n. 2) I 216, 218 f.

[157] Cf. Endzelin, *Lettische Grammatik* (n. 71) 311.

*-ĕ-} coming into effect, variation (1) presupposes that if
*-i̯- is to be kept, then *i̯ek- becomes /i̯ak-/; hence *jăknos*; if,
on the other hand, *-e- is to be kept, then *i̯ek- has to
become /ek-/: hence *ĕknos*. As for variation (2), an original
exertion of word-final *-i̯ by a following word *ek- becomes
abolished, but not before the collocation *...i̯#ek- is reinterpreted as */...i̯#ak-/ or */...ø#ek-/, whence ultimately
ăknos, as well as *ĕknos* again. Variations of the type *àš/èš*
can be explained in the same formula, *sandhi*-variation (2):
the crucial link is the proposed Baltic merger of *-i̯ĕ- and
*-ĕ- into *-i̯ĕ- (followed by depalatalization into *-ĕ-).
Furthermore, as already suggested, it is the latter development, the merger into *-i̯ĕ-, which could bring about the
resegmentation of *...#i̯ek- as *...i̯#ek-, parallel to the
type *...i̯#ež- yielding *àš/èš*.[158] In sum, I suggest the following order of rules for the Baltic languages:

(1) *-ĕ- and *-i̯ĕ- > *-i̯ĕ-
(2) *-i̯ĕ- > *-ĕ-
(3) *-i̯ĕ- > *-i̯ĕ-
(4) *-ĕ- > *-ă̯-.[159]

[158] Similarly with the Baltic reflex of the IE verbal formant *-i̯e/i̯o-: from
the standpoint of IE, we might expect *-i̯e- in the Baltic third person; but,
with {*-i̯ĕ- > *-ĕ-} coming into effect, the potential development of 3rd
*-e- vs. e.g. 1st plural *-i̯a-me (< *-i̯o-me) would exert a disruptive effect
upon the whole paradigm. If, however, *-i̯- were to be kept in the 3rd person,
then original *-i̯e- would have to become *-i̯a- instead: the latter, in relation
to e.g. 1st plural *-i̯a-me, would serve to level and solidify rather than disrupt
the verbal paradigm. In other words, the 3rd ending in e.g. Lithuanian *liẽčia*
need not necessarily be traced back to IE *-i̯o-: an original *-i̯e- could be
posited instead. Likewise with Lithuanian 3rd person *dìrba*: instead of recon-
structing IE *-o- from -*a*, we could treat the latter as a secondary development:
3rd person -*a* could have spread from bases with palatalized final consonant
(-*C'a*, < *-*Ci̯a*) to bases with non-palatalized final consonant (-*Ca*, replacing
*-*Ce*). For a similar argument, cf. W. R. Schmalstieg, "A Balto-Slavic Structural Parallelism," *Word* 20 (1964) 35–39.

[159] For processes 3–4, I propose an indirect typological parallel from dialectal Russian:

-*C'a*- > -*C'e*-   e.g. *p'aták* > *p'eták*
-*Ce*- > -*Ca*-   e.g. *žen'ix* > *žan'ix*.

Cf. Jakobson, *Principes de phonologie historique* (n. 152) 206.

§29. We can add to this chronological ranking the following essential corollary, simultaneous with the just-mentioned processes 3–4:

*-ii̯æ- > *-ī-
*-ii̯ǣ- > *-ǣ-.[160]

These two developments can be described as contractions, in the sense that a disyllabic segment has in both cases become monosyllabic. If indeed genuine contractions are involved here, we should be able to show the original presence of syllabic *-i- in the reconstructed *-ii̯ǣ̆-. The most decisive test emerges from the evidence of Lithuanian, in the development of *-č'-/-dž'-* from *-ti̯-/-di̯- vs. *-t'-/-d'-* from *-t-/-d- before front vowel *-i-. Hence e.g. in such dialectal contrasts as *vertẽ*, *verčià* and *kándė*, *kándžia*, the very survival of *t/d* in *-tė/-dė* predicates the reconstruction *-tii̯ā/-dii̯ā as opposed to the *-ti̯ā/-di̯ā resulting in *-čia/-džia*. Put another way, *-Ci̯ǣ > *-C'ǣ while *-Cii̯ǣ > *-Cǣ. Contraction is also implied by the exemption of e.g. standard Lithuanian nominative singular *-ė* from the process of shortening into *-e, despite its position in the word. Likewise with nominative singular *-ys* (= *-īs*, < *-ii̯æs < *-ii̯as), shortening into

[160] For possible positional constraints affecting these rules, cf. the tentative remarks of Stang, *Vergleichende Grammatik* (n. 2) 115, 202. However, the diverse declensional developments in e.g. Lithuanian *gaid-ỹ-s/gaidž-iá-ms* ("rooster") vs. *kat-ė̃/kat-ė́-ms* ("cat") need not necessarily mean that the phonological process {*-ii̯æ- > *-ī-} had been suspended in word-medial position. The just-cited contrasts between nominative singular and dative plural can actually mislead, since the declensional pattern of nouns in *-is(-ỹs)* differs greatly from that of nouns in *-ė*. With the latter, there is only one slot in the paradigm where contraction did not occur because etymological *-ā- did not follow *-ii̯-, namely the genitive plural: hence *kačių̃*. With the former, etymological *-ā̆- or *-ē̆- did not follow *-ii̯- in e.g. the singular dative/instrumental, and the plural genitive/accusative/locative: hence no contraction in *gaĩdžiui/gaidžiù* and *gaidžių̃/gaidžiùs/gaidžiuosè* respectively. Here alone we see five parallels with the declension of simple thematic stems without *-ii̯-, such as in *vargas* "hardship": *vargui/vargù* and *vargų̃/vargùs/varguosè*. Thus intraparadigmatic leveling may well be the sole cause of the type *gaidžiáms*, modeled on the type *vargáms*.

-*is* is regularly obviated in such East *Aukštaičiai*-dialects as those of Kupiškis, Skapiškis, Rimšė, etc., as also in North-West *Žemaičiai*-dialects; but in e.g. standard Lithuanian, there has occurred a distortion of the original distribution because of an apparently late phonological shortening of -*īs* (hence -*is*), except when -*īs* = -*ys* was stressed (hence -*ỹs*).[161] A further argument for the original presence of syllabic *-i- in e.g. what ultimately yielded Lithuanian -*ys* we find in such metatonic morphological relationships as *ragúotas/ raguõtis*, where the original ictus of the type *raguõtis* can be etymologically reconstructed over *-i-, in the following sequence: ˜*is* < *˜*īs* < *-i̯i̯as.[162] It is even possible to make a direct comparison between such formants as Baltic *-i̯i̯as in the types *raguõtis*, *vandẽnis*, etc., and the IE-inherited formant *-íi̯os reconstructed for the Sanskrit type *udaníyaḥ* and the Greek type γομφίος.[163] Finally, a prehistoric configuration *-i̯i̯as in Baltic can still be seen in Finnic borrowings: e.g. Estonian *takijas* "thistle, bur" < *dagii̯as > Lithuanian *dagỹs*, Latvian *dadzis*.[164]

§30. We must still examine the successive rearrangements triggered by the order of rules proposed in § 28. To

---

[161] Cf. Stang, *Vergleichende Grammatik* 189 f. The Latvian type *brālis* "brother" (rather than *brāls) is further proof that the -*is* of the standard Lithuanian type *brólis* should be derived from *-īs. That the standard Lithuanian nominative plural ending of *i*-stem nominals (-*ys*) had not been phonologically shortened (to *-is) can be explained on the grounds of morphological counterpressure: cf. again Stang, *Vergleichende Grammatik* 189 f. An argument which we might add to those adduced by Stang is that the formal opposition between nominative singular and plural would have been canceled if -*ys* became *-is in *i*-stems.

[162] Cf. Stang, *Vergleichende Grammatik* 146 f.

[163] *Ibid.*; the IE-inherited formant *-íi̯os is probably a secondary configuration—a morphological reflex of more basic *-éi̯os; cf. chap. iv n. 79.

[164] Cf. Stang, *Vergleichende Grammatik* 190; *dagii̯as = "stinger" ⇐ "inflamer" (← *dèg-ti* "burn"): cf. *gaidii̯as, § 9 *supra*; cf. also Fraenkel, *LEW* (n. 2) s.v. *dègti*. For Stang's views on the circumflex in Lithuanian -*ỹs/-ẽ* as a compensatory feature resulting from contraction, cf. esp. 127. On the etymology of e.g. attested Lithuanian -*ijas* as *-īi̯as, cf. *Vergleichende Grammatik* 190 f.

make clear the correlations, here again is the suggested sequence:

(1) *-ĕ- and *-i̯ĕ- > *-i̯ẽ-
(2) *-i̯ẽ- > *-ĕ-
(3) *-i̯ĕ- > *-i̯æ̃-
(4) *-ĕ- > *-æ̃-.

Such an order implies the following repertory of configurations at different stages:

stage I, before process 1.   *-i̯ã- *-i̯ĕ- *-ĕ-
stage II, after process 1.   *-i̯ã- *-i̯ĕ-
stage III, after processes 3–4. *-i̯æ̃- *-æ̃-.

In *Žemaičiai*-dialects of Lithuanian, the original three variants of stage I are by stage III further reduced from two (*-i̯æ̃-/-æ̃-) to one (*-æ̃-).[165] As for those Lithuanian dialectal areas where Baltic *-ā- becomes -ō- (and the standard language falls into this category), the allophonic realization of this original */-ā-/ as *[-æ̃-] after *[-i̯-] has been suspended, whence the development of -C'ō- from inherited *-Ci̯ā-, as in -es-nióji = /-es-n'ó-ji/. Elsewhere too, there are drastic rearrangements beyond stage III, especially in Latvian. Here the -æ̃- (= -ẽ̦-) undergoes, in most dialects, *Umlaut* to -ĕ- before front vowel in a successive syllable, so that e.g. -ẽ̦-...-i- becomes -ĕ-...-i-.[166] Such a trend as {-æ̃- > -ĕ-} in Latvian would in turn help promote a reversal like {*-i̯æ̃- > *-i̯ã-}. But a much more important factor contributing to the stabilization of *-æ̃- to *-ã- before original *-i- is the fate of palatalized consonants, as in e.g. standard Latvian: *-ti̯-/-di̯- > -š-/-ž-, *-ki̯-/-gi̯- > -c-/-dz-, *-si̯-/-zi̯- > -š-/-ž-, etc.[167] The loss of palatality in such instances could be a

---

165 Cf. § 27.
166 Cf. Stang, *Vergleichende Grammatik* (n. 2) 31, 45.
167 For a survey of such developments, cf. Stang, *Vergleichende Grammatik* 102 ff.

crucial impetus for the reassertion of *-ă- after etymological
*-i̯-. With original *-ti̯a- as an example, the sequence might
be this: *[-ti̯æ-] vs. *[-tæ-] = */-ti̯a-/ vs. */-te-/; then *-ti̯-
(> *-ti̯- > *-tš-) > -š-; with loss of *-i̯-, the allophonic
realization of /-a-/ as [-æ-] is suspended, whence standard
Latvian -ša-. Nevertheless, traces of *[-i̯æ-] are indeed found
in Latvian, with the preservative mechanism provided by a
second factor, the already-mentioned *Umlaut* of [-ẵ-] to
[-ĕ-] before front vowel in the successive syllable.[168] Endzelin
has described the relevant facts as follows: "Daselbst
findet man suffixales *e* statt *a* hinter *r* < *ŕ*, *m* < *mi̯*, *p* < *pi̯*
(und wohl auch *b* < *bi̯*) in der Stellung vor -*s* < -*si* und
-*mę̄s*."[169] Hence e.g. *veres* (< *veŕasi) and *veremę̄s* (<
*veŕamę̄s), vs. the types *plę̄šas* and *plę̄šamę̄s* respectively.[170]

§31. There is an interesting side-effect to the reflex
of IE *-ii̯ā-/-i̯ā- as e.g. Lithuanian -*ė*-/-*io*-: the combination
*-ii̯ā- has become indistinguishable from *-ii̯ē- in the
Baltic languages. The latter segment is attested as a nominal
formant in Latin: e.g. *māter-iēs* vs. *māter-ia*. Nevertheless,
in order to posit a corresponding Baltic *-ii̯ē(s) vs. *-ii̯ā,
we would have to assume tentatively that the Latin fifth
declension is not an internal development independent of IE.
That issue will not be taken up here.

§32. Even if e.g. the opposition {*-ii̯ā- : *-i̯ā-} were
the sole IE factor reflected by {*-ē- : *-'ā-} in the Baltic
languages, we still have to account for other factors, non-IE,
which influenced the eventual distribution of e.g. postconsonantal -*ė*-/-*io*- as observed in standard Lithuanian.
A striking instance is the prevalence in Lithuanian of nominal
formant -*ė*- after the labials *p*, *b*, *v*, *m*.[171] This pattern

---

168 Cf. n. 166.
169 *Lettische Grammatik* (n. 71) 92.
170 *Ibid.*
171 Cf. Sommer, *Stämme* (n. 1) 78, 214.

suggests that labials could generate vocalic *-i- from a simple off-glide *-i̯-: with B used as cover-symbol for *p*, *b*, *v*, *m*, we can represent the process as follows: *-Bi̯V- > *-Bii̯V-. A relevant circumstance is that *-i̯- in the Baltic languages lost its phonemic status after labials later than after e.g. dentals, whence such Lithuanian spellings as *kùrpjū* (genitive plural of *kùrpė* "shoe");[172] the standard representation *kùrpių̄* indicates *p*', whereas *kùrpjū* reflects the *j* regularly spelled in intervocalic position, in which slot Baltic *-i̯- had always remained: e.g. Lithuanian *kójų̄*, genitive plural of *kója* "foot." We may posit, then, that during the period when *-Cii̯ā- was distinct from *-Ci̯ā-, such an opposition was suspended wherever C = B, so that original unproductive *-Bi̯ā- and productive *-Bii̯ā- could not remain distinct: both became *-Bii̯ā-, whence -*Bė*-/-*Be*- in Lithuanian/ Latvian. In Old Prussian too, the *Elbing Glossary* shows a contrast between -*i* (< *-i̯ā) and -*e* (< *-ii̯ā) after non-labial consonants, while after labials only -*e* apparently occurs.[173]

---

[172] Cf. Sommer, *Stämme* 78 f and Stang, *Vergleichende Grammatik* 103; also Otrębski, *Gramatyka* (n. 2) I 339 f.
[173] Cf. Schmid, *Verbum* (n. 2) 19.

CHAPTER III

THE DEVELOPMENT OF *ι* AND *ι̯*
IN GREEK, AND THEIR
DISTRIBUTION[1]

§1. Works cited in Chapter III:

W. S. Allen, "Some Problems of Palatalization in Greek," *Lingua* 7 (1958) 113–133.

A. Bartoněk, "Outline of the Phonemic System in Mycenaean Greek," *Sborník Prací Filosofické Fakulty Brněnské University*, A 12 (1964) 195–209.

—— "The Phonic Evaluation of the *s*- and *z*- Signs in Mycenaean," *Sborník Prací Filosofické Fakulty Brněnské University*, E 4 (1964) 89–102.

—— *Vývoj konsonantického systému v řeckých dialektech: Development of the Consonantal System in Ancient Greek Dialects* (Opera Universitatis Purkynianae Brunensis, Facultas Philosophica 77 [Praha 1961]).

R. Coleman, "The Dialect Geography of Ancient Greece," *Transactions of the Philological Society* (1963) 58–126.

W. Cowgill, "Ancient Greek Dialectology in the Light of Mycenaean," *Ancient Indo-European Dialects*, ed. H. Birnbaum and J. Puhvel (Berkeley and Los Angeles 1966) 77–95.

W. Diver, "On the Prehistory of Greek Consonantism," *Word* 14 (1958) 1–25.

A. Heubeck, "Zur dialektologischen Einordnung des Mykenischen," *Glotta* 39 (1960–1961) 159–172.

---

[1] In this section, Linear B forms will be cited from the *Mycenaeae graecitatis lexicon* (Roma 1963) of A. Morpurgo (-Davies). In reconstructions of Greek with roman characters, *ị and *ụ will be rendered as *j and *w, mainly because of the general convention in transcribing the Linear B syllables

-ja-, -je-, -jo-, -wa-, -we-, -wi-, -wo-.

F. W. Householder, "Early Greek -*j*-," *Glotta* 39 (1960–1961) 179–190.

P. Kretschmer, "Der Wandel von τ vor ι in σ," [*A. Kuhn's*] *Zeitschrift für vergleichende Sprachforschung* 30 (1890) 565–591.

C. Lambert, *De dialecto aeolica quaestiones selectae ad grammaticam pertinentes* (Dijon 1903).

M. Lejeune, "Les sifflantes fortes du mycénien," *Minos* 6 (1958) 87–137.

W. Porzig, "Sprachgeographische Untersuchungen zu den altgriechischen Dialekten," *Indogermanische Forschungen* 61 (1954) 147–169.

E. Risch, "Die Gliederung der griechischen Dialekte in neuer Sicht," *Museum Helveticum* 12 (1955) 61–76.

M. Scheller, *Die Oxytonierung der griechischen Substantiva auf -ιᾱ* (Zürich 1951).

Chr. S. Stang, "Quelques remarques sur le système consonantique du grec commun," *Symbolae Osloenses* 33 (1957) 27–36.

§2. On the basis of the independently developed arguments of Diver[2] and Stang,[3] we may posit, for a remote stage of Greek,[4] the gemination of a single consonant originally preceded by a short vowel and followed by *-j-; i.e., -V̆CjV- > -V̆ĈĈjV-; e.g., *aljos > *aĨĨjos (> *aĨĨⁱos > finally ἄλλος in e.g. Ionian, upon depalatalization). Once such a shift took place, it could automatically suspend Sievers' Rule (-V̄CijV- vs. -V̆CjV-),[5] since it entails the presence of *-j- instead of *-ij- after a heavy syllable (as produced by the newly-geminated simple consonant); the result is that the pattern -V̄CjV- instead of -V̄CijV- is now possible, and that it too can undergo consonantal gemination: -V̄CjV- > -V̄ĈĈjV-.

[2] "Greek Consonantism" (§ 1) 8 ff.

[3] "Système consonantique" (§ 1) 28 ff.

[4] This development is common to a prehistoric period of all Greek dialects, but it does not belong in the period of Common Greek: cf. the stages *a/b*.2 in the diachronic chart of § 6, posited for the genesis of the -σ- in e.g. Attic/Ionic ὅσος; on this same chart, gemination is represented as beginning only at stage *c*.

[5] Q.v. in chap. i § 1.

Next to be ascertained is the effect of gemination on the IE-inherited morphological opposition {-V̆C‖ijV- : -V̆CjV-}.[6] In some morphological categories, it is evident that productivity notwithstanding, original -V̆C‖ijV- becomes -V̆C‖jV- (> -V̆ĈĈjV- > -V̆ĈĈʲV-). For example, the etymological relationship of ἕλιξ/-ἑλισσα[7] and of ἕλιξ/ἑλίσσω suggests that at the time when postconsonantal *-j- was still an autonomous phonological element in Greek, it was a component in such productive categories as feminine nominals in *-jă̆/*-jās (nominative/genitive singular) and denominative verbs with stem in *-je/jo-: hence e.g. *Ϝελικ-ιᾰ̆ and *Ϝελικ-ιω respectively. Moreover, on the basis of the attested reflexes in classical Greek (here -ἑλισσᾰ and ἑλίσσω), it seems that the ultimate development was this: -V̆C‖ijV- became -V̆C‖jV- because of gemination in the unproductive counterpart -V̆CjV- (thus -V̆CjV- > -V̆ĈĈjV-), and then -V̆C‖jV- came to undergo gemination likewise: -V̆C‖jV- > -V̆ĈĈjV- (> -V̆ĈĈʲV-); the latter pattern emerges in e.g. -ἑλισσᾰ (< *Ϝελικ-ιᾰ̆ ← *Ϝελικ-s > ἕλιξ), or, with heavy syllable preceding *-jă̆, in θῆσσᾰ (< *θητ-ιᾰ̆ ← *θητ-s > θής). In other words, the morphological opposition {-V̆C‖ijV- : -V̆CjV-} was obliterated because the nature of the elements contrasted had been altered: whereas before gemination the unproductive pattern -CjV- had been the *raison d'être* for the productive -CijV- (in that the syllabic/vocalic nature of the *-i- in the latter could set it off as distinct from the former, with its non-syllabic/consonantal *-i-), now, after gemination in the unproductive forms, the opposition {vocalic : consonantal} in *-i- (i.e., {*-ij- : *-j-}) could become blurred because it ceases to be the sole distinguishing factor; thus synchronically motivated forms

---

could come to be felt as no longer presupposing *-ij(V-) vs.
*-j(V-) after a morpheme-boundary.

§3. The obliteration in Greek of the morphological
opposition {-V̆C‖ijV- : -V̆CjV-} by the phonological mechanism of gemination may be represented thus:[8]

$$
\text{I} \quad
\begin{cases}
\text{-V̆CjV-}_a > \text{-V̆ĈĈjV-}_a > \text{-V̆ĈĈʲV-}_a \\
\text{-V̆C‖ijV-}_b \Rightarrow \text{-V̆Ĉ‖jV-}_b
\end{cases}
$$

II -V̆Ĉ‖jV-$_b$ > -V̆ĈĈjV-$_b$ > -V̆ĈĈʲV-$_b$.

§4. If, as posited here, the denominative verb-formant
*-je/jo- was still productive by itself just before the period
when postconsonantal *-j- ceased to be autonomous in
Greek, then we still have to ask how it is that its reflex in
attested classical Greek is phonologically divergent from
that of the denominative adjective-formant originally in
*-je/jo-. For example, from a base μειλιχ- (as in μείλιχος),
there are attested the historically derivative configurations
μειλίσσω and μειλίχιος, respectively the denominative
verb and adjective in *-je/jo-.[9] The more basic question,

[8] The downward direction of stages I-II approximates the vector of time.
Qualification: original Greek -V̆C₁C₂jV- and -V̆C₁C₂‖ijV- could not undergo
gemination; the respective results would therefore be -V̆Ĉ₁Ĉ₂ʲV-$_a$ and
-V̆Ĉ₁Ĉ₂ʲV-$_b$, corresponding to stages I and II. The raised *-j- is meant to
represent loss of status as autonomous phoneme. The need for subscripts $_a$
and $_b$ after -V̆ĈĈʲV- will be justified in § 6 *infra*.

[9] For a list of such pairs, cf. A. Fick/A. Führer, "Die suffixlosen Nomina der
griechischen Sprache: II," [*A. Bezzenberger's*] *Beiträge zur Kunde der indogermanischen Sprachen* I (1877) 129. Among the entries submitted are ἀτασθαλία/
ἀτασθάλλω, βασκάνιον/βασκαίνω, καθάριος/καθαίρω, μαλθακία/μαλθάσσω,
ναυτιλία/ναυτίλλομαι, πλημμυρία/πλημύρω, στωμυλία/στωμύλλω, etc. Another list
is compiled by Fick in section III of the same article, pp. 312 f of *Bezzenberger's
Beiträge* I: this time, more complex configurations are considered, such as
διπλάδιος/διπλάζω, συγ-κοιτάδιος/συγ-κοιτάζω, λιβάδιον/λιβάζω, νοσφίδιος/νοσφίζω,
προικίδιος/προικίζω, ἐγ-χειρίδιος/ἐγ-χειρίζω, ἁρμόδιος/ἁρμόζω, etc.
    Especially interesting is the pair κουρίδιος/κουρίζω. From the context of
passages where κουρίδιος is attested, we can extract the sense of "(lawfully)
wedded" or "nuptual"; to be added is κουρίδιον·παρθένιον, καὶ τὸν ἐκ παρθενίας
ἄνδρα (E 414). Λάκωνες δὲ κουρίδιον καλοῦσι ⟨τὸν⟩ παρὰ [δὲ] αὐτοῖς τετράχειρα
'Απόλλωνα (Hesychios). The concept of παρθένιος ἀνήρ and κουρίδιος πόσις is

then, is why original *-j- entailed gemination of the preceding consonant in the former case but not in the latter, where its reflex is vocalic. I propose that the answer involves the factor of accent, and the accentual principles which I apply in an attempt to demonstrate this are essentially those drawn up by Kuryłowicz.[10]

Specifically, the crucial mechanism is the development in Greek of accent-limitation: $\{\text{\'-X}\breve{X}\breve{X}\# \Rightarrow \text{-}\acute{X}\breve{X}\breve{X}\#\}$ and $\{\text{\'-XX}\bar{X}\# \text{ or -}\acute{X}X\bar{X}\# \Rightarrow \text{-}X\acute{X}\bar{X}\#\}$. Here $\bar{X}/\breve{X}$ = a syllable with long/short vowel; the acute-sign (´) can be used in these representations because it was the unmarked prosodic element of Greek:[11] the opposition {unmarked ´ : marked ˆ} was phonologically relevant only within the final ensemble, $\text{-}\breve{X}\breve{X}$ or $\text{-}\bar{X}$.[12] Now the effects of accent-limitation by the

discussed by F. Bechtel, *Lexilogus zu Homer* (Halle an der Saale 1914) 200 f. As for the Homeric κουρίζων (χ 185), it is interpreted as ἀκμάζων or νεάζων in e.g. the Kyrillian Συναγωγὴ λέξεων χρησίμων, while the entry κουριζόμενος is defined in the Hesychian tradition as ὑμεναιούμενος, διὰ τὸ γαμουμέναις λέγειν σὺν κούροις τε καὶ κόραις (Aischines, fragment 43) ὅπερ νῦν παρεφθαρμένως ἐκκορεῖν λέγεται. Cf. K. Latte, *Hesychii Alexandrini Lexicon* II (København 1966) 521.

[10] *Accentuation* 106–113.

[11] Cf. Jakobson, *Selected Writings* I ("On Ancient Greek Prosody" [1937]) 266 f:

A marked category tends to be interpreted in relation to the unmarked one as a compound, complex category opposed to a simple one. The circumflex, as testified both by its original graphic symbol, ˆ, and by its traditional interpretation on the part of the grammarians, was viewed as being composed of two simple tones—a high one and a low one (the acute and the grave). It is interesting that the complexity of a long syllable under the acute accent (a low mora followed by a high one) was not noticed: the obligatory raising of the last mora in a long vowel was evaluated as the simplest, unmarked variety of the accent. Therefore, the raising of the second mora of a long vowel and the only mora of a short vowel was indicated by one and the same sign.

The raising of the initial mora of a long vowel is more striking than the raising of the final mora—such an interrelation is most natural for a language in which the basic determinant of the place of the accent is the end of the word.

[12] As shown by Kuryłowicz, *Accentuation* 111; cf. also n. 10.

final ensemble are apparent in the cited from μειλίχιος (not *μείλιχιος, despite μείλιχος), and e.g. its dative singular, μειλιχίῳ: here, then, are illustrations of {X́XXX̆ ⇒ XX́XX̆}, and, more significantly for the present discussion, of {X́XXX̄ ⇒ XXX̆X̄}. If, as herewith posited, this accent-limitation was already operative in Greek even before the obliteration of the morphological opposition {-V̆C‖ijV- : -V̆CjV-}, then the accentual pattern of denominative adjective-suffixes in *-je/jo- would involve e.g. nominative singular *-íijos vs. dative singular *-íjōi.[13] But the accentuation of the latter type, in -V̆C‖íjV-, means that the later process {(-V̆C‖ijV- ⇒) -V̆Ĉ‖jV- > -V̆ĈĈjV- > -V̆ĈĈʲV-ъ}[14] was subject to interference. Thus in a paradigm where originally -V̆C‖ijV- and -V̆C₁C₂‖ijV- alternated with -V̆C‖íjV- and -V̆C₁C₂‖íjV- respectively, as e.g. in {*-íijos : *-íjōi}, the ultimate results of -V̆ĈĈʲV-ъ and -V̆Ĉ₁Ĉ₂ʲV-ъ[15] could be prevented; instead, there would ensue this distribution: -V̆ĈjV-/-V̆ĈíjV- and -V̆Ĉ₁Ĉ₂jV-/-V̆C₁C₂íjV-, in a paradigm now showing e.g. *-íjos/*-íjōi. Henceforth, this posited original pattern will be symbolized {-í̯ı-/-í-}. Then, during the process of depalatalization (i.e., when -VĈĈʲV- > e.g. -VCCV-), the paradigmatically-conditioned non-geminating *-í̯ı- of grammatical categories with original {-í̯ı-/-í-} could be displaced in Ionian, for one, by vocalic -í̯ı-, in a generalization due to the by-form -í- (hence μειλίχιον/μειλιχίῳ and πότνιἄν/ποτνίᾳ[16]).

In Greek dialects where depalatalization did take place, there is at least one other condition, besides that of accentuation, which could be operative in ultimately preventing

---

[13] The alternation is made possible by the recessive accentuation of Greek nominals with formant *-(i)j-e/o-, for which cf. P. Chantraine, *La formation des noms en grec ancien* (Paris 1933) 38.

[14] As outlined in § 3 *supra*.

[15] Q.v. in § 3.

[16] Q.v. in § 5 *infra*.

gemination of -Ĉ- in original -V̆Ĉ‖jV-, or even in -V̆ĈjV-;
that is, if the pattern -V̆Ĉ(‖)iC- had coexisted in the same
paradigm with -V̆Ĉ(‖)jV-, as in πόλις, πόλιος (originally
with *⸍is, *⸍jos). In the latter case, however, the alternation
{-ιV-/-ιC-} is only one of two factors preventing the gemination of a preceding consonant, since in *i*-stem nouns, the
accentual alternation { ⸍ι-/-í-} is also present, as seen e.g. in
πόλιος/πολίων. Of course, gemination of -Ĉ- in -Ĉj- was
prevented not only by accentual patterns, but also by this
circumstance—when -Ĉ- is immediately preceded by still
another consonant.[17]

In returning to the subject of the alternation { ⸍ι-/-í-},
I suggest that this old pattern, later replaced in e.g. Ionian
by { ⸍ι-/-í-}, is probably the source for the metrical license, as
early as in the Epic, of devocalizing ι in the classically-
attested slot -CιV-: e.g. πόλιος in Φ 567 and πόλιας in θ 560
can be scanned only as ◡ -,[18] so that the rendering must be
πόλι̯ος and πόλι̯ας respectively. In some instances of such
devocalization, the spelling of ι has even been omitted in the
textual tradition, as in M 213: δῆμον (with hypercorrect
accentuation) for δήμιον.[19] Of course, as in all poetic conven-
tions which through the medium of precedent perpetuate
archaic linguistic conditions, the artificially-inherited mechanism involved can become subject to overextension, from
the standpoint of the original, purely linguistic, factors.
Thus after depalatalization in the Ionian dialects, a bard
belonging to this linguistic group could become unaware
that a poetically-transmitted distribution {-ι̯-/-í-} was originally accent-conditioned, so that from his standpoint,
the poetic license of devocalizing -ι- could be extended to

---

[17] Cf. note 8 *supra*.
[18] The second syllable here is long because it makes position with the consonant which follows in the text, q.v.
[19] Cf. Schwyzer, *GG* I 244 f.

-ι- as well; hence e.g. in δ 229, the scansion of Αἰγυπτίη
is - - -, not - - ◡ -, which would be impossible in dactylic
hexameter; in fact, if it were not for an inherited metrical
licence of substituting -ι̯- for -ι- in prevocalic position, the
word Αἰγυπτίη as it stands would have been rejected from
the Epic altogether.[20]

In the Aiolian dialects, on the other hand, it seems that
depalatalization did not take place: whereas in Ionian the
alternation { ´ι̯-/-í-} becomes { ´ι-/-í-}, the ultimate result in
Aiolian is apparently { ´ι̯-/´ι̯-}. That is, while in Ionian there
is the innovation of generalizing -ι- over -ι̯-, Aiolian shows
likewise an innovating feature, but with the reverse generalization of -ι̯- over -ι-. Hence the gemination in an epigra-
phically-attested Thessalian form like πολλιος (*DGE* 558.13:
genitive singular of πολις);[21] the writing-out of prevocalic
-ι̯- in e.g. πολλιος is probably prompted by the preconsonantal -ι- in the nominative; in e.g. other forms like Thessalian
κυρρον (*DGE* 590.20; = Ionian κύριον), however, it is
apparently felt unnecessary to include ⟨ι⟩: presumably,
⟨CC⟩ is adequate for representing both /ĈĈj/ and /ĈĈʲ/,
though in deference to panhellenic spelling-conventions,
⟨Cι⟩ is the regular practice,[22] even in the inscription which
contains the form κυρρον, *DGE* 590. Sporadic though the
spellings ⟨CCι⟩ and ⟨CC⟩ (for /ĈĈj/ = Ionian /Cι/) may
be in the presently-attested Thessalian evidence, the implication is clear: by classical times, the Aiolian equivalent
of Ionian -CιV- is -ĈĈι̯V-, even if -ι- in the latter was originally accented.

Against the claim that Aiolian did not undergo depalatalization, there might be this objection: that a form like πολλιος

---

[20] For a very important and useful list of instances where -CιV- is scanned
-Cι̯V- in early Greek poetry, cf. Scheller, *Oxytonierung* (§ 1) 99 ff.

[21] For several such examples in Thessalian and Lesbian, cf. Scheller,
Oxytonierung 108–113.

[22] Cf. Scheller, *Oxytonierung* 110.

is a relatively late development, possibly well within the classical period. This much might be tentatively accepted, but nevertheless, it does not follow that the direct ancestor of e.g. πολλιος was a trisyllabic πόλιος which later became πόλιος, which in turn underwent gemination as seen in πολλιος. Rather, the separate development in Aiolian may have started with the same patterns as in Ionian, {˝ι̯-/-ί-}. That is, the crucial forms of the word under discussion, from the accentual standpoint, would have been e.g. (1) πόλις, (2) πόλιος, (3) πολίων. Thus gemination in type 2 could be prevented in both Ionian and Aiolian by the accent-pattern -VCίV- in type 3 (and by the paradigmatic by-form -VCιC- in type 1).

However, such accent-conditioned prevention did not take place in all productive categories with *-∥j-:[23] we have already observed that in both Ionian and Aiolian, there is also the development -ĈjV- > -ĈĈjV- > -ĈĈjV-ᵦ. It is at a time when the latter type is already -ĈĈjV-ᵦ[24] that divergence between Ionian and Aiolian could have set in. In Ionian, there is depalatalization, so that -ĈĈjV-ᵦ may survive as e.g. -CCV-ᵦ, while paradigmatically-conditioned -ĈjV- (as in πόλιος) becomes -CιV- (πόλιος: e.g., Herodotos I 26). In Aiolian, on the other hand, there seems to be no depalatalization in -ĈĈjV-ᵦ};[25] but here too, there is eventual innovation, since paradigmatically-conditioned -ĈjV- (as in πόλιος) becomes -ĈĈιV- (hence Thessalian ⟨πολλιος⟩). Since gemination had previously been prevented in this slot by accentual patterns within the paradigm, a form like πολλιος suggests that this conditioning was finally removed in Thessalian. Thus in a paradigm where the accentual

---

[23] Cf. the detailed discussion in § 5.
[24] I.e., after stage II, as outlined in § 3, when {*-j- = *-ι̯-} is no longer an autonomous phonological entity.
[25] With Boiotian probably excluded: cf. § 6.

pattern originally involved { $\acute{\underset{\chi}{\iota}}$-/-$\acute{\iota}$-}, as in * $\acute{\iota}$jos/*-íjōi, * $\acute{\underset{\chi}{\iota}}$- becomes generalized over *-ι-, with gemination accompanying the generalization; hence e.g. the Thessalian-type genitive singular [αρ]‖γυρροι[26] (= Ionian ἀργυρίου), presumably accented ἀργύρροι.

This Aiolian result of { $\acute{\underset{\chi}{\iota}}$-/ $\acute{\underset{\chi}{\iota}}$-} from { $\acute{\underset{\chi}{\iota}}$-/-$\acute{\iota}$-} has already been mentioned, but it now becomes apparent that there are other possibilities; for example, in an original accentual contrast of genitive singular -ίᾱς vs. genitive plural -ιάων. Once contraction set in, so that -άων becomes potential *-ᾶν, recessive accentuation becomes a factor in the rearrangement of nominals with original -ίᾱ, in that the Aiolian system rejects accentuation on the final ensemble[27] (thus *-ᾶν ⇒ Aiolian $\acute{}$ᾶν, from the synchronic standpoint): since -ιάων could give rise to -$\underset{\chi}{\iota}$άων, unlike e.g. genitive singular -ίᾱς, the newly-contracted genitive plural of nouns in -ίᾱ, now $\acute{\underset{\chi}{\iota}}$ᾶν, could again produce the alternation { $\acute{\underset{\chi}{\iota}}$-/-$\acute{\iota}$-}. Here too, then, * $\acute{\underset{\chi}{\iota}}$- could become generalized over -ι-, with gemination accompanying the generalization: hence in Thessalian, for one, the accusative singular ιδδιαν[28] (= Ionian ἰδίᾱν), presumably accented ἴδδ$\underset{\chi}{\iota}$ᾶν.[29] As for types such as Lesbian πέρροχος (Sappho 106 [Lobel/Page]),[30] probably an -$\underset{\chi}{\iota}$- in e.g. *περ$\underset{\chi}{\iota}$όχῳ replaced the -ι- in e.g. *περίοχος; then, just as ἀνθρώπῳ : ἄνθρωπος, so also *περ$\underset{\chi}{\iota}$όχῳ : *πέρ$\underset{\chi}{\iota}$οχος (> *περρόχῳ : πέρροχος). Here, then, is an instance where *-$\underset{\chi}{\iota}$$\acute{}$ is generalized over *-ι-, from an original alternation {-$\underset{\chi}{\iota}$$\acute{}$/-$\acute{\iota}$-}. So much for the proposal that in the Aiolian dialectal group, there was no depalatalization in

[26] Q.v. in Bechtel, *GD* I 35; the inscription involves the consultation of the oracle at Dodona by the people of Mondaia. Cf. also Scheller, *Oxytonierung* 109.

[27] Cf. Kuryłowicz, *Accentuation* 157.

[28] Bechtel, *GD* I 35.

[29] To be contrasted with Schwyzer's version (*GG* I 274): ἰδδίαν.

[30] The first word of a line in dactylic hexameter.

/ĈĈʲ/ and /Ĉj/; hence the eventual gemination of the latter
into /ĈĈj/, as in πολλιος, and even the generalization of
-ι̯- over -ι-, as in ιδδιαν.

Now the latter type of glide-prevalence ultimately happened
in the general Ionian dialectal group also, and it can still
be seen in latter-day Dhimotikí; e.g. accusative singular
kardhyán, corresponding to classical καρδίαν. In fact, such
generalization of -ι̯- over -ι- must have taken place at
least as early as in the era of Alexandrian scholarship, since
the structure -ιά̯ even found its way into the Homeric textual
canon.[31] Briefly put, -ία̅ becomes -ιά̯ in the Ionian group (here
specifically the Attic form is given) at least before the Aristar-
chean era. Outside of occasionally-preserved Epic textual
heritage, however, the acceptance of the accentual pattern
-ι̯ά is generally restricted in the grammatical tradition to
substandard words, as convincingly shown throughout
Scheller's *Oxytonierung*.[32] It is possible, then, that instances
of the accentuation -ιά̯ in the surviving Homeric tradition
reflect a mistaken attempt by Alexandrian textual critics
to reconcile a recent linguistic phenomenon, the replacement of -ι- by -ι̯´ in e.g. Ionian, with the metrically-preserved traces (like the above-mentioned πόλι̯ος and Αἰγυπτι̯η)
of a time when { ´ι̯-/-ι-} had not yet been replaced by { ´ι-/-ι-},
at a much earlier stage of Ionian. More likely, however, is
that the pronunciation -ιά̯ became permissible in the rhapsodic tradition of recitation, but not in the canon of what was
contemporaneously considered correct conversational pronunciation. Thus the attempted reconciliation of two chronologically disparate linguistic conditions might have been
simply a relatively late poetic, not exegetic, convention,
arising from such inherited scansions as in Αἰγυπτι̯η, which
may well have been pronounced in the rhapsodic tradition

---

[31] Cf. Scheller, *Oxytonierung* 12 *et passim.*
[32] § 1.

as Αἰγυπτιή. What little there is left of direct Epic textual tradition regarding an accentual pattern -ιά[33] may actually reflect the scrupulous adherence of Alexandrian exegetes to the traditional rhapsodic pronunciation of their times.[34]

But a more crucial question still remains: whether the replacement of e.g. -ιᾱ by -ι̯ά in later Ionian is a purely phonological change. This does seem to hold for {-ι- > -ι̯-},[35] but not entirely for the actual accentual shift. Morphology too probably has a rôle here, by way of internal paradigmatic pressures. In oblique cases such as genitive singular -ιᾱς (by redundant accentual description, -ιᾰ̃ς), the shift {-ι- > -ι̯-} could result in -ι̯ᾶς (= -ι̯ᾰ̃ς); perhaps only thereafter did the following type of proportion set in: -ῆς : -ή = -ι̯ᾶς : -ι̯ά.

Granted, then, that in Ionian as in Aiolian, -ι̯- could ultimately become generalized over -ι-; but the point insisted upon is this important difference: that in the second dialectal group, this generalization entailed gemination, but not in the first. Hence the original contention, however tentative, that depalatalization did not take place in early Aiolian, unlike Ionian, and that in the attested evidence of the former, the secondary gemination (resulting in /ĈĈjV/) as in Thessalian πολλιος is a direct extension from the kind of primary gemination (resulting in /ĈĈʲV/) which is a phenomenon common to all Greek dialects.[36]

§5. In a comparison of forms like μειλίσσω and μειλίχιος, the question still to be answered is why original *-j- entailed gemination of the preceding consonant in the former instance, whereas in the latter, its attested reflex is vocalic.

---

[33] E.g. ἁρμονιῇσιν in ε 248, 361; cf. Scheller, *Oxytonierung* 130, 133 ff.

[34] For further discussion of rhapsodic pronunciation, cf. § 5 *infra*.

[35] Q.v. in Scheller, "Konsonantisches ι im nachklassischen Griechischen," *Oxytonierung* 117–123, and "Zur Konsonantisierung des ι im Neugriechischen," pp. 123–125.

[36] As a typological parallel of Thessalian πολις/πολλιος cf. Oscan *aeteis* (Latin alphabet) "partis"/[a]*ittiúm* (native alphabet) "partium"; q.v. in C. D. Buck, *A Grammar of Oscan and Umbrian*[2] (Boston 1928) § 162.

The proposed solution is this: at the time when accent-limitation was already operative in Greek (so that X́XX̄ ⇒ XX́X̄), non-enclitic finite forms of denominative verbs in *-je/jo-, as a productive category, were still accented on the thematic vowel of the inflectional suffix.[37] Thus the factor of accentuation could not enact an -i- coexisting with -i̯-, and therefore the latter in turn could not ultimately be generalized as -ι- in Ionian, for example. Now it has been argued by Kuryłowicz[38] that upon the convergence of a morphological and a phonological factor, namely univerbation and accent-limitation respectively, non-enclitic finite forms of verbs with original suffixal accentuation, such as the type λιπεῖν, underwent recessive accentuation. To accommodate the present theory on the type μειλίσσω, we therefore have to suppose that accent-limitation was already operative before univerbation; then by the time that univerbation too became operative (whence the recessive accent in e.g. μειλίσσω), original non-enclitic finite -VC₁‖-jé/jó- and -VC₁C₂‖-jé/jó- had already become -VĈ₁Ĉ₁ʲ-é/ó- and -VĈ₁Ĉ₂ʲ-é/ó- respectively.[39] In other words, with recessive accentuation in the type μειλίσσω finally resulting from univerbation, the continuing factor of accent-limitation could no longer entail the alternation { ´i̯-/-i- }, since original *-i̯- was by then irrevocably entered into the combinations -Ĉ₁Ĉ₁ʲ- and -Ĉ₁Ĉ₂ʲ-.[40]

As for deverbative verbs in *-je/jo-,[41] productivity must have been lost generally before the onset of accent-limitation, unlike the denominative verbs in *-je/jo-. In unproductive

---

[37] Cf. the parallel evidence of the Indic denominative verb-formant -yá-: chap. i § 9.2 *supra*. For the recessive accentuation of the denominative nominals in *-je/jo-, cf. again n. 13.

[38] *Accentuation* 151 f.

[39] I.e., stage II had already been reached: cf. § 3.

[40] Q.v. in § 3 again.

[41] With recessive accent; cf. the parallel evidence of the Indic deverbative verb-formant ´ya-: chap. i § 9.2 *supra*.

forms, $\{-\breve{V}CjV_{-a} > -\breve{V}\hat{C}\hat{C}^jV_{-a}\}$ (stage I) preceded the same progression in productive forms, $\{-\breve{V}\hat{C}\|jV_{-b} > -\breve{V}\hat{C}\hat{C}jV_{-b}\}$ (stage II).[42] The example of the ancestral form producing classical στέλλω we may then describe as follows: once productivity ceases in the formant of a verb like *stél-ije/ijo-, there is a reversion to *stél-je/jo-.[43] With such an onset of unproductivity and its phonological results, the former morpheme-boundary in the present tense between base and suffix can no longer be perceived; thus *stél-je/jo- can become synchronically resegmented as *stélj-e/o-, a simple thematic-stem verb. Hence *stélj-ō > *stéĺĺj-ō > *stéĺĺj-ō (the pattern $-\breve{V}\hat{C}\hat{C}^jV_{-a}$: stage II)[44] > e.g. Ionian στέλλω. At a time when στέλλω was *stéĺĺj-ō, a verb like ἀγγέλλω was a then-productive denominative in *-jé/jó-, thus *angel-jó (originally *angel-ijó); a corresponding nominal would have been *ángel-jos/*angel-íjōi and *angel-íjā in the nominative/dative singular masculine and nominative singular feminine respectively. Because of the suffixal accentuation in non-enclitic forms of the verb, the following chain of phonological developments becomes possible: *angel-jó > *angeĺĺjó > *angeĺĺjó (the pattern $-\breve{V}\hat{C}\hat{C}^jV_{-b}$: stage II);[45] next, with univerbation and subsequent recessive verbal accent, the development proceeds to e.g. Ionian ἀγγέλλω. But in the corresponding adjective, the alternation $\{-\mathfrak{i}-/-\acute{\iota}-\}$ (involving the mechanism of accent-limitation) prevented the development of stage II: hence the Homeric noun ἀγγελίη (as in Γ 206), not *ἀγγέλλη. So much, then, for the disparate developments resulting in μειλίχιος and μειλίσσω. The axiom meant to be derived from this discussion is that stage II is reached by once-productive categories in *-‖jV-, unless prevented by accent-limitation.

[42] Cf. § 3 and § 6.
[43] This is the process described in chap. i § 3 as attrition.
[44] Cf. § 3.
[45] *Ibid.*

Now besides denominative verbs in *-je/jo-, another such once-productive category in *-‖jV- has been mentioned, namely the feminine nominal in *-jă/*-jās.[46] Already compared[47] have been *welik̂-jō and *welik̂-jă, as reflected in ἑλίσσω and ἀμφιέλισσά respectively. On the basis of such still-productive participial formants as classical -ουσά, < *-oñt̂jă, and -(σ)ᾱσά, < *-(s)añt̂jă, we can infer that the ancestral constituent *-jă/*-jās must itself have been a productive formant as long as *-j- was capable of segmentation (here symbolized with the hyphens). Granted, the two just-mentioned participial formants are productive in the classical period only as composite structures; still, the inherited foundations {-ουσά ← -ων} and {-(σ)ᾱσά ← -(σ)ᾱς} are decisive: they must be traced back etymologically to {*-oñt̂-jă ← *-ont-s} and {*-(s)añt̂-jă ← *-(s)ant-s}: that is to say, etymology shows that these synchronically-attested foundations go back to a period when *-j- was still a functional unit. This in turn suggests that in common Greek, at a time before the stages I–II,[48] there was a productive formant *-‖ijă/*-‖ijās. Thus besides a *welik-ijō, there could once be a *welik-ijă.

The attested formal reflexes ἑλίσσω and -ἔλισσά, then, indicate that the latter type had undergone, with a productive formant *-ijă-, the stages I–II[49] and that there was no interference by accent-limitation; otherwise, the attested result would have been *ἑλίκιά/*ἑλικίᾱς. Hence the possible

---

[46] Homeric ʹτειρα/-τειρῆς, compared with the Attic ʹτρια/-τρίᾱς, betrays an original quantitative apophonic alternation in the declension of nominals in *-jă/*-jās: the four components just mentioned must have resulted from a paradigmatic split of an original *-t-ér-i-ə₂/*-t-r-i-é₂₂-s; likewise, the types ʹυια/-υίᾱς and -εῖα/-εῖᾱς reveal an original *-u̯-és-i-ə₂/*-u-s-i-é₂₂-s (cf. Schwyzer, *GG* I 474 f).

[47] § 2.

[48] § 3.

[49] *Ibid.*

conclusion that the original accentuation of such nominals was *-ijă̆-/-ijā̆-,[50] as indeed suggested e.g. by Schwyzer,[51] who compares Sanskrit *staríḥ, takṣṇí, satí, pṛthví* with what he proposes are accentual innovations in the corresponding Greek στεῖρᾰ, τέκταινᾰ, οὖσᾰ/ἔασσᾰ, πλατεῖᾰ. But in contrast to such Indic forms in -í/-yáḥ, there is also the type *pátnī/pátnyāḥ*. I propose that the corresponding Greek πότνιᾰ/ποτνίᾱς also had original root-accentuation throughout its paradigm, a feature inherited by Common Greek as by Indic for what must have been an unmotivated form in both. Now this question remains: why a productive category of nominals in *-jă̆/*-jā́s, with originally suffixal accentuation in e.g. the genitive singular, should later have undergone accentual recession in Greek. The answer can be postponed until we make this crucial point: the preservation of syllabic -ι- in a form like πότνιᾰ was not due to "Sievers' Law," as is usually claimed, if indeed the phonological opposition {-V̄CijV- : -V̆CjV-} had become obliterated by gemination;[52] rather, syllabic -ι- is preserved because of the alternation {-ι̯-/-í-}, which in turn was made possible by the circumstance that ever since the period of Common Greek, πότνιᾰ had been root-accented, hence subject to accent-limitation. Thus stage II[53] (in this case -V̄C̆₁C̆₂‖jV- > -V̆C̆₁C̆₂ʲV-) was prevented in the word πότνιᾰ by the alternation {-ι̯-/-í-}, i.e. *póĩnjă̆/*potníjās. Then, during the period of depalatalization, *-j- could become vocalized (hence classical πότνιᾰ, -◡◡). A reflex, however, of earlier *póĩnjă̆ (-◡) has been preserved by the Homeric meter, in ε 215, ν 391, υ 61, with even the spelling

---

[50] As we will see later, this accentuation need be assumed only for *-ijā̆-, not for *-ijă̆-: cf. *infra* in this same section.

[51] *GG* I 381.

[52] Cf. § 2.

[53] As described in § 3.

πότνα introduced into the textual tradition, in order to accommodate the scansion -◡.[54]

But the same process of depalatalization which brought about the vocalization of *-j- in -Ĉ₁Ĉ₂j- (as in πότνιᾰ) also triggered this change: -Ĉ₁Ĉ₂ʲ- (the final product of stage II)[55] > -C₁C₂-. An often-quoted example is the classical reflex of an original and no longer motivated form *werĝjō: namely, > *werdĵō > *werdʲō > ἔρδω, vs. ῥέζω < *wredẑʲō < *wredẑjō < *wreĝjō;[56] the neutralization of the opposition *g/*d in favor of *d could become irrevocably perpetuated only before the type of *-j- seen in *werĝjō/*wreĝjō, not before the *-j- which belongs to the alternation {-ι̯-/-ί-}. Indeed, the absence of *-ί- and the generalization of *-ι̯- after *γ/*δ is the etymological essence of the classical Attic/Ionic ζ itself.[57] The unit spelled ⟨ζ⟩ is a product of gemination, possible only when original *γι̯ and *δι̯ had not been preceded by another consonant; hence the divergent developments in ῥέζω and ἔρδω. The δ instead of etymological γ in the latter is the sign of an original pattern -Ĉ₁Ĉ₂ʲ-. Whereas after depalatalization Ionian (*d̂dj >) *d̂ẑʲ becomes ζ,[58] it appears that *Ĉd̂ʲ becomes Cδ. The important point, then, is that -V̆Ĉ₁Ĉ₂ʲV-, as seen in both stages I and II,[59] is the regular development from -V̆Ĉ₁Ĉ₂jV-, unless accent-limitation interferes. The classical Ionian reflex of such a pattern, furthermore, would be -V̆C₁C₂V-, not -V̆C₁C₂ιV-. Thus the productive type in *-jă/*-jắs, if preceded by

---

[54] Cf. also the spelling δῆμον for δήμιον in M 213, as discussed in § 4.

[55] Cf. § 3.

[56] Cf. also § 6. As for Linear B wo-ze (Pylos/Ea 309, etc.), it probably represents *wordẑʲei; for the transcription with *-d̂ẑʲ-, cf. § 9. I propose that the etymological sequence is the following: e.g. *wordẑʲō < ...*wr̥d̂djō < *wr̥ĝjō, ø-grade counterpart of e-grade *werĝjō.

[57] The specific phonological manifestations will be discussed further in § 6, with reference to dialectal divergence.

[58] Cf. § 6.

[59] Cf. § 3.

-C_1C_2-, is reflected in classical Ionian Greek as -C_1C_2ă/ -C_1C_2ης. A list of such forms is given by Lambert,[60] some of the most certain examples being πρόλιμνἄ (< *pro-limn-jă), ἔπιβδᾰ (< *epi-bd-jă < *epi-pd-jă), ἔχιδνᾰ (< *ekhidn-jă);[61] so also with the participial types like λύουσᾰ, i.e. < *luonsă < *luoñŝʲă < *luoñŝjă < *luont-jă.[62]

In contrast to πότνιᾰ, δέσποινα might have been suffix-accented in e.g. the genitive singular, as if it were a motivated formation, so that it could undergo stage II[63] because the alternation {-ɪ̯-/-ί-} (prompted by accent-limitation) was not there to interfere. From a proposed juxtaposition like {*pótñjă/*potníjās} vs. {*déspoîñʲă/despoîñʲás}, then, we might surmise that *-oîñj-/*-otní- became -οτνι-, while *-oîñʲ- (> *-oññʲ-) became e.g. Ionian -οιν-.

In the proposed nominative form *déspoîñʲă, the accentual interpretation has not yet been specifically discussed: nor yet, for that matter, in the nominative of other Greek forms in original *-jă/*-jās with proposed suffixal accentuation in e.g. the genitive singular. The complication is this: the Greek nominative singular in *-jă is not a direct phonological development from IE. Kuryłowicz has observed[64] that in Indic and Greek, there had occurred a remodeling of the IE nominative/accusative singular in *-iə₂/*-iə₂m. In Indic, the direct phonological development would be *-ī/*-iyam, but the second member is remodeled as -īm on the basis of the nominative. In Greek, the direct phonological development would be *-ī/*-ijă(n); by homalized anticipation in external *sandhi*, *-ăn#(V-) is generalized over *-ă#(C-), so that *-ăn# can precede both V- and C-; then *-ī becomes replaced by *-ijă on the formal precedent

---

[60] *Quaestiones* (§ 1) 44 f.
[61] Cf. also Schwyzer, *GG* I 475.
[62] For the proposed details of phonological development, cf. § 6.
[63] Cf. § 3.
[64] *Apophonie* 195.

III.§5

of the accusative, *-ijăn.[65] Now the matter of accent can be considered, with an adjustment on Schwyzer's relevant formulation.[66] As far as we can reconstruct on the basis o surviving apophonic distributions, the nominative/accusative/genitive singular of the IE nominal class under discussion may well have involved this pattern: * ´iə/* ´iəm̥/*-i̯éəs.[67] Now this accent-distribution could have been perpetuated as a polarizing feature in secondary, productive forms,[68] while becoming relinquished in primary forms; hence in Indic, there survives in e.g. the genitive singular an accentual contrast such as {motivated *devyā́ḥ* : unmotivated *pátnyāḥ*}. Yet with the new formal distribution in Indic of the three cited paradigm-members N -ī A -īm G -yāḥ, no productive apophonic distribution between N/A and G could be synchronically perceived—that is, before the inherited apophonic relation {ā : ī} was replaced in certain morphological categories by a productive newly-created relation {ā : ī}.[69] Before such a period, however, the final accent on forms like the G could be generalized on the -ī- of the N/A as well, because there would be no synchronic perception of an apophonic mechanism between -ī- and -iyā-; hence e.g. Indic *devī́* (/*devyā́ḥ*). In Greek, however, the distribution of N *-ijă A *-ijăn G *-ijās could synchronically persist in implying a functional apophony of {reduced grade *-jă- : full grade *-jā-},[70] which in turn could perpetuate in productive categories an accentual pattern of N * ´ijă A * ´ijăn G *-ijás: hence the divergent historical developments

---

[65] For possible instances where the same factor of external *sandhi* actually becomes the cause of divergent dialectal development in word-final syllables, cf. § 8.
[66] *GG* I 381; cf. again nn. 50 and 51.
[67] Cf. n. 46 *supra*.
[68] Applicable here is Kuryłowicz's axiom I, quoted in chap. i n. 5.
[69] For further discussion of this restructuring, cf. Kuryłowicz, *Apophonie* 258.
[70] Cf. W. Cowgill, "Evidence in Greek," *Evidence for Laryngeals* 150.

119

of e.g. *pótn̄jǎ/*potníjās vs. *lúoñŝjǎ/*luoñŝjás.[71] After depalatalization, the original productive type in *ˊijǎ/*-ijás finally became unproductive, with *ˊjǎ/*-jás becoming ˊǎ/-ῆς, while the even previously unproductive *ˊjǎ/*-íjās survived as ˊιǎ/-ίᾱς. Furthermore, since unproductivity in ā-stem nouns entails accentual recession in Greek,[72] the ultimate result from ˊǎ/-ῆς is ˊǎ/ˊης, as in λύουσᾰ/λυούσης. However, even though through phonological changes *-jǎ ceased to be a productive ending vis-à-vis *-ont- (as in *lú-ont- vs. *lú-ont-jǎ), classical -ουσᾰ persisted in productivity vis-à-vis -ων (as in λύων : λύουσᾰ).

Also to be noted is that there are, still in classical times, traces of the older pattern in ˊǎ/-ῆς. For example, there is μίᾰ: since the accentual pattern *ˊja was here impossible, the alternation {-ι-/-ι̯ˊ} in e.g. *smíja/*ŝm̄jás could cause the retention of syllabic ι; as Kuryłowicz observes,[73] the accentuation of μίᾰ(ν) represents a syncretism of two possible patterns in a corresponding three-syllable word, namely ×ÚU and ×̀UU; thus, since μίᾰ(ν) from the synchronic standpoint does not solely imply recessive accentuation, the latter is not generalized for oblique forms like μᾶς either. Then too, nouns in original *ˊijǎ/*-ijás with the specialized semantic function of place-names could retain the end-accent (thus here again an example of the perpetuation of an archaic feature in a secondary function),[74] whence such attested forms as Μελαιναί, Πλαταιαί, etc. Besides, there is a transmission in the Epic of such forms as καυστειρῆς (Δ 342, M 316), ἀγυιῆ (ο 441; vs. the varia lectio ἀγυίη), θαμειαί (A 52, etc.), ταρφειαί (T 357, etc.). It has been said of these forms: "Gerade die Schwierigkeit, die schon die

[71] For the later morphological development, irrelevant here, of *-ås from *-ás, cf. Kuryłowicz, Accentuation 126 ff.

[72] Cf. Kuryłowicz, Accentuation 115.

[73] Accentuation 120.

[74] Applicable is Kuryłowicz's axiom IV, quoted in chap. i n. 7.

alten Homerkritiker in diesen Formen fanden, und die
falschen Nachbildungen der spätern Dichter, beweisen ihre
Echtheit."[75] Furthermore, a cogent argument can be made
that such transmitted accentual patterns were not derived by
the Alexandrian exegetes from spoken dialectal pronunciation, but rather, from intense research in recited rhapsodic
pronunciation.[76] For this possibility, it is worth quoting the
following exploratory statement:

Mihi in his rebus versanti iterum iterumque occurrit, etiam in
obsoletioribus vocabulis aliquam de accentu traditionem fuisse.
Etenim etiamsi ponamus in versibus recitandis accentum voce
non notatum esse, quam saepe extra versum etiam Homericorum
vocabulorum proferendi occasio erat, partim coram discipulis
in ludo, partim in rhapsodorum et philosophorum confabula-
tionibus: ut facile cogitari possit multorum vocabulorum accentus
quasi per manus traditos usque ad Alexandrinos pervenisse.
Et cum idem sensus, qui ab initio vocibus suos accentus imper-
tierat, qui in quibusdam a regula defecerat, etiam postea valeret
in hominibus Graecis, eo magis ad verum et genuinum in hac re
inclinasse censendi sunt: quamquam poterat subinde fieri (de
hoc iudicandum erat grammatico) ut formis certae genti regioni-
que propriis animo obversantibus ab eo, quod antiqua et com-
munis lex et consuetudo Graecae linguae suaderet, deflecterent.
... Ad ea quae de traditione et de sensu Graecis insito diximus,
hic addere necesse, quod sane memorabile, de οὐτάμενος, βλήμενος
et plurimis quae adhuc recensuimus, Herodiano Aristarchi
argumenta videri ignota fuisse. Nonne inde licet concludere
haec pleraque Aristarcho et aequalibus ne dubitabilia quidem
fuisse, quae et posteriores regulae scrutatores et nos hodie mirantes
vix assequimur? Attendant haec ingeniosiores. Memorabilis
res est et olim fortasse huic rei plus lucis allatura, quam nunc
per nos licuit.[77]

[75] J. Wackernagel, "Akzentstudien III," Nachrichten von der Gesellschaft der
Wissenschaften zu Göttingen (1914) = Kleine Schriften II 1176.
[76] Cf. J. Wackernagel, Beiträge zur Lehre vom griechischen Akzent (Basel 1893)
= Kleine Schriften II 1072–1107, esp. 1103.
[77] K. Lehrs, De Aristarchi studiis Homericis³ (Leipzig 1882) 258. Cf. also
Scheller, Oxytonierung (§ 1) 9, for speculation about possible mechanisms of
preserving in recited poetry certain accentual patterns no longer in current
spoken usage.

In short, then, traces of Alexandrian commentary show that there was an awareness of a tradition-preserved pronunciation of the type ʹἄ/-ῆς. For example, in scholiastic commentary[78] on the line Z 422, the reading ἄγυιαν in Υ 254 is specifically ascribed to Aristarchos, as also ἀγυιάς in Z 391; a report to the same effect is found in Eustathios 652.53. In later grammatical traditions, an awareness of only the latter type of accentual variation in a word like ἄγυιᾰ could lead to the mistaken postulation of suffixal accentuation throughout: hence the false accent in nominative singular ἀγυιά, as in the Etymologicum Magnum 14.21, etc. Then too, there is the false accentuation transmitted for accusative singular ἀγυιάν, in Pindar, Olympia 9.34, though in Nemea 7.92, the correct ἄγυιαν is attested in the codices uetustiores. That Pindaric exegesis in the era of Alexandrian scholarship did take into account an accentual tradition of the type ʹἄ/-ᾶς is shown by the reading γλωσσᾶι in a papyrus-fragment (Parthenia 2 [= fr. 94b].35 [Snell]).[79]

So much, then, for the reasons why productive Greek denominative verbs in original *-ijé/ijó- and the productive nominal formation in *ʹija/*-ijás both underwent stage II (q.v. in § 3); there was no accentual interference in either category. In the case of the latter, however, we must still examine a further problem: why syllabic ι was preserved in feminine agent-nouns of the type ʹτριᾰ/-τρίᾱς. As with πότνιᾰ, the answer does not involve Sievers' Law, but rather, previous accent-pattern. I submit that an original *ʹtrijᾰ/*-trijás became *-tríjᾰ/*-tríjās on the model of coexisting feminine agent-nouns in *-trís/*-tríjos, later replaced by *-trís/*-trídos (as in πλυν-τρίς).[80] Then, after depalatalization, when endings in original *-ijᾰ/*-ijās

---

[78] Σ Veneti 454 (A).

[79] Cf. Schwyzer, GG I 474: from Attic: Ionic γλῶσσα:γλᾶσσα, we may even postulate a paradigm-split from *{γλῶσσα/γλᾱσσᾶς}; cf. n. 46 supra.

[80] For the productive replacement in Greek of i-stems by ίδ-stems, cf. Schwyzer, GG I 464 f.

were no longer independently productive, there could be accentual recession; hence ^{2}τρια/-τρίᾱς (as in πλύν-τρια). Unlike the early formant *-ijă/*-ijās, however, the composite formant originally in *-trijă/*-trijās, taken as a whole, continued to preserve its productivity even as ^{2}τριᾰ/-τρίᾱς. As for the residual type ^{2}τειρᾰ in the Epic, its original accentuation was apparently unaffected by -τρίς: hence *-téřjă/*-teřjás > *-téřřjă/*-teřřjás, whence ultimately-τειρᾰ/ -τειρᾶς (with the morphological rearrangements of accent-recession/circumflex);[81] and the accentuation of the second member given here is actually attested in the above-mentioned καυστειρῆς (Δ 342, M 316).

§6. There is yet to be cited an actual instance in Greek where the product of stage I, $-\breve{V}\hat{C}\hat{C}^{j}V$-$_a$, is perceptibly different from that of stage II, $-\breve{V}\hat{C}\hat{C}^{j}V$-$_b$.[82] I propose here the Ionian -σ- as in τόσον (< *toîjon) and μέσον (< *meîjon < *methjon) for the former category, and -σσ- as in μέλισσᾰ (< *melîtja) and πλάσσω (< *plaîjō < *plathjō) for the latter. In a representation where the vector of time runs from left to right,[83] the intervocalic developments can be described as follows:[84]

	a	b	c	d	e	f	g	
1.	sj	hj	jj			iʲ	i	(diphthongal)
2.	tj	ŝj	ŝŝj			ŝŝʲ	s	
3.	t‖ij	ĵ	îĵj	îtĵj	îŝj	îŝʲ	ts	
4.	kj	îtĵj			îŝj	îŝʲ	ts	
5.	k‖ij	ĵ	îtĵj	îŝj	îŝʲ	ts		
6.	dj	d̂d̂j		d̂ẑj	d̂ẑʲ	dz		
7.	d‖ij	d̂j	d̂d̂j	d̂ẑj	d̂ẑʲ	dz		
8.	gj	d̂d̂j		d̂ẑj	d̂ẑʲ	dz		
9.	g‖ij	d̂j	d̂d̂j	d̂ẑj	d̂ẑʲ	dz		
10.			ts	ss	ss	s		

[81] Cf. again nn. 72 and 71 respectively; also n. 46.

[82] For stages, see § 3.

[83] Several of the stages might be simultaneous: e.g. c and d, d and e.

[84] The opposition between aspirated/non-aspirated voiceless stops had been neutralized in favor of the latter before *-j- (cf. Allen, "Palatalization" [§ 1]

Column *c* represents the results of stage I, column *d*, those of stage II.[85] It should be noted that the neutralization of *k/*t and of *g/*d in favor of *t and *d respectively in column *c* could be perpetuated only if *j was not the first member of the accent-conditioned alternation {-i̯-/-í-}.[86] Even more, as discussed in § 4, stages I and II were actually prevented by this alternation {-i̯-/-í-}; hence e.g. μειλίχιος vs. μειλίσσω. As for the above representation, it is crucial that in Attic/Ionic (as also in Arcado-Cypriote), the expected *ss of *g*.2 was simplified into σ, just as with the expected *ss (< *ts) in *g*.10; hence e.g. μέσος, κατεδίκασαν respectively;[87] in Lesbian, on the other hand, σσ, as derived originally from *tj, is retained just as σσ derived from *ts; hence e.g. μεσσος, κατεδικασσαν respectively.[88] But in Attic, even though *ts (*d*.10) becomes σ, *ts (*g*.3/4/5) becomes

---

119); there is likewise neutralization of *kʷ/*k and *gʷ/*g into *k and *g within the same environment. Hence the opportunity to reduce the repertory of symbols in column *a*.

Also, word-initial *j- has collapsed with the word-initial *dj- (as in n. *a*.6), whence e.g. ultimately ζεύγνυμι (< *i̯eu-; cf. Sanskrit *yoktár*-) vs. Ζεύς (< *di̯eu-; cf. Sanskrit *dyáuḥ*). For a typological parallel, cf. Italian *giorno* (< *diurnum*) vs. *Giove* (< *Iouem*). As for instances where *j- did not merge with *dj- in Greek, one reason may be that the former is actually a reflex of *əj-; for a critical discussion, cf. W. Cowgill, "Evidence in Greek," *Evidence for Laryngeals* 162. Then too, the typology of contrasts like Latin *diū* (< *di̯eu) vs. *Iūppiter* (< *di̯eu-p-pater) is misleading: the primary factor operative here is the presence/absence of morpheme-boundary after the *di̯-; cf. chap. i § 6.

85 That the types ὅσον/μέλισσα involved two different stages conditioned by the absence/presence of morpheme-boundary has been suggested before: cf. Allen, "Palatalization" (§ 1) 119 n. 31, with bibliography. As for the palatal affricates in column *f*, they might be described in a variety of ways: e.g., instead of *-îŝi̯-/*-d̂ẑi̯-, the representation could be *c'/*ʒ'; cf. Byelorussian *c'/ʒ'* < *t'/d'*, as discussed by Jakobson, *Selected Writings* I (*Principes de phonologie historique* [1931]) 203. Nevertheless, the complex transcriptions *-îŝi̯-/*-d̂ẑi̯- are preferable for Ionic, because of such ultimate reflexes (after depalatalization) as geminated -*ss*- for the former and metathetized -*zd*- for the latter.

86 Cf. the discussion on ἔρδω in § 5.

87 For a comparison with Boiotian, cf. § 7.

88 Q.v. in Bechtel, *GD* I 33, 91.

ττ; hence e.g. μέλιττᾰ. The reason for this divergence from Ionic can be explained on the basis of Boiotian phonology. In the prehistory of the latter dialect, $a.2/3/4/5$ evolved identically: i.e., $b.2$ did not occur, so that *îtj holds for $d.2$ as well as for $d.3/4/5$. Thereupon *îtj > *ît̂ʲ > *ttʲ > *tts > ττ, just as *ts > (*tts > ? *tts >) ττ: hence e.g. μεττω (= Ionian μέσου), οποττα (= Ionian ὁπόσα), διαφυλαττι (= Ionian διαφυλάσσει), εψαφιττατο (= Ionian ἐψηφίσατο), etc.[89] On the other hand, where no gemination is possible, i.e. in a non-intervocalic slot, Ĉtj > Ĉt̂ʲ > Ctʲ > Cts > Cs, just as Cts > Cs. Hence e.g. πασαν (< *pansan < *pantjan), *πασι (< *pansi < *pantsi) as in Πασαρετος, etc.;[90] also in word-final position, gemination did not occur, so that *-ts# > -s, instead of *-ττ; e.g., καταβας (< *katabans < *katabants), παις (< *paits < *paids).[91] I likewise posit that the development in Boiotian from $d.6/7/8/9$ onwards was as follows: *d̂dj > *d̂d̂ʲ > *ddʲ > *ddᶻ > δδ,[92] where the onset of depalatalization is marked by the change {*ʲ > *ʲ}.[93] If, then, Boiotian is to be called a representative of Aiolian at all,[94] it is in this respect apparently

[89] Q.v. in Bechtel, *GD* I 248 f.

[90] Q.v. in Bechtel, *GD* I 241; cf. also Thumb/Scherer, *GD* II 35, 83. The type *πασι is later replaced by the type παντεσσι, since Boiotian is among those classically-attested dialects where a new dative plural desinence -εσσι has infiltrated the declension of consonant-stem nominals. For a discussion of this areal feature and its possible sources of diffusion, cf. Coleman, "Dialect Geography" (§ 1) 96 f, who concludes that there is no need to assume this extended distribution of -εσσι to be a mark of Aiolian substratum.

[91] Q.v. in Bechtel, *GD* I 241 and in *DGE* 456 n. 1 respectively.

[92] For the close phonological relationship between aspirates (here the unvoiced *ʲ, namely *ʲ, in *ttʲ and *ddʲ) and fricatives (here the *s and *z in later *tts and *ddᶻ), cf. Allen, "Palatalization" (§ 1) 119 ff and also n. 37, where further bibliography is given. As Allen points out, "the acoustic correlate of the masking factor" is apparently the feature of stridency; cf. R. Jakobson, C. G. M. Fant, M. Halle, *Preliminaries to Speech Analysis* (Cambridge/Massachusetts 1963) 23–26.

[93] I do not assume the same impetus for the development of affricates in e.g. Ionic, as seen from the discussion preceding.

[94] Cf. § 7.

divergent from Thessalian and Lesbian, where depalatalization does not seem to have been realized.[95] Now the effect
of Boiotian on the Attic development of $g.3/4/5$ can be formulated: under the influence of Boiotian *tt^s > $\tau\tau$, Attic
*ts $(g.3/4/5)$ became $\tau\tau$ also, instead of *ts > $\sigma\sigma$, as in
Ionic proper.[96] According to Allen's perceptive evaluation,[97]
the identity here of ultimate development in Attic and Boiotian can be attributed to a partial *phonologisches Sprachbund*,
resulting from geographical proximity:[98] "Attic and Boeotian
being both then at the affricate stage, both would have followed the typical Boeotian development to a stop rather
than a fricative (as in Ionian)."[99] As for $g.6/7/8/9$ of Attic,
we may ask why it is that under the influence of Boiotian
dd^z > $\delta\delta$, there was no corresponding Attic evolution
*dz > *$\delta\delta$. The likely explanation seems to be that in Attic,
*dz already underwent metathesis into *zd, spelled ζ;[100]
cf. e.g. Ἀθήναζε (< *-ănsde), as discussed by Lejeune:
"pareille chute de la nasale ne s'observe que devant sifflante

---

[95] Cf. § 4.
[96] For a discussion of $\sigma\sigma/\tau\tau$ representing [ss]/[tt], cf. W. S. Allen, *Vox Graeca*
(Cambridge 1968) 57 f. There are instances in Old Ionic where even *ts seems
still extant: e.g. ἐλάσσονος is attested with the spelling ελαTονος (Erythrai),
q.v. in Bechtel, *GD* III 80. Cf. also n. 116.
[97] (§ 1) 126.
[98] For a typological discussion, cf. Jakobson, *Selected Writings* I ("Über
die phonologischen Sprachbünde" [1931]) 137–143.
[99] Allen, "Palatalization" (§ 1) 126; cf. also Bartoněk, *Vývoj* 147. The same
development of $\tau\tau$ is touched off in the contiguous dialects of Euboia and
Oropos.
[100] That *-dz- > -zd- was not accompanied by *-ts- > *-st- must have
been influenced by this factor: [-z-], unlike [-s-], had not been an autonomous
phonological element, but rather, a combinatory variant; e.g., $s + b \Rightarrow$ -zb-,
$s + d \Rightarrow$ -zd-, etc. Cf. Allen, "Palatalization" (§ 1) 121 n. 40. Metathesis from
*-dz- to -zd- in e.g. Attic would have been facilitated by the pre-existing availa-
bility of the latter combination, even in such inherited forms as ὄζος [ozdos]
< *osdos; cf. Gothic *asts*, German *Ast*. For the possibility that early ⟨ζζ⟩
represents a [dz] in place-names such as Κλαζζομενιοι, cf. Allen, *Vox Graeca*
(n. 96) 55 n. 3. The spelling *⟨δσ⟩ would not be adequate for [dz], "since
voice-assimilation in Greek is normally regressive rather than progressive":
Allen, *Vox Graeca* 55.

suivie d'occlusive (§ 121): le traitement *-νζ- > -ζ- suppose donc pour ζ . . . la valeur *zd*."[101] On the other hand, as Bartoněk points out,[102] this metathesis of *dz to *zd* is not a phenomenon common to all dialects: in fact, there is even the strong possibility that some Ionian dialects underwent *dz > *zz*, parallel with *ts > *ss*. In Attic too, from the fourth century B.C. onwards, ζ comes to be used for the transcription of Iranian *z*, whereas previously, it had approximated Iranian *zd*, as in *mazdara-/Μαζάρης*.[103] The new pronunciation may be due not to forward-assimilation, but to a dialectally-caused ouster of Attic *-zd-* (< *-dz-) by the *-zz-* (< *-dz-) of the now prevailing Koinē, the constitution of which was not Attic exclusively but Attic-Ionic in a wider sense;[104] parallel would be the replacement in Koinē of Attic ττ (*-tt-*) by Ionic σσ (*-ss-*).

§7. The Boiotian reflexes ττ and δδ arising from the etymological configurations proposed in § 6 are shared by e.g. central Cretan, as seen in forms like μεττον (*tj), αποδαττασθαι (*ts), δικαδδεν (*dj), etc.[105] Hence the following comment by Diver: "The usual analysis is that Boeotian represents an original Aeolian dialect that was heavily infiltrated from the west subsequent to the Doric invasion, and indeed it would appear that the ττ-δδ development itself is a Doric feature."[106] That is, Diver would add the reflexes ττ/δδ to all the other Dorian features of Boiotian.[107]

---

[101] *Traité* 95 f; cf. also the relatively late *testimonium* from Dionysios of Halikarnassos, *De compositione uerborum* 53.1–7, on the pronunciation of ζ as [zd] by the educated, apparently even in his time (first century B.C.).

[102] *Vývoj* 150 ff.

[103] Cf. Lejeune, *Traité* 310.

[104] For an interesting discussion of dialectal pedigree in Koinē, cf. e.g. Schwyzer, *GG* I 128 ff.

[105] Q.v. in Bechtel, *GD* II 694, 698.

[106] "Greek Consonantism" (§ 1) 22.

[107] As listed e.g. by Thumb/Scherer, *GD* II 18, and Buck, *GD* § 217.

It should be pointed out, however, that the term "Dorian" will now be used not in the sense applicable to the attested official languages of communities understood to be Dorian in classical times; rather, I define it here simply as the ancestor-dialect which, upon being superimposed in preclassical times on the earlier dialects of certain communities, produced features in their attested official languages which cannot be explained as derived from the ancestor-dialects of attested Attic-Ionic, Arcado-Cypriote, and Aiolian. Furthermore, on a tentative basis, no overall *terminus post quem* will be set for the beginning of Dorian superimposition. More clarification is also needed in reference to the designation "Aiolian": in the opinion of Porzig[108] and Risch,[109] original Aiolian is reflected more closely by the western variety (the most representative being the East-Thessalian dialect in the Pelasgiotis) than by its counterpart in the East (represented by Lesbian); thus in a contrast like Pelasgiotic -τι- vs. Lesbian -σι-, according to this theory, the former is genuine Aiolian, the latter, an ionicism diffused from the contiguous areas—in contrast to the older theory according to which the latter is genuine Aiolian, the former, a doricism resulting from an outright superimposition of Dorian upon Aiolian.[110] Left for the time being as a moot question, this issue has been raised at this particular point only to illustrate the difficulty in determining what features in West-Aiolian are actually Dorian, and not originally Aiolian.

Risch too argues that Boiotian shows clear traces of Dorian influence,[111] and thus Diver's quoted suggestion[112] that Boiotian ττ/δδ is a Dorian feature is not to be ruled out in terms of the Risch/Porzig theory, especially since ττ/δδ is also attested in central Cretan, as already seen. Diver's

---

[108] "Sprachgeographische Untersuchungen" (§ 1) 149–155.
[109] "Gliederung" (§ 1) 70.
[110] Cf. e.g. Buck, *GD* 5; also § 210.
[111] "Gliederung" (§ 1) 70.
[112] Cf. n. 106.

statement, however, still requires an important qualification: ττ/δδ is not *the* Dorian development, but *a* Dorian development from an earlier *îtj/*ddj (vs. the *îŝj/*dẑj posited for Ionian, q.v. in *e.*3/4/5 and *e.*6/7/8/9, § 6). The phonological evolution would involve at least the following stages:

	A	B	C	D	E
1.	îtj	îtʲ	ttʲ	ttˢ	ττ *or* σσ
2.	ddj	ddʲ	ddʲ	ddᶻ	δδ *or* ζ.

Besides the already-quoted central Cretan forms showing stage E, namely μεττον, αποδατταθθαι, δικαδδεν,[113] there are also attested earlier forms of the same local provenience, revealing stage D: e.g., οζοι (= Ionian ὅσοι), ανδαζαθαι (= Ionian -δάσασθαι), εδικαζε (= Ionian ἐδίκασε);[114] this spelling with *zayin* (ζ, with the shape I) in the most archaic extant inscriptions of central Crete[115] implies an affricate stage, corresponding to the *ttˢ and *ddᶻ of stage D. From a historically graphic standpoint, *zayin* as seen in the early Cretan alphabet might have originally been integrated into a schema of expressing stop + sibilant. With D = dental, G = velar, B = labial, S = sibilant, and with merely general rather than epichoric connotations intended, such a pristine schema can be outlined thus:

$$
\begin{aligned}
I\ \text{zayin} &= D + S & \zeta \\
\text{Ⅼ såmękʰ} &= G + S & \xi \\
\Psi &= B + S & \psi.[116]
\end{aligned}
$$

From such an early affricate stage (cf. again column D) of *ttˢ and *ddᶻ as actually attested in central Cretan, there

---

[113] Cf. n. 105.
[114] Q.v. in Bechtel, *GD* II 694, 698; all six of these forms are from Gortyna.
[115] Again, cf. Bechtel, *GD* II 694.
[116] Originally, the opposition voiced/unvoiced could have been ignored in such an orthographic system, whence e.g. the archaic Theran spelling of [dzeus] as ⟨ξευς⟩, not ⟨ζευς⟩—apparently caused by a confusion of voiced dentals and velars: cf. L. H. Jeffery, *The Local Scripts of Archaic Greece* (Oxford 1961) 317. Nevertheless, the spelling-mechanism of ζ/ξ/ψ for D + S/G + S/B + S

are different possible developments; the one shared by the later variety of central Cretan itself and by Boiotian has already been discussed, namely $D + S > D + D$, as in ττ and δδ. But the extant dialects of many communities with Dorian ancestry show alternate possibilities; where $*t + *s$ develops into σσ, so too $*tt^s$ into σσ, as in the official idiom of Argolis:

$*t + *s > *tt^s > ss$ e.g. ησσαντο, ισσατο, etc.[117]

$*tt^j > *tt^s > ss$ e.g. οσσα, γλωσσαι, etc.[118]

$*dd^j > *dd^z > zd$ e.g. νοσφιζεσθαι, χρειζον, etc.[119]

That $*dd^z > *dz > zd$ here is suggested by the spelling δικασζοιτο.[120] A likely motivation for the metathesis into *zd* is the synchronic lack of a correlate $*ts$ for $*dz$; the crucial impetus, however, may well be the *Sprachbund*-pressure of an areal feature, with locus of diffusion left undetermined in the present discussion.[121]

An important factor to consider in any further investigation is that metathetized *zd* or assimilated *dd* are not the two inevitable alternatives that develop phonologically from $*dd^z$. Another possibility is *zz* ($< *dd^z$), parallel to *ss* ($< *tt^s$). Still another is the simple retention of *dz*, without metathesis. Whether ⟨ζ⟩ represents *zz* or *dz* in the official language of a particular area with Dorian pedigree is often difficult, if not impossible, to decide directly. Nevertheless, the use of ⟨ζ⟩ (i.e., I) for an affricate *ts* in the Oscan

---

is unstable because the underlying phonological hierarchy lacks symmetry: Greek preserves no voiced/unvoiced opposition like *ks/gz* or *ps/bz* to match a *ts/dz*. For a discussion of the graphemic problem from the standpoint of a specific area, cf. J. Brause, *Lautlehre der kretischen Dialekte* (Halle an der Saale 1909) 152 ff. On the representation of unvoiced $D + S$ by the Ionian *T* and the Pamphylian *Ψ*, cf. Bartoněk, *Vývoj* 149.

[117] Q.v. in Bechtel, *GD* II 465 f.

[118] *Ibid.*

[119] Q.v. in Bechtel, *GD* II 466 f.

[120] *Ibid.*

[121] Cf. also n. 100.

native alphabet, or the report by Velius Longus (*GLK* 7.51.1–20) on the *testimonium* of Verrius Flaccus that the first component of ζ is a *d*—these are the kinds of factors which at least point to an areal feature *dz* in e.g. Italiotic Greek, thus perhaps putting into perspective such facts as this: after the colonization of Taras (Tarentum) and Herakleia by Lakonia, ζ-spelling persists in the first two areas mentioned, while δδ-spelling prevails in the third.[122] We may derive very important additional perspective from some latter-day dialects of Greek:[123] for example, the pronunciation *dz* is still extant in the Greek enclaves of Terra d'Otranto (Salento) in South Apulia, as also of Bova and Condofuri in South Calabria—though at Ruchudi and Roccaforte *z* has prevailed;[124] furthermore, there are enough vestiges from Siceliotic Greek, in the form of borrowings, to indicate original *dz* there too: e.g. *madza* "Erdscholle" < μάζα.[125] The pattern *dz* is also attested for e.g. the islands Kos and Syme; likewise for the remote community of Ἔλυμπος ("noch heute nur auf Maultierpfaden zugäng- lich-")[126] on Karpathos, while *zz* (geminated, < *dz*) prevails on the rest of this island.

In sum, ττ/δδ, belonging to the relative stage E, is a reflex of Common Dorian *tt^s/*dd^z, but it is by no means the sole reflex possible. A dialect apparently showing half of the same development in stage E is Elean, with σσ and δδ. Certain orthographic idiosyncrasies in archaic inscriptions from Olympia (sixth-fifth centuries B.C.) seem even to betray the earlier stage D, when *ss* and *dd* had still been *tt^s and *dd^z. In word-initial position, the latter would have been

---

[122] Cf. Bartoněk, *Vývoj* 147.
[123] As pointed out by G. Rohlfs, "Die Aussprache des *z* (ζ) im Altgriechi- schen," *Das Altertum* 8 (1962) 3–8.
[124] *Ibid.* 6 f.
[125] *Ibid.* 7.
[126] *Ibid.* 6.

Attic/Ionic

	1	2	3	4
a	*-ehe-[129]	*-ee-	-ḗ-	/-ē-/ -ei-
b	*luhō[130]	*lusō	lusō	/lusō/ λύσω
c	*wepessi	*wepesi	*wepessi	/epesi/ ἔπεσι
d	*possi	posi	posi	/posi/ ποσί
e	*epsāphisse[131]	*epsāphise	*epsāphise	/epsēphise/ εὐήφισε Ionic
f	*phulatŝiei[132]	*phulatŝiei	*phulatsei	/phulassē/ φυλάσσει Ionic /phulattē/ φυλάττει Attic
g	*meŝŝloho	*meŝŝioo	mesǭ	/mesǭ/ μέσου
h	*tojjo[133]	*tojjo	toio	/toio/ τοῖο
i	*dokimadẑiei	*dokimadẑiei	dokimazdei	/dokimazdē/ δοκιμάζει

Boiotian

	1'	2'	3'	4'
a'	*-ehe-[129]	*-ee-	-ē-	/-ē-/ -ei-[134]
b'	*luhō[130]	*lusō	*lusō	/lusō/ λούσω
c'	*wepessi	*wepessi	*wepessi	/*wepessi/ *Ϝεπεσσι[135]
d'				[136]
e'	*epsāphitse[131]	*epsāphitse	*epsāphitˢe	/*epsāphitte/ *εψαφιττε[137]
f'	*phulatŝiei	*phulatŝiei	*phulattˢei	/*phulattē/ *φυλαττει[138]
g'	*mettˢoho	*meŝŝioo	*mettˢō	/mettō/ μεττω[139]
h'				
i'	*dokimaddˢiei	*dokimaddˢiei	dokimaddˢzei	/dokimaddē/ δοκιμαδδει[140]

*t^s- and *d^z- at that time. Later, during stage E when *-tt^s-/ *-dd^z- had already become -ss-/-dd- in word-medial and s-/d- in word-initial position, the original distinction between a word-initial affricate *d^z- and a simplex stop *d- of course collapses in favor of the latter, d-. Thus a word-initial orthographic contrast between e.g. ζ- and δ- becomes redundant, whence such hypercorrect spellings as ζαμον (for δαμον = Ionic δῆμον);[127] the precedent of such hypercorrection can then spread even into word-medial position, whence e.g. ολυνπιαζον.[128]

On page 132 is a tentative diachronic outline juxtaposing the relevant phonological problems in Attic/Ionic and Boiotian (as heretofore discussed) with the outcome of intervocalic *s/*ss.

[127] Q.v. in Bechtel, GD II 831 f; also 839 f.
[128] Ibid.
[129] Originally *-ese-.
[130] The distribution of a morphologically-induced *-ū- in *lūsō is left out of the present discussion.
[131] Originally *epsāphidse; that the morphological extension of *-e into the 3rd singular active of the sigmatic aorist has already taken place at this stage is only a presupposition; the focus here is simply on *ts + vowel.
[132] Originally *îīj, then > *îŝʲ (stage f in the outline of § 6); the latter reconstruction seems supported by such variant orthographic representations in Linear B as pa-sa-ro, wa-na-so-i (cf. classical Ionic πάσσαλος, ἄνασσα), as discussed in § 9; the presumed syllabic division was *paî-ŝʲalō and *wanaî-ŝʲoin: hence the spelling of the syllabic coda *-î- was omitted in both instances. For a summary of the orthographic treatment of syllabic codae in Linear B, cf. F. W. Householder, "A Morphophonemic Question and a Spelling Rule," Mycenaean Studies, ed. E. L. Bennett (Madison 1964) 71–76.
[133] Originally *tohjo, from *tosjo: cf. stages 1.a-c in the outline of § 6.
[134] Q.v. in Bechtel, GD I 236 f.
[135] Predicated by such attested Boiotian forms as δαιμονεσσι, q.v. in Bechtel, GD I 269.
[136] For the spread in e.g. Boiotian of a new consonant-stem desinence -εσσι at the expense of -σι, cf. n. 90.
[137] Attested is 3rd singular middle εψαφιττατο, q.v. in Bechtel, GD I 248; cf. n. 89.
[138] Attested with itacized spelling: διαφυλαττι, q.v. in Bechtel, GD I 249; cf. n. 89.
[139] Q.v. in Bechtel, GD I 248; cf. n. 89.
[140] Q.v. in Bechtel, GD I 250.

Notes:

In $d(1)$ and $e(1)$, *ds (> *ts) > *ss already, whereas $e'(1')$ still shows *ts. During stage (1), intervocalic *h is a combinatory variant of preconsonantal or postconsonantal *s; e.g. *eh-mi, *eh-i, *es-ti (becoming ultimately εἰμι, εἶ, ἐστι in e.g. Attic). Intervocalic /ss/ as in $cde(1)$ is felt as the geminate of intervocalic /s/; the latter is pronounced [h], as in a and b. By stage (2), intervocalic [h] disappears in $ag(2)$, whence also the loss of motivation for differentiating geminated intervocalic /ss/ with simplex /s/, so that *ss can now be reduced to *s, as in $cde(2)$. Likewise *ŝŝ^j can be de-geminated as soon as it is depalatalized, whence the /s/ of $g(3)$. The stage of depalatalization is of course $(3/3')$, as shown in $fghi/f'g'i'$. Meanwhile, there had occurred a mor-phological restoration of intervocalic *s, restricted to such specific categories as the sigmatic future; the mechanism was furnished on the model of consonant-base verbs, e.g. *agō : *aksō = *luō : *lusō.[141] On the other hand, in stage (2'), geminated intervocalic *ss is retained in e.g. c' as an effective contrast with *ts as in e'.

An indirect reflex of stage (1) can be found in the Epic, where formulaic interplay brings about the optional reten-tion of geminated intervocalic *ss in types like cd: e.g. ἔπεσι $(A\ 150, \text{ etc.})$ vs. ἔπεσσι $(I\ 113, \text{ etc.})$, ποσί $(N\ 617, \text{ etc.})$ vs. ποσσί $(N\ 579, \text{ etc.})$, etc. Such coexistence causes the poetic precedent producing e.g. Ὀδυσεύς $(\beta\ 246, \text{ etc.})$ besides Ὀδυσσεύς $(a\ 57, \text{ etc.})$, in a proportion like ποσσί : ποσί = Ὀδυσσεύς : Ὀδυσεύς.

The *Sprachbund*-pressure of neighboring Boiotian *tt^s > tt, stages $(3')$ to $(4')$, touches off Attic *ts > tt as opposed to Ionic *ts > ss in stages (3) to (4).[142] However, the Boiotian development of *dd^z to dd in stages $(3')$ and $(4')$ exerts no

---

[141] For a morphological category showing hesitation in restoring intervocalic *s, cf. 2nd singular middle *-sai, *-so, as in μέμνη-αι vs. μέμνη-σαι, δαίνυ-ο vs. κεῖ-σο: cf. Lejeune, *Traité* 81; cf. further in n. 184.

[142] Cf. nn. 96, 99, 100.

Sprachbund-effect on Attic, since already in *i*(3) *dz had become metathetized to *zd*.[143]

Stages (1–2) of the schema are valid for Arcado-Cypriote as well as for Attic/Ionic; stage (2) can even represent the attested situation in the standard dialect of the Linear B texts.[144] Stages (1'–2') in turn are valid for the prehistory of the Dorian idiom, as defined in § 6.

§8. At this point, the opportunity to re-examine the isogloss {-τι- : -σι-} finally arrives. In answer to the question posed in the introduction to this work, we must determine what the phonological conditions are for the assibilation of *-τι- to -σι- in e.g Attic/Ionic. For word-medial position, as with adjectives in -τ-ιος (e.g. Dorian) and -σ-ιος (e.g. Ionian), the essential prerequisite for assibilation is that *ti must be followed by V: hence the possibility of *j, in *-t̂jV-. But with productive adjectives in -ιος, as discussed in § 4, the accent-conditioned alternation {-i̯-/-í-} was originally operative, and that is why stage II (q.v. in § 3) is here averted. Thus after stage II, e.g. the nominative/ dative singular masculine in the instance now under consideration would involve the pattern *´t̂jos/*-tíjōi. The chronological table of § 6 indicates that after stage II, there was this pertinent development: *t̂îj (n. *d*.3/4/5) > *t̂ŝj (n. *e*.3/4/5). Such a change, it is proposed, was accompanied by e.g. {*´t̂jos > *´ŝjos}, which in turn could trigger an extension throughout the rest of the paradigm: hence *´ŝjos/*-ŝíjōi. After depalatalization in Ionian, of course, with {-i̯-/-í-} having become leveled to {-ι-/-í-} as outlined in § 4, the phonological motivation for a no longer obligatory process {*-τi̯V- > -σi̯V-} in a form like ´σιος/-σίῳ could not be synchronically operative: hence the possibility now of contrasting e.g. newly-generated αἴτιος (← *αἶτος, as in ἔξαιτος) with αἴσιος (← αἶσα < *aitjă).[145] Hence also

---

[143] Cf. n. 100.
[144] Cf. § 9.
[145] Cf. Schwyzer, *GG* I 270, and Frisk, *GEW* s.v. αἶσα.

such synchronic/inherited formations as Attic ναυτία/Ionic ναυσίη (← ναύτης).[146] Schwyzer lists[147] several synchronic formations of the former type, e.g. φιλοχρηματία, νότιος, μαθητιάω, ἱμάτιον, etc.; hypercorrect spellings like ἱμασιοπωλου[148] even suggest an awareness of grammatical (and artificial) stricture again -τιV-, based on a synchronic appreciation of the inherited distribution of -σιV- in the Attic/Ionic lexical repertory. In cases where a structure of an original pattern A (*-τ-‖{-ι-/-ί-}) persists in functionally coexisting with a by-form of pattern B (*-τ-‖ {no -ι-}), the following ultimate development is possible: even though *-τι- became *-σι- previously, the *-τ- of pattern A is nevertheless reinstated after depalatalization (while *-σ- in turn is ousted) on the basis of pattern B; for example:

A	B
μῆτις, μήτιος[149]	μῆτις, μήτιδος[150]
δολόμητις[151]	δολομήτης[152]
μάντις, μάντιος[153]	potential *μαντεύς[154]
μάρπτις[155]	μάρπτω.[156]

146 For the forms, cf. Scheller, *Oxytonierung* (§ 1) 41.

147 *GG* I 270.

148 In a papyrus dated to the ninth year in the reign of Ptolemy Philometor: *Urkunden der Ptolemäerzeit*, ed. U. Wilcken (Berlin/Leipzig 1922 ff) 7.8.

149 As in *Hymn to Aphrodite* 249.

150 As in Aischylos, *Hiketides* 61.

151 As in α 300.

152 As in *A* 540.

153 As in *N* 663.

154 Presupposed by e.g. μαντηος, as in μ 267: such a genitive can correspond to a nominative in *μαντεύς as well as μάντις. The former type of nominative is also implied by e.g. μαντεύομαι, as in *A* 107. Syncretism of -τεύς and -τις in this instance could be perpetuated because μάντις was no longer endowed with the function of *nomen actionis*. For a typological discussion of shifts from *nomen actionis* to *nomen agentis*, cf. chap. ii § 11.

155 As in Aischylos, *Hiketides* 826; "ravisher": here too as with μάντις, the semantic function of *nomen actionis* has been lost, in contrast with e.g. κάμμαρψις· μέτρον σιτικόν, τὸ ἡμιμέδιμνον. Αἰολεῖς (Hesychios).

156 The morpheme-boundary in μάρπτις had probably switched from μάρπ-τις to μάρπτ-ις, even though the -πτ- of μάρπτω (in contrast with that of μάρπτις) is not etymologically genuine: *marp̂jō > *marp̂ᵗʲō > μάρπτω; cf. Allen, "Palatalization" (§ 1) 119 f n. 36.

Furthermore, it has already been mentioned in § 6 that before
*j, the distinction between e.g. *t and *th was neutralized in
favor of *t.[157] Just as *τ > σ, then, it is possible that *θ > σ
before the alternation {-ị-/-í-}. Thus e.g. * ⸜ị̂jos/*-tíjōi >
* ⸜ṣ̂jos/*-tíjōi ⇒ * ⸜ṣ̂jos/* ⸜ŝíjōi could be paralleled by * ⸜ị̂jos/
*-thíjōi > * ⸜ṣ̂jos / *-thíjōi ⇒ * ⸜ṣ̂jos/*-ŝíjōi > ⸜σιος/ -σίῳ,
after depalatalization. Hence the following examples of
inherited relationships, as attested in Attic/Ionic: Προβάλινθος:
Προβαλίσιος, Τρικόρυνθος : Τρικορύσιος, σμίνθος : Σμισιών;[158]
besides the inherited type 'Αμαρύσιος, there is also attested
the newly-created (after depalatalization) synchronic type
'Αμαρύνθιος.[159] Another inherited form with -σι- (from
*-θι-) is ἐπ-ηλυσ-ίη, etymologically but not synchronically
a derivative of the adjectival stem ἐπηλυθ-.[160]

Still to be outlined are the circumstances for the innovation
{*-τι- > -σι-} in absolute word-final position, as with δίδωσι.
Here too, in external *sandhi*, *τ was followed by the alternation {-ị-/-ι-}; the second counterpart *-ι- was in this instance
motivated not by being accented, but rather, by the possibility of its being followed by C: i.e., *-ị#V- vs. *-ι#C-. To
the formulation of this pattern, an important qualification
must be added: before depalatalization, the pattern *-ι#V-
might also have existed, but only when *-ι was morphologically motivated, as seen in locative singular οἴκοι. Now the
attested accentuation of e.g. Attic/Ionic nominative plural
οἶκοι indicates that -οι here, despite its attested diphthongal
status, has to be considered etymologically a short vowel: apparently the accentual patterns *oîkoj#V-/*oíkoi#C- had
been homalized in favor of οἶκοι after depalatalization.

---

[157] Cf. again Allen, "Palatalization" 119.
[158] Cf. Thumb/Scherer, *GD* II 336, and Heubeck, "Einordnung" (§ 1) 164.
[159] Discussion of the forms by Heubeck, "Einordnung" 164.
[160] For an analysis of this derivation, cf. O. Szemerényi, *Syncope in Greek and Indo-European and the Nature of Indo-European Accent* (Napoli 1964) 15. Cf. also the important article of W. Burkert, "Elysion," *Glotta* 39 (1960–1961) 208–213.

Not so with locative singular οἴκοι, where -ι was apparently segmented like the -ι of consonant-stems: hence *oíkoi ≠ V-/ C- becomes οἴκοι.

That word-final position should become subject to restricted phonological conditioning by a following ≠V- to the exclusion of ≠C- seems to be a special Attic/Ionic trend of homalization in external *sandhi*—a trend that may be responsible for several phonological developments which at first seem unrelated; e.g.:

(1) An original alternation *ánthrōpoj ≠ V-/*anthrṓpoi ≠C- in the nominative plural results in ultimate prevocalic generalization in Attic/Ionic, whence ἄνθρωποι (cf. also the already-discussed οἴκοι). To be contrasted is Doric ἀνθρώποι,[161] seemingly showing preconsonantal generalization.

(2) Despite {*-V̄iC- > -ViC-} in Greek, the Attic/Ionic dative singular of *o*-stems is -ωι, as in ἀνθρώπωι. Some other dialects, most Doric, show -οι; summary by Buck, *GD* § 106.2.

(3) Despite {*-VnsC- > -VsC-} in Greek, the Attic/Ionic accusative plural of *o*-stems is -ους (< *-ons), as in ἀνθρώπους. Some other dialects, most Doric, show -ος; summary by Buck, *GD* § 78.

(4) In Attic/Ionic and Doric, *-n̥C- > -aC- and *-n̥V- > -anV-. An original particle *kn̥ (ø-grade of κεν) survives as ἄν in Attic/Ionic (the κ has been segmented out) and generally as κα in the Doric dialects; summary by Buck, *GD* § 134.2.[162]

---

[161] For *testimonia* from the Greek grammatical tradition, cf. H. L. Ahrens, *De Graecae linguae dialectis* II (Göttingen 1843) 27 f. For a different evaluation of this Doric divergence from Attic/Ionic, cf. Kuryłowicz, *Accentuation* 158.

[162] The poetic attestations of κα as also κᾱ can be ascribed to metrical lengthening of the type described by Kuryłowicz, *Apophonie* 276–285; for a discussion of the resegmentation whereby καν ⇒ ἄν in Attic/Ionic, cf. e.g. L. R. Palmer, "The Language of Homer," *A Companion to Homer*, ed. A. J. B. Wace and F. H. Stubbings (London 1963) 90 ff.

(5) Attic/Ionic -σι vs. Doric -τι. There will be further discussion, as the argument proceeds, on the assibilation of original *-ti, prompted by prevocalic occurrence in word-final position.

In this incomplete list of contrasts, the signal inference concerns the prevocalic generalization in Attic/Ionic; such an innovation does not automatically presuppose a reverse preconsonantal generalization in e.g. Doric; although there are signs of just such a parallel innovation, n. 2 and n. 3 in the present list can definitely not be applied to all Doric dialects. Furthermore, in central Cretan, the *sandhi*-alternation -Vns≠V-/-Vs≠C- is actually still extant, though perhaps already inoperative and only artificially restored in the conservative epigraphic tradition; the latter possibility is suggested by the attested instances of orthographic inconsistency in the application of the rule just cited.[163]

In sum, the same conditions prevailed for assibilation in absolute-final position as in word-medial: i.e., the alternation {-ι̯-/-ι-}. Thus *-t̂j≠V- > *-ŝj≠V-, and just as *ˊŝjos/ *-tíjōi ⇒ ˊŝjos/*-ŝíjōi, so also *-ŝj≠V-/*-ti≠C- ⇒ *-ŝj≠V-/ *-ŝi≠C-. Hence the type δίδωσι after depalatalization. Likewise in absolute word-final position, a structure of an original pattern A (*-τ-‖{-ι̯-/-ι-}), if it continued to coexist after depalatalization with a by-form of pattern B (*-τ-‖{no -ι̯-}), could drop *-σ- in *-σι≠ (< *-σι̯≠ < *-τι̯≠) and restore *-τ- on the basis of pattern B: hence e.g. the proclitic preposition ἀντί (A) vs. ἄντα (B).[164] So much, then, for the causes of the assibilation from original *-τι- to -σι-. Dialects which internally underwent this innovation would be expected likewise to exhibit the change *t̂îj > *t̂ŝj (nn. *d*.3/4/5 and *e*.3/4/5, as outlined in § 6); where on the other hand *t̂îj remained, developing ultimately into *tt^s

---

[163] Cf. e.g. Thumb/Kieckers, *GD* I 156 and Bechtel, *GD* II 718.
[164] Q.v. in Frisk, *GEW* s.vv.

after depalatalization (nn. A.1, D.1, as outlined in § 7),
in these dialects -τιV- could remain also. What has been
inferred all along this section can now be fully stressed:
assibilation of *-τι- to -σι- was not a haphazard process,
though such may be the impression gained even from the
older epigraphical evidence of classical Dorian communities. Thus e.g. in Korinthian, if besides forms like δίδωτι
there exists an *ethnikon* like Φλειασιος[165] instead of *Φλειατιος,
the two forms cannot be reconciled phonologically, and the
latter type is due either to direct linguistic pressure from
the outside (as even from the Epic) or to the continuing
inside-influence of a substratal dialect (as indicated by the
rubric "Vordorisches" in the individual treatments of classical Dorian idioms in Thumb/Kieckers, *GD* I); here, then,
is an illustration of why Dorian was defined in § 7 from a
negative viewpoint: for an analysis of common Dorian, one
first has to subtract elements acquired in the cultural
stratifications from other dialects. A survey of Bechtel's
GD II will show that the classical dialects of Dorian communities often have forms in -σιV-, but generally in onomas-
tic and technical contexts only, while in basic grammatical
structures -τιV- and -τι# prevail. Dorian, then, can definitely be classified as a τι-dialect, while Attic/Ionic and Arca-
dian/Cypriote, as σι-dialects. Whether genuine Aiolian had
been a τι- or a σι-dialect is not decided here; instead, the
problem will be investigated in a projected work utilizing
historiographical arguments.

§9. Some features discernible from the texts of Linear
B apparently have a direct bearing on the matters thus far
discussed. Gemination seems clearly attested in the reflex
of etymological *sj ($>$ *jj; cf. line n.1 in the chronological outline of § 6); as Householder notes,[166] there is a

[165] Cf. Bechtel, *GD* II 232, 233.
[166] (§ 1) 183.

spelling mechanism capable of making a distinction between words with this etymology and those with originally simple intervocalic *j; /-CVjjV-/ can be spelled ⟨-CV-i-jV-⟩, vs. ⟨-CV-jV-⟩ for /-CVjV-/: cf. *e-te-wo-ke-re-we-i-jo* (as in Pylos/ Sn 64.15) vs. *e-re-pa-te-jo* (as in Pylos/Ta 642.3), with the former presupposed by an *s*-stem (e.g. nominative *Etewok-lewēs), the latter, by a non-*s*-stem (e.g. genitive *elephan-tos). Whenever there is less likelihood of confusing a word in /-VjjV-/ with one in /-VjV-/, however, no need is then felt to make a graphemic contrast: thus the participle (*ararusjă >) *ararujjă is simply spelled *a-ra-ru-ja* (e.g., Knossos/Sd 4401); likewise with *o*-stem genitives of the Homeric type -οιο, showing *-ojjo (< *-osjo) spelled ⟨-o-jo⟩, as in *do-e-ro-jo* (Knossos/C 912r.1). We may also note here that *jj must have been operative in the etymology of the classically-attested productive adjectives in -ειος and -αιος, derived from *o*-stem and *ā*-stem nouns respectively. At the onset of the process designated here as depalatalization, when intervocalic *j in e.g. *-ejos and *-ājos was about to disappear, the *jj of *-ejjos and *-ajjos (< *-esjos and *-asjos) replaced the *j of *-ejos and *-ājos by dint of the former's capacity as redundant feature $(j + j)$ in terms of the latter (j).[167] Thus *-ejos and *-ājos become transformed into *-ejjos and *-ajjos (< *-ājjos) just before (and contingent upon) the deletion of simplex intervocalic *j, so that the productive classical reflexes show -e̯ios and -a̯ios = -ειος and -αιος, structurally still parallel with -Cιος.[168] During the displacement of intervocalic *j by *jj in such productive categories, the phonological development of the latter could already be reaching the diphthongal stage (i.e., it might have already become a diphthongal component). As for the actual

---

[167] Applicable here again is Kuryłowicz's axiom I, quoted in chap. i n. 5.
[168] For classical -V̯iV- < -VjjV-, cf. *g*.1 in the chronological outline of § 6.

stage of development in the time of attested Linear B, with the entire chronological outline of § 6 taken into consideration, I suggest that the closest approximation can be represented by column f. Hence the aftermath of stage II (q.v. in § 3) and the consequences of the alternation $\{-\underline{\iota}\text{-}/\text{-}\iota\text{-}\}$ (q.v. in § 4) might be discernible. The following patterns relevant to the preceding discussion seem to be involved:

a (-CV$_A$)-$\hat{C}_1\hat{C}_2{}^j$V$_B$- (where $\hat{C}_1 = \hat{C}_2$ optionally):
spelled $\langle$-C$_2$V$_B$-$\rangle$,[169] $\langle$-C$_1$V$_B$-C$_2$V$_B$-$\rangle$,[170] possibly also $\langle$-C$_2$V$_A$-jV$_B$-$\rangle$.[171]

β -$\hat{C}$jV-/-C$\underline{i}$jV-:
spelled not only as $\langle$-Ci-jV-$\rangle$ but also possibly as $\langle$-CV-$\rangle$.

γ -$\hat{C}$j$\#$(V-)/-Ci$\#$(C-):
both spelled $\langle$-Ci$\rangle$, for syntactical clarity.

For the rare occurrences, examples are in order:

a $\langle$-C$_2$V$_A$-jV$_B$-$\rangle$:
o-ro-jo (Pylos/Eq 213.2–6), = apparently *oř̄^{j}ōn; cf. classical Cypriote οιρων.[172]
to-so-jo (Pylos/Er 312.2, 8), = apparently *tośś^{j}on; cf. τόσον.[173]

---

[169] Cf. e.g. *to-so* (Pylos/Er 312.5, etc.) for *tośś^{j}on (classical Attic/Ionic τόσον).

[170] Where $\hat{C}_1 \neq \hat{C}_2$. For a summary of the factors motivating general spelling of consonantal clusters in Linear B, cf. Householder (n. 132) 71–76.

[171] The spelling of an empty vowel -V$_A$- tends to prove that the following -*j*- is an off-glide, not an on-glide.

[172] Attested as *i-to-i-ro-ni* = ιν τόιρονι in ll. 8, 31 of the *Edalion Bronze* (217 in *Les inscriptions chypriotes syllabiques*, ed. O. Masson; Paris 1961); likewise as οἰρών·ἡ ἐκ τῆς καταμετρήσεως τῆς γῆς εὐθυωρία (Hesychios). Cf. J. Puhvel, "Mycenaean *o-ro-jo*," *Minos* 6 (1958) 61–63, and Householder, "Early Greek -*j*-" (§ 1) 180.

[173] Cf. Householder, "Early Greek -*j*-" 180. The spelling *to-so-jo* in ll. 2 and 8 of Pylos/Er 312 coexists with the normal spelling *to-so*, in l. 5 of the same tablet (cf. also *to-so-de* in l. 6), and even in the same contextual slot (modifying *pe-ma* + GRANUM-symbol + number):

l. 2: *to-so-jo pe-ma* GRANUM 30
l. 5: *te-re-ta-o to-so pe-ma* GRANUM 30
l. 8: *to-so-jo pe-ma* GRANUM 6.

III. §9

pa-ra-wa-jo (Pylos/Sh 737), = apparently *parāẅẅʲō, nominative/accusative dual of *parāẅẅʲon; cf. παρήϊον.[174]

β ⟨-CV-⟩:

ku-ru-so (Pylos/Ta 716.1, etc.), = apparently *khrūsíjō, dual adjective, meaning "golden."
a-sa-ti-ja (Pylos/Mn 162.4), = alternate spelling of *a-si-ja-ti-ja* (Pylos/Ae 134, etc.); toponym.

[174] Cf. Householder, "Early Greek -*j*-" 188. The etymology seems to involve the following stages: *parāẅẅʲo- < *parāwyo- < *par-āus-jo- "by the ear"; cf. Old Irish *arae* "temples" < *par-aus-jos, perhaps also the Gaulish place-name *Arausio* = Orange. Q.v. in Frisk, *GEW* s.v. παρειαί; also Schwyzer, *GG* I 349. The Attic forms παρεV- reveal the expected phonological shortening from παρηV- (< παρηιV-), which persists in Ionic. As for Attic παρειV-, cf. O. Szemerényi, "Attic οὖς and its compounds," *Studi Micenei ed Egeo-Anatolici* 3 (1967) 64 f, n. 68. The views here otherwise differ.

As for the formulation of {-VwjV- > -VẅẅʲV- (> ultimately -VjjV- > -ViV-)}, cf. the similar arguments of Allen, "Palatalization" (§ 1) 116 f n. 23, positing a labiopalatal glide as a feature involved in the diachronic transition from e.g. *-bowjos to -βοιος. Likewise -VtwV- > -Vtẅ V- > -Vt̂t̂ʷV- > -Vt̂ŝʷV- > -Vt̂ŝʲV-, henceforth integrated into stage *f* of the chronological table in § 6, so that e.g. Ionic τέσσερες can be derived ultimately from *kʷet-weres in terms of the same table and of the conditions here appended.

Because of the inherent nature of -*iẅ*-, it is possible that even further orthographical variations are involved: I propose that -CVₐẅẅʲVв- may be spelled in the following additional ways:

(1) ⟨-CVₐ-jVв-⟩
(2) ⟨-CVₐ-wi-jVв-⟩
(3) ⟨-CVₐ-u-jVв-⟩
(4) ⟨-CVₐ-wVв-⟩ possibly.

Examples:

(1) *i-je-re-ja* (Pylos/Eb 317.1, etc.) vs. *i-je-re-u* (Pylos/An 218.2, etc.); cf. ἱέρεια vs. ἱερεύς. For a list of such nominals with suffix spelled ⟨-(C)e-ja⟩, cf. Householder, "Early Greek -*j*-" (§ 1) 183 f. For a similar emphasis as here on the possibility of a preserved *w*-constituent underlying the orthography, cf. A. Bartoněk, "Diphthongs in Mycenaean," *Minos* 8 (1963) 57. On the basis of context, *pa-ra-jo* in Pylos/Sh 740 has been cited as a possible graphic doublet of *pa-ra-wa-jo* (the already-discussed entry of Pylos/Sh 737) by M. Lejeune, *Mémoires de philologie mycénienne* I (Paris 1958) 119 n. 30. I propose that *pa-ra-wa-jo* and *pa-ra-jo* are both approximations of *parāẅẅʲō.

(2) *me-wi-jo* (Knossos/Ak 611.2, etc.); to be transcribed as *meẅẅʲōn; cf. classical μείων.

(3) *me-u-jo* (Knossos/Ak 612, etc.) = *me-wi-jo*.

(4) *a-ke-re-wa* (Pylos/Ac 1277, etc.) vs. *a-ke-re-u* (Pylos/Cn 441.3, etc.); cf. Lejeune, *Philologie mycénienne* I 142 f n. 52.

143

po-pu-ro₂ (Knossos/L 758), = apparently *porphuríō, dual adjective, meaning "purple."[175]

Now if the stage symbolized as *f* had already been reached in the time of the attested Linear B tablets, then *-t͡sʲV- of n. *f*.3/4/5 could be spelled ⟨-sV-⟩. This indeed seems to be the case with such rare spellings as *pa-sa-ro* (Pylos/Ta 716.1), = apparently *pat͡sʲalō (dual of *pat͡sʲalos < *pat͡t͡jalos < *pakjalos;[176] *pat͡sʲalos > ultimately πάσσαλος); also *wa-na-so-i* (Pylos/Fr 1222, etc.), = apparently *wanat͡sʲoin (dual genitive/dative of *wanat͡sʲă < *wanat͡t͡jă < *wanakjă; *wanat͡sʲă > ultimately ἄνασσα).[177] Another way of writing *-t͡sʲV- was apparently with ⟨-zV-⟩: e.g., *za-we-te* (Pylos/Ma 225.2) = *t͡sʲāwetes "this year" (modeled on *t͡sʲ-āmeron "today"; *t͡sʲ- here is derived from proclitic *t͡t͡j- < *kj- < *ki-, as also seen in Latin *ci-s*, Gothic *hi-*, Old Slavonic *sь*; *t͡sʲāmeron/*t͡sʲāwetes > ultimately σήμερον/σῆτες).[178] The spelling ⟨-zV-⟩ also approximated *d͡ẑʲ (n. *f*.6/7/8/9), as in *to-pe-za* (Pylos/Ta 642.1, etc.) = *torped͡ẑʲă (cf. classical τράπεζα); for the graphemic ambivalence here, we may cite the typological parallel of central Cretan ⟨ζ⟩, as

---

[175] Cf. H. Mühlestein, "L'adjectif mycénien significant 'en or'," *Études mycéniennes*, ed. M. Lejeune (Paris 1956) 93–97. As for the graphemes ⟨-ro₂-⟩ and ⟨-ra₂-⟩, standing for *-r͡rʲŏ-/*-r͡jŏ-/*-ríjŏ- and *-r͡rʲă-/*-r͡jă-/*-ríjă- respectively, it should also be noted that there are known cases where e.g. both ⟨-ra-⟩ and ⟨-ra₂-⟩ are at different occasions spelled for the same name by the same scribe: *ta-ra-to* (Pylos/Eo 247.6)/*ta-ra₂-to* (Pylos/Eo 351; 471): cf. M. Lejeune, "Doublets et complexes," *Proceedings of the Cambridge Colloquium on Mycenaean Studies*, ed. L. R. Palmer and J. Chadwick (Cambridge 1966) 146 f; Lejeune also gives a list of attested nominals with endings spelled ⟨-ro₂⟩, showing classical parallels in -ριος and -ρίων ("Doublets et complexes" 147 n. 1).

[176] Q.v. in Frisk, *GEW* s.v. πάσσαλος; cf. Latin *păc-īscor*.

[177] Cf. Lejeune, "Sifflantes fortes" (§ 1) 132, and Heubeck, "Einordnung" (§ 1) 166. For a more recent defense of the etymology {ἄνασσα < *wanakjă}, cf. G. R. Hart, "The effects of the palatalization of plosives in Mycenaean Greek," *Cambridge Colloquium* (cf. n. 175) 131 f.

[178] Cf. Lejeune, "Sifflantes fortes" 123; also 134 f.

discussed in § 7. Yet in a few isolated instances, ⟨-zV-⟩ also seems to represent e.g. *giV and *kiV,[179] as in a_3-za (Pylos/Ub 1318.7) = ? *aigíjā (cf. classical αἴγ-ειος, αἰγ-εία) and su-za (Knossos/F 841.5) = ? *sūkíjai (cf. Herakleian συκια[180]). Now since *giV/*kiV (or even *gjV/*kjV) cannot be reconciled phonologically with *dẑⁱV/*t̑ŝʲV,[181] the circumstance that the graphemes ⟨-za-⟩, ⟨-ze-⟩, and ⟨-zo-⟩ could straddle such a phonological gap might suggest an archaic spelling-mechanism which had outlived its initial function. According to such a theory, ⟨-zV-⟩ once represented e.g. n. a.3/4/5/6/7/8/9 in the chronological outline of § 6. Then, after stages I and II (q.v. in § 3), the graphemes ⟨-zV-⟩ would be left covering two disparate phonological combinations: (1) the products of stage II, *t̑ŝʲV and *dẑʲV, and (2) those forms which had not undergone stage II, because of the alternation {-ι̯-/-ι-}: thus *k(h)-i/j-, *g-i/j-, *t(h)-i/j-, *d-i/j-. It could then be posited that spellings like a_3-za and su-za reflect archaisms in the script-tradition, surviving by the medium of traditional mnemonic associations with particular words and rubrics adopted by a scribal school. More plausible, however, is the alternative theory that a_3-za and su-za are archaic in morphology, not in orthography. That is, we may reject the transliterations *aigíjā and *sūkíjā, and propose instead *aidẑʲā and *sūt̑ŝʲā, or even *aidẑʲă and *sūt̑ŝʲă: such forms would suggest that the morpheme-boundary between base and suffix had broken down, so that development of the alternation {-ι̯-/-ι-} was prevented; thus the direct classical reflexes, if attested, would have been *αἴζη and *σύσση (or *αἴζă and *σύσσă), not *αἰγία and *συκία.[182] Examples of

---

[179] Cf. Lejeune, "Sifflantes fortes" 128, 133.
[180] Q.v. in Bechtel, GD II 387.
[181] Cf. the chronological outline of § 6.
[182] Similar conclusions on the morphology have been reached by C. J. Ruijgh, "Observations sur la tablette Ub 1318 de Pylos," $Lingua$ 16 (1966)

actual coexistence between such inherited and synchronic formations respectively are still extant in classical times: e.g. γλύσσων/γλυκίων,[183] showing the morpheme-boundary lost/restored.[184]

Such spelling-alternations as the following, however, might involve an entirely different phenomenon:

a-ze-ti-ri-ja (Knossos/Ap 694.3, etc.)
a-ke-ti-ri-ja (Knossos/Ai 739.1, Pylos/Aa 85, etc.)

ze-i-ja-ka-ra-na[(Pylos/Xa 70)
ke-i-ja-ka-ra-na (Pylos/Nn 228.3)

a-no-ze-we (Pylos/Cn 600.13)
a-no-ke-we (Pylos/An 192.13, Knossos/Db 1261).[185]

The seemingly free interchange of ⟨-ze-⟩ and ⟨-ke-⟩ is symptomatic here of something more immediate than inherited spelling, and perhaps it involves synchronic phonological similarity. Genuine /ke/, during the period before

---

151 f; cf. also Bartoněk, "Phonic Evaluation of the s- and z-Signs" (§ 1) passim. By the same reasoning, the comparative ka-zo-e (Pylos/Va 1323) is to be interpreted as *kaȋsⁱoes, not *kakijoes. For further perspective on the breakdown of the morpheme-boundary between the base and the suffix *-(i)j-ŏn/ŏs-, cf. n. 183.

183 For a list of such pairs, cf. Schwyzer, GG I 538: θάσσων/ταχίων, βράσσων/ βραχίων, βάσσων/βαθίων, etc. It is difficult to find similar instances of coexistence between e.g. reflexes of suffixal formations involving nominals with original *ʹjos vs. *ʹijos, mainly because base-forms (X-) are lacking for extant reflexes of X̂ + jos, so that no new X + ιος can be synchronically generated. For example, there is no base-form *μεθ- from which a synchronic *μέθιος could be generated, destined to oust μέσος (< *methjos). By contrast, the positive base-forms γλυκύς, ταχύς, βραχύς, βαθύς can prompt the new comparatives γλυκίων, ταχίων, βραχίων, βαθίων, destined to oust γλύσσων, θάσσων, βράσσων, βάσσων.

184 For a parallel to such a precarious coexistence (precarious in that it implies the eventual ouster of the inherited form), cf. the barely surviving occurrences of the type μέμνη-αι (Φ 442) besides μέμνη-σαι (Ψ 648) in the Homeric corpus, as already mentioned in n. 141; for details, cf. P. Chantraine, Grammaire homérique I³ (Paris 1958) 474 f.

185 For further possibilities, cf. Lejeune, op. cit. (§ 1) 136. A critical discourse on the relative certainty of these correspondences is offered by Hart, "Palatalization of plosives" (n. 177) 130 f.

III. §9

depalatalization, could have been pronounced [k̂ʲe],¹⁸⁶
in the standard dialect of the Linear B texts. Now if a particular scribe who heard this segment was the native speaker
of a τι-dialect, then [k̂ʲe] in an unfamiliar lexical entry
would sound to him much like [t̂ʲe], or perhaps already
[t̂ʲe]; hence he might approximate [k̂ʲe] with e.g. his
/t̂ʲe/, written ⟨-ze-⟩;¹⁸⁷ to a speaker of a σι-dialect, on
the other hand, the latter grapheme would be read /t̂ŝʲe/.

¹⁸⁶ There are several reasons for postulating a palatal onset-glide before
*ĕ (hence *ʲĕ) in the standard language of the Linear B texts; among these are:
   (1) *jV-, where it did not collapse with *djV- (cf. n. 84), would have become
*ʲV- by stage f in the chronological outline of § 6. As for *jĕ, however, a merger
with *djĕ- might have been prevented already in stage a, because of an early
syncretism with *ʲĕ. It even seems that inherited *jĕ- could become *djĕ-
only through morphological conditioning: i.e., through coexistence with an
o-grade or ø-grade variant. Such a conclusion is prompted by an examination
of entries beginning with ζε- in Frisk's GEW: e.g. ζεά vs. -ζοος, ζευγ-/ζυγ-,
Ζεν-/Δι(ϝ)-, ζέφυρος/ζόφος, ζέω/ζόη.
   (2) Already at stage b of the outline in § 6, *(e)pet-ʲe > *(e)peŝʲe; because
of the pivotal nature of the 3rd singular (cf. chap. i n. 76), an alternation like
(e)peton/(e)peŝʲe becomes leveled to *(e)peŝʲon/*(e)peŝʲe, whence ultimately ἔπεσον/ἔπεσε, aorist 1st/3rd singular of πίπτω in Attic/Ionic.
   (3) *kʷĕ > *kʷʲĕ > *tʷ̂ĕ; after depalatalization, > t̂ĕ in e.g. Attic/Ionic,
tŝĕ in e.g. Arcadian (whence the usage of an affricate-sign И, as in ειИε "εἴτε,"
etc.: cf. Thumb/Scherer, GD II 124f). The configuration *tʷ̂ĕ might be
assigned to as early a stage as c in the outline of § 6. For a detailed discussion of
ẅ-palatalization, cf. Allen, "Palatalization" (§ 1) passim, esp. 116 f.
   (4) In Linear B, whereas -(C)iV- is regularly spelled ⟨-(C)i-jV-⟩, the specific
combination -(C)ie- is approximated by ⟨-(C)i-e-⟩ as well as ⟨-(C)i-je-⟩, as
if the traditional j-spelling were superfluous because of the automatic presence
of a palatal on-glide before -e-: i.e., -ʲe-; hence e.g. the noun reflected as ἱερεύς
in Attic/Ionic shows a Linear B spelling i-e-re-u (Pylos/En 74.16, etc.) besides
i-je-re-u (Pylos/An 218.2, etc.). Cf. also classical Cypriote -i-je-re-u-se- (Masson,
ICS [note 172] n.91.2) = ἱερεύς, besides -i-e-re-u-se- (Masson, ICS n.90.2)
= idem. In fact, Masson reports (ICS p. 54) that the Cypriote grapheme
⟨-je-⟩ is very rare, and that it is not even a constituent of the common syllabic
repertory, appearing instead to have been a localized innovation in the New
Paphian tradition, to which belong both the cited texts n.90 and n.91. The
former inscription shows further evidence for an automatic palatal onset-glide
before ĕ in Cypriote, as seen from the following formula of l. 5: -ta-i-te-o-i-
ta-e-ra-i = τᾶι θεῶι τᾶι "Ηραι; Masson's transliteration (ICS p. 146), as here
cited, expresses the divergent spelling of the diphthong-component -ι before
-ta-/-e- by means of iota adscript/subscript.
   ¹⁸⁷ For a clear instance of orthographic confusion because of t/k neutralization,
cf. the following Knossian variants: o-da-ke-we-ta (So 4446, etc.), o-da-ku-we-ta

147

The last issue to be raised is contingent: namely, the problem concerning the dialectal texture of the idiom represented by the Linear B tablets now extant, on the basis of the isogloss {-τι- : -σι-}. It appears that *⁻ᵗĵV-/*-tíjV- > *⁻ˢĵV-/*-tíjV- ⇒ *⁻ˢĵV-/*-ŝíjV- and that *⁻ᵗĵ≠V-/*-ti≠C- > *-ŝĵ≠V-/*-ti≠C- ⇒ *-ŝĵ≠V-/*-ŝi≠C- (as also in e.g. Attic/Ionic, q.v. in § 8) on the basis of forms such as the following:[188]

e-qe-si-jo (Pylos/Eb 847.1) = *hekʷeŝjoi: ← *e-qe-ta* (Knossos/As 821.2, etc.) = *hekʷetās
ra-wa-ke-si-jo (Pylos/Ea 814) = *lāwāgeŝíjōi: ← *ra-wa-ke-ta* (Pylos/ Un 718.9, etc.) = *lāwāgetās[189]
di-do-si (Pylos/Ma 365.2, etc.) = *didonŝi
e-ko-si (Pylos/Eb 847.1, etc.) = *ekhonŝi
a-pu-do-si (Knossos/B 818, etc.) = *apudoŝis
ko-ri-si-ja (Pylos/Eb 347.1, etc.) = Korinŝíjā: ← *ko-ri-to* (Pylos/ Ad 921) = *Korinthos.[190]

The tentative conclusion, then, is that the entries just submitted represent a selection from the repertory of a σι-dialect. But if the pronunciation [ŝĵ] or [ĺĺĵ] instead of [ŝŝĵ]

(So 4435, etc.), *o-da-tu-we-ta* (So 894), *o-da-*87-ta* (So 4430, etc.): in the first three entries, the -*ke*-, -*ku*-, and -*tu*- obviously contain empty vowels; in the fourth, *87 = probably -*kwe*-; cf. Lejeune, *Mémoires* (n. 174) 287 f. Conversely to /ĵĵe/ spelled ⟨-ze-⟩, if *me-za-na* in Pylos/Cn 3.1 can possibly be interpreted as the same place-name as *Μεσσήνη*, then it would have to be transliterated as *Meĵĵānā, compared with standard *Meŝŝjānā, which would have been spelled *me-sa-na; cf. *to-sa* (Pylos/En 609.1, etc.) = *toŝŝja. For a discussion of *me-za-na*, cf. F. Kiechle, *Lakonien und Sparta* (München 1963) 12 n. 4.

[188] For a more exhaustive list, cf. E. Vilborg, *A Tentative Grammar of Mycenaean Greek* (Göteborg 1960) 50.

[189] Possibly *lāwāgētās; cf. Lakonian *Λαναγητα*, q.v. in *Wörterbuch der griechischen Eigennamen*,³ ed. W. Pape and G. E. Benseler (Braunschweig 1875) s.v.

[190] Cf. Attic *Προβάλυνθος* → *Προβαλίσιος*; for the mechanism of assibilation here, cf. § 8; for more examples, cf. Heubeck, "Einordnung" (§ 1) 164.

can really be ascribed to some scribes, as already suggested, then such scribes would be speakers of a $\tau\iota$-dialect,[191] and one might expect them to revert occasionally to the spelling $\langle$-ti-jV-$\rangle$ for what was to them /tiV/. There seem to be some examples available which can be checked against a careful analysis by E. L. Bennett[192] of the scribal hands which were responsible, so to speak, for the entries to be examined presently. In other words, the selection here is made from among the Aa, Ab, and Ad tablets of Pylos only because in the case of these texts there is effective control, on the basis of Bennett's cited work, over exactly which scribe wrote what. Now one Pylian official, the so-called "scribe of Ad 290," writes the following forms:

ti-nwa-ti-ja-o (Pylos/Ad 684)
mi-ra-ti-ja-o (Pylos/Ad 380, 689).

Another official, the "scribe of Ab 186," writes

ti-nwa-si-ja (Pylos/Ab 190)
mi-ra-ti-ja (Pylos/Ab 573).

Why the spelling of e.g. what one would have expected to be *Milāŝijai actually turns out to be approximated by *mi-ra-ti-ja* is a circumstance which seems to have no intrinsic phonological motivation in terms of a $\sigma\iota$-dialect: even the pattern *-tíjai/*-ŝjáōn cannot be postulated, because of the alternation *ti-nwa-si-ja/ti-nwa-ti-ja-o*. The random fluctuation of $\langle$-ti-$\rangle$ and $\langle$-si-$\rangle$ here would suggest that the pronunciation [-tiV-] might have been appreciated as non-standard or perhaps even substandard, from the scribal standpoint. It is more plausible to posit from such evidence the existence of at least two dialectal elements in Linear B, rather than a

---

[191] Cf. the arguments in § 8.
[192] "Correspondances entre les textes des tablettes pyliennes des séries Aa, Ab et Ad," *Études mycéniennes*, ed. M. Lejeune (Paris 1956) 121–136.

conflict between archaism and innovation within one dialect, simply because on the basis of the conditions for assibilation outlined in § 8, there seems to be no cogent phonological mechanism which could counteract such a linguistic innovation, once it occurs within one dialect. The apparent isogloss {-τι- : -σι-} is involved in the Linear B texts to such an extent that even personal names are subject to analysis with this criterion; hence e.g. the following two formations of the type τερψίμβροτος:[193] ma-na-si-we-ko (Pylos/ Jn 431.3) = *Mnā-si-wergos[194] vs. o-ti-na-wo (Pylos/Cn 285.14) = *Or-ti-nāwos.[195]

§10. There remains to be accomplished in a projected work the extensive application of the dialectal criterion here developed to Kretschmer's cited work.[196] An important consideration will be the problem of whether genuine Aiolian was a σι- or a τι-dialect, and contingent historiographical arguments will have to be introduced. Related to this issue is the circumstance that in the Homeric corpus, there are compound-formations of the type *τερπτίμβροτος as well as τερψίμβροτος, and that the one definite instance, βωτιανείρῃ (A 155), is an epithet of the Thessalian region Phthia, homeland of Achilles; furthermore, the name of Achilles' mother, Θέτις, reveals the nomen actionis θέσις, within the framework of a τι-dialect.[197] Another related point in the Homeric tradition is that the grandfather of one Ὀρσίλοχος (E 542, etc.) was Ὀρτίλοχος (E 547, etc.); from

---

[193] For which cf. Th. Knecht, Geschichte der griechischen Komposita vom Typ τερψίμβροτος (Teildruck: Biel 1946).

[194] Μνησίεργος is actually attested in classical times: cf. Pape/Benseler, Eigennamen (n. 189) s.v.

[195] Cf. Ὀρτίλοχος/Ὀρσίλοχος, as discussed in § 10.

[196] Cf. § 1.

[197] Cf. Kretschmer, "Wandel" (§ 1) 571. Perpetuation of -τι- here instead of -σι- could be enhanced in the Epic tradition of a σι-dialect by the extension of an ιδ-declension at the expense of an older ι-declension: hence e.g. genitives Θέτιδος (Δ 512, etc., Alkman 5.2 ii. 15 [Page], etc.) vs. Θέτιος (Pindar, Isthmia 8.27, Paianes 6.84 [Snell], etc.).

the historical and dialectal standpoints, it is crucial here that the provenience of Orsilochos was Messenian Phera (E 543).[198] The conclusions reached will be applied to an evaluation of what specific dialect the traces of morphologically unmotivated [-tiV-] in Linear B might represent, which in turn will lead to a dialectal criterion applicable all the way to the Bronze Age.

[198] For perspective on the significance of this correlation, cf. F. Kiechle, "Pylos und der pylische Raum in der antiken Tradition," *Historia* 9 (1960) 1–67, esp. 13 ff, 41 f, 50 f (and n. 1), 63.

CHAPTER IV

MARGINALIA TO BENVENISTE'S ORIGINES

§1. In *Origines* 98 f, Benveniste has suggested that with locative endings in *-i, "ce que l'on dénomme 'locatif' repose comme un bon nombre de nominatifs-accusatifs, sur un 'cas indéfini' qui avait en indo-européen la forme même du thème neutre." As for the "thème neutre," he argues that its locus of diffusion involves an original type with radical ending in *-i̯, such as nominative/accusative *ói̯i,[1] genitive *oi̯i-ós—attested, with gender altered, in several IE languages: e.g., Sanskrit *áviḥ* : *ávyaḥ*, Greek *ŏ(F)ις* : *ŏ(F)ιος*.[2] Now the formation of adjectives in *-(i)i̯o-, the production of which eventually spread to most nominal types, started apparently within the category of those nominals where the ending in *-i̯ had still been part of the root; hence the etymological segmentation *-i̯-o- in e.g. Sanskrit *ávy-a-* "ouīnus" (... ← *ói̯i), Greek *ἄλι-o-* (... ← *sáli̯). But the problem remains how to explain the extension of *-(i)i̯o- to roots without final *-i̯. The crucial factor appears to be that there also developed, from primary nominals with radical ending in *-i̯, a secondary group which Benveniste classifies as the derivatives in *-éi-, where the element *-i̯-[3] was no longer a constituent suffix[4] of the

---

[1] From *ə₃ei̯-i̯-; cf. Luwian *ḫawi-* "Hammel."

[2] *Origines* 60; on the accentuation of *ávyaḥ* and of *ŏ(F)ιος*, cf. n. 18.

[3] I.e., the *-i- in *-éi-.

[4] As the discussion proceeds, there will be further elaboration on this term, as used by Benveniste; cf. especially § 2–§ 5. This suffix is "constituent" in that it is a constituent of the root, causing the latter's basic structural variations.

root; in Sanskrit, for example, we can illustrate the etymological distinction thus: nominative *mat-íḥ*, genitive *mat-éḥ* (derivative type) vs. nominative *ávi-ḥ*, genitive *ávy-aḥ* (primary, radical type).[5] I propose that the former type, with the extra-radical derivative morpheme *-éi-, had been the founding category of the IE nominal formant *-(i)i̯o-.

§2. Before further development of this subject, it is necessary to consider F. B. J. Kuiper's important critique[6] of Benveniste's presently-discussed analysis of the IE *i*-declension.[7] In the following evaluation of the conflicting arguments, I intend to avoid polemic for its own sake, so that only those factors cited by either Benveniste or Kuiper which are relevant here will be discussed. Crucial is Kuiper's objection to Benveniste's formulation of nouns with the structure CₑCi̯, CₑCu̯.[8] Significantly, it does not seem justifiable to assert, as does Kuiper, that "nominatives like *ǵónu̯, *dóru̯, *dhḗlu̯, *pōi̯u̯ ([*Origines*] 53) are unacceptable from the standpoint of [IE] phonology."[9] Only if Benveniste's theory of the IE root (as propounded in *Origines* chapter IX) were disproved or seriously qualified could Kuiper's objection to the formulations CₑCi̯ and CₑCu̯ prevail, since the latter are consistent with the general positing of an IE root-structure CₑC-C'-, a pattern-formulation which can be applied with success to other attested nominal formations, i.e. to those with constituent suffix (-C'-) other than *-i̯- and *-u̯-.[10] From the standpoint of the early morphological system of IE, the elements *-i̯- and *-u̯- can indeed be described as fitting into the consonantal slot of a constituent

[5] Benveniste, *Origines* 60.

[6] *Vedic noun-inflexion* 6–9 *et passim*.

[7] As also of the structurally kindred *u*-declension; thus all of *Origines* chap. iv is involved.

[8] Throughout chap. iv from here on, the symbol ε will represent the thematic vocalism *-e/o-, in accordance with the practice of scholars like E. P. Hamp.

[9] Kuiper, *Vedic noun-inflexion* 7.

[10] Benveniste, *Origines*, *passim*.

suffix, even if they became vocalized *-i- and *-u- in the respective positional slots -Cj̥-($\#$)C- and -Cu̥-($\#$)C-.[11] Certainly Benveniste's formulation of CₑCj̥ and CₑCu̥ was based primarily on an extension of his overall theory of the IE root and not, as Kuiper seems to ascribe,[12] on the proposition that the genitival ending involved the phonologically-conditioned distribution of *-s after a vowel and *-ₑs after a consonant.[13] The latter formulation was intended to account for the desinential contrast in e.g. the genitival formations *ávy-aḥ*[14] ($<$ *...-ₑs) vs. *maté-ḥ* ($<$ *...ɛ́i-s) or *mádhv-aḥ* ($<$ *...-ₑs) vs. *sūnó-ḥ* ($<$ *...ɛ́u-s).[15] Yet Benveniste's effort to differentiate *-ɛ́i- and *-ɛ́u- from *-ɛ́y- and *-ɛ́w-[16] respectively is not really necessary; what is more, an originally coexisting genitival formation in -ₑCs besides the supposedly exclusive -Cₑs appears to be clearly attested: e.g. Sanskrit *gnā́ḥ* ($<$ *...-ₑə₂s), Avestan *xᵛə̄ng*, *də̄ng*, ($<$ *...-ₑns), etc.[17] Kuiper seems justified, then, in not accepting the proposition that from the IE standpoint, *-ₑs was the obligatory genitive desinence, to the exclusion of *-s, in postconsonantal position. Nevertheless, rejection of the latter notion does not necessarily damage the formulation of structures like CₑCj̥ and CₑCu̥, much less of course Benveniste's theory of the IE root; indeed, just the opposite: the admissibility of both *-s and *-ₑs can be explained in terms of the selfsame theory.

§3. Before such an explanation can be attempted here, we must note an important statement into which Kuiper

---

[11] Cf. chap. i § 1.

[12] Kuiper, *Vedic noun-inflexion* 7.

[13] Benveniste, *Origines* 64, 68.

[14] The desinence *-s evidenced in the nominative, *ávi-ḥ*, reflects a much later phenomenon: the metastasis from inanimate to animate gender; cf. Benveniste, *Origines* 61.

[15] Benveniste, *Origines* 52.

[16] That is, *-ɛj- and *-ɛu-.

[17] Kuryłowicz, *Apophonie* 63, 97; *idem, Inflectional Categories* 195; Kuiper, *Vedic noun-inflexion* 7 f.

had been prompted because of Benveniste's citing e.g. the Sanskrit genitive singular *mádhvaḥ* (<*medhu̯és)[18] in order to justify the positing of an original nominative *médhu̯ (> Sanskrit *mádhu*),[19] with constituent suffix (*-u̯-) in original consonantal slot; Kuiper's remark is worth repeating:

It may be stated as a fundamental objection to this theory that it is based upon a rather normal type of inflexion *mádhu/ mádhvaḥ*, though there is no evidence whatever that this type is older than the others and reflects any more the original inflexional system. Accordingly Benveniste is unable to account for the interesting type *dáru/dróḥ, sánu/snóḥ*, though this archaic type admittedly preserves some scanty relics of the prehistoric inflexion: on account of *mádhu/mádhvaḥ* he assumes an original paradigm *dóru̯/*dóru̯-os, and likewise *ĝónu̯/*ĝónu̯-os (cp. Gr. δόρυ/δουρός, γόνυ/γουνός). But the Greek genitives can easily be explained as new formations, since in Greek owing to a rearrangement of the noun-inflexion nearly all substantives of the *u*-declension have a genitive in -vos (-Fos). As compared with the anomalous genitives *dróḥ, *jñóḥ* they cannot be old and must evidently be innovations of Greek.[20]

Kuiper's point, that the relationship of *dáru* (from *déru̯)[21] with *dróḥ* (< *dréu̯s) seems to be a more archaic type than the one between *mádhu* (< *médhu̯) and *mádhvaḥ* (< *medhu̯es), is indeed cogent and will be evaluated further in the discussion. But his characterization of these relatively earlier and later relationships as paradigmatic (witness the above expressions "the original inflexional system," "the prehistoric inflexion," "an original paradigm," and, later on,[22] "the really antique paradigms") can mislead. Clearly,

---

[18] The accentual leveling evident in *mádhu/mádhvaḥ* is an outgrowth of formal declensional constitution; further discussion follows in the present § 3 *et passim*.

[19] Benveniste, *Origines* 60 *et passim*.

[20] Kuiper, *Vedic noun-inflexion* 7.

[21] Specifically, *dáru* from *dóru̯; for the Indo-Iranian morphological shift from IE *-o- to -á-, cf. Kuryłowicz, *Apophonie* 336.

[22] Kuiper, *Vedic noun-inflexion* 8.

Benveniste had proposed[23] that the link between e.g.
dáru and *dróḥ* was originally not inflectional, that is to say
paradigmatic, but rather, derivational. Kuiper sees in this
proposal an argument for indiscriminate heteroclisis,[24]
as if the latter had to be suggested by Benveniste merely in
order to claim anteriority for the relationship of *mádhu/*
mádhvaḥ over that of *dáru/dróḥ*. Yet it is possible to object
that positing a process whereby derivational categories of
IE become transformed into inflectional categories is not
merely an isolated conjecture invoked *ad hoc* by Benveniste
for the sake of explaining the type *dáru/dróḥ*, but rather, a
theory that pervades the entire extent of the work *Origines*.
What is more, this theory is supported *passim* by citations of
actual structural evidence, in that originally derivative
IE formants can be shown to have developed into inflectional formants, be they indirect case-markers or direct
ones; an instance of the former type we see in Benveniste's
discussion of the derivational suffix *-ɛn-, which evolves
into a case-marker *-n-[25] preserved e.g. by the Sanskrit
genitive *asth-n-áḥ* of nominative *ásth-i*;[26] an instance of the
latter type, on the other hand, is evident from Benveniste's
synoptic remarks on the ultimate fate of the IE suffix *-ɛs-:

La spécialisation de *-nt- abstrait-collectif comme indice de
pluriel en luwi et en tokharien évoque curieusement le sort de
*-es-, lui aussi suffixe d'adjectif et suffixe d'abstrait, qui a fourni
en allemand le pluriel en *-er*.[27]

Our attention here will be confined to *-ɛs-, to the exclusion
of the equally interesting morpheme *-nt- as reflected in

[23] *Origines* 54.
[24] *Vedic noun-inflexion* 8.
[25] For an evaluation of ø-grade suffixal formants, cf. § 5.
[26] *Origines* 176–178, esp. 177.
[27] *Origines* 128. The same trend {abstract *-ɛs ⇒ nominative plural *-ɛs}
can be posited for IE as a whole; this subject will be developed further in the
discussion which follows.

Luwian and "Tocharian." The implication of the quoted passage seems clear: once a suffix formerly derivational has become specialized as inflectional, of the type designated as a direct case-marker, it can then be characterized as an actual desinence. Yet, the metastasis of derivational morpheme into inflectional morpheme could be the result of a split. In other words, the shift from abstract suffix *-es to nominative plural desinence *-es could still have left behind a residual category of abstract suffixal formations. Even formal polarization could accompany the functional, manifested in the distributional split of the apophonic vocalism *-e-; hence perhaps the development in Greek, for one, of such a qualitative opposition as between the endings of abstract type γέν-ος and plural type φρέν-ες. Aside from this question, the crucial point remains this: that an originally derivational segment like *-es- can become an inflectional segment, a desinence. Instead of citing from Benveniste's *Origines* further examples of this phenomenon called grammaticalization,[28] it would be preferable to quote here about this subject one single general statement in *Origines*, which had been prompted by a previous discussion of heteroclitics with elements in *-r/n-, like Greek οὖθαρ/οὔθατος, Sanskrit *údhar/údhnah*, Latin *femur/feminis*:

Considéré sous ce jour, la flexion hétéroclitique apparaît pour ce qu'elle est: une tentative faite pour intégrer aux cadres nouveaux de la flexion les multiples dérivés anciens qui se constituaient sur la racine, sur les thèmes radicaux ou sur des formes déjà dérivées. Ce n'est pas une flexion organique, mais un assemblage de formes empruntées à des systèmes très différents, unifiées après coup, et souvent sans cohérence. Malgré leur aspect rigide, ces ensembles nouveaux ne doivent plus être transposés tels quels en indo-européen. Il faut les dissocier pour les comprendre.

---

[28] A term used by Kuryłowicz, among others; cf. his important typological comments in *Inflectional Categories* 35–38.

Alors, pris séparément, les éléments de cette flexion révèlent autant de choses que, par leur liaison, ils ont offusqué.[29]

Thus the type *dáru/dróḥ* shows a heteroclitic declension too, to the extent that the genitive was once a derivative of what later became the nominative (-accusative), whereas in nouns of the type *-r/n-, the *-r- of the nominative (-accusative) and the *-n- of the genitive had both been derivative formants of a simpler base, and were only later to become specialized as case-formants of one paradigm. But in the sense that the type *dáru/dróḥ* is heteroclitic, so too is *mádhu/ mádhvaḥ*, in that the *-es reconstructed for the genitive singular can also be considered the original derivative-formant of what later became the nominative (-accusative), *mádhu*.

§4. As already seen,[30] Benveniste has suggested that the IE suffix *-es- had been a formant of adjectives and abstract nouns;[31] it was then proposed that in the latter function, the following shift could take place: abstract suffix *-es ⇒ nominative plural desinence *-es;[32] as for the earlier function, that of adjective, we can now add a similar proposition for another shift: singular adjectival suffix *-es ⇒ singular genitive desinence *-es. I also propose tentatively that with the advent of formal declension, the still-productive morpheme just described as an old adjectival suffix *-es shifts to become marker of animate singular nominative. In effect, then, this theory implies that *-es does not remain suffixal either, but rather, is resegmented so that only *-e- persists as derivative-marker while *-s becomes the singular

---

[29] Benveniste, *Origines* 187.

[30] Cf. n. 27.

[31] We may surmise that the second is a semantic extension of the first.

[32] Not just the separate Germanic extension is taken into account here, but the general IE phenomenon. For the later animate adjective-formant *-es derived from inanimate abstract-suffix *-es, and the possible formal connection of the former with thematic-stem nominative plural *-es, cf. n. 85.

nominative desinence in what is now the declension of the productive nominal formation *par excellence* in the IE dialects, namely the so-called thematic-stem nouns and adjectives. To describe *-es in such a way is admittedly controversial; the thematic vowel is generally defined as an enlargement of the root or suffix,[33] that is to say, it is deemed to be a predesinential element. But such an evaluation is not disputed here, and is indeed adequate for a synchronic description of the IE dialectal stage when *-e- is really a derivational formant, so that we can formulate an opposition

{thematic-stem animate nominative *-o-s, accusative *-o-m, etc.

vs.

athematic-stem animate nominative *-s or -ø, accusative *-m (*-m̥)};

nevertheless, a diachronic perspective may well require, on structural grounds, an older segmentation *-eC (thus e.g. *-os, *-om, etc.). Derivational relationships of the type seen in Latin *modus/modestus* (< *mod-os/*mod-es-tos), *ager/ agrestis* (< *agr-os/*agr-es-tis), and *domus/domesticus* (< *dom-os/*dom-es-tikos) might be traced back to an early period in IE dialects when the formal split between adjective-suffix *-es and abstract-suffix *-es had not yet taken place; the positing of such a phase could perhaps account for the absence (in *modus* and *domus*) of the usual differentiating qualitative apophony which later developed in the specialized and productive abstract-formations as seen in Greek νέφ-ος / Old Slavonic *neb-o*, Latin *gen-us* / Greek γέν-ος; perhaps the types *mod-es- and *dom-es- show an earlier stage than that of the expected *med-os- and *dem-os-. But in *modus, ager, domus*, the segmentation *-e-s had ultimately

[33] Cf. e.g. Benveniste, *Origines* 172.

prevailed. The reverse holds for *pondus*, with the segmentation *-es- as in the synchronically-generated ablative singular *pondere* of classical Latin, to be contrasted with residual *pondō* (attested in e.g. the *Twelve Tables*). Comparable to the Latin type *agr-os/*agr-es-tis: Lithuanian *gaĭlas* "compassion" vs. *gaĭlestis* "*idem*"; also Old Slavonic *nagъ* "naked" vs. *nagostь* "nudity," *mrъtvъ* "dead" vs. *mrъtvostь* "mortality," etc.[34] Likewise, there is structural evidence to warrant at least the tentative proposal that in an attested IE language like classical Greek, the genitive singular *-os* of the athematic declension and the nominative singular *-os* of the thematic can be described historically as descendants of one and the same IE formant.[35] Most important for such a claim is the fact that on the basis of the attested IE dialects, there is no common formant which can be reconstructed for the genitive singular of the thematic-stem nominal category; as C. Watkins points out,[36] even within a single dialectal group of IE such as Baltic, there are divergent formations marking the thematic genitive singular, as with Old Prussian *deiwas* (< *-oso) and Lithuanian *diẽvo* (< ablative *-ōd). Then too, there are such IE-inherited formal pairs as the reinforced genitive (⇒ ablative) *-tos and the adjectival (/participial) *-tos, or again genitives

---

[34] Cf. A. Meillet, *Études sur l'étymologie et le vocabulaire du vieux slave*[2] (Paris 1961) 280–285. E. Benveniste has argued (*Hittite et indo-européen* [Paris: Adrien Maisonneuve, 1962] 94 f) that the Baltic suffix *-estis* shows no internally-established original connection with an inanimate suffix *-es-. As for not only Old Slavonic *-ostь* but also Hittite *-ašti*, they are abstract-formants synchronically motivated by adjectives (Benveniste, *ibidem*); this productive foundation by adjectives may reflect a very ancient derivational relationship, wherein an archaic motivation by inanimate-formant *-es- is seen bypassed in favor of a still more archaic motivation by an adjective-formant *-es-, before the latter had been resegmented (cf. § 6). In Hittite, inanimate nouns in *-os- have not even survived.

[35] A like proposal has been offered by van Wijk, *Genetiv Singular* (*passim*), though on the basis of arguments different, often also divergent, from those assembled herewith.

[36] "Italo-Celtic Revisited," *IE Dialects* 38.

*-nos, *-inos, *-īnos and adjectival *-nos, *-inos, *-īnos.[37]
What is more, the descendant of the thematic-stem paradigm
in Hittite nominals regularly shows identical forms for the
nominative and genitive singular: -aš for both.[38] Reflected
here are, for the former category, an originally adjectival
suffix *-ɛs,[39] later resegmented as derivative formant *-ɛ- +
nominative singular desinence *-s, and, for the latter, the
same adjectival suffix *-ɛs, left unsegmented and having
become specialized as genitival desinence by the process
of grammaticalization; in this instance the functional split
of the originally adjectival suffix *-ɛs is not yet accompanied,
even within the same paradigm, by newly-imposed formal
differentiation; hence Hittite -aš/-aš (< *-os/*-os), as
opposed to the situation in e.g. Latin, where the type -us/-ī
(< *-os/*-ī) replaced -us/*-us (< *-os/*-os). In the latter
language, there is evidence not only for the formal intra-
paradigmatic innovation of introducing the ending -ī into
the slot of genitive singular in the ɛ-stem declension, but
also apparently for an extra-paradigmatic differentiation of
the original adjectival suffix *-ɛs, in that the e-vocalism of
thematic *ɛ is generalized for the function of genitival
desinence in e.g. the third, athematic, declension (hence
-is < *-es), as opposed to the o-vocalism in the nominative
singular of the second, thematic, declension (-us < *-os);
Latin genitives of the type nominus (instead of nominis), as
found e.g. in the Senatusconsultum de Bacchanalibus, are residual.
Seemingly comparable:

{adjectival suffix *-ɛs ⇒ genitive desinence *-ɛs ... ⇒ e.g.
Latin *-es, in opposition to *-os of the nominative singular}

---

[37] Cf. Schwyzer, *GG* I 490 f; also Kuryłowicz, *Apophonie* 130 and *Inflectional Categories* 220.
[38] Cf. J. Friedrich, *Hethitisches Elementarbuch* I² (Heidelberg 1960) 44, 46; cf. also Kuryłowicz, *Inflectional Categories* 196 f, n. 15.
[39] For further discussion of the later resegmentation, cf. § 6 *infra*.

{abstract suffix *-ϵs ⇒ nominative plural desinence *-ϵs ... ⇒ e.g. Greek -ϵς, in opposition to -ος of the residual abstract suffix}.[40]

§5. It is now possible to resume consideration of the proposition that, as ultimate components of a genitive desinence, both *-s and *-ϵs are admissible in postconsonantal position from an IE standpoint. I have also claimed[41] that the removal of a restriction on postconsonantal genitive *-s can actually be justified in terms of Benveniste's theory of the IE root. In essence, then, the task here will be to show that the Sanskrit type dā́ru/dróḥ can be derived from an original IE variation *dérṵ/*dréṵ-s, not necessarily *dérṵ/*dréu-s. If we leave out of focus, for the moment, the ultimate desinence-formant *-s seen in the reconstructed *dréṵ-s, so that only *dérṵ- and *dréṵ- are compared, then the two variants correspond to Benveniste's well-known formulation of radical states I (CϵC-C'-) and II (CC-ϵC'-).[42] What seems crucial is that the formal opposition between state I and state II has a functional correlation. As an example, one can cite the concise statement of Watkins:

It is hardly a coincidence that the second state of the root, e.g., TR-eT- [T = C], is itself in many verbs the only formal mark of the aorist, in opposition to the present built on a state

[40] The results of such a differentiation as the latter have already been illustrated with the contrast seen in {γέν-ος: φρέν-ϵς}; cf. § 3 supra.

[41] Cf. § 2 supra.

[42] As propounded in the crucial chap. ix of Origines. The locus of diffusion for the alternation CϵC-C- : CC-ϵC- may have been restricted originally to the specific structure CϵR-C-/CR-ϵC-, as Kuryłowicz implies in the equally crucial § 14 ("Les racines biformes") of Apophonie, 130–134. Granted, some attested instances of the pattern CϵR-C- may reveal simply a relatively late, even dialectal, stage of IE, when an original CRϵC- could be refashioned into a new CϵRC- on the basis of a zero-grade CR̥C- (after the -R̥- in the latter had become -iR-, -uR-, etc.; cf. Apophonie 131 et passim). But the point on which to insist, as Kuryłowicz has done, is that there definitely seems to be an early stage of IE where the patterns CϵR-C- and CR-ϵC-, instead of being indirectly related as just described, show rather a direct and original morphological opposition to each other; and, what is more, the same opposition is found in the general context of CϵC-C- and CC-ϵC- (cf. nn. 43, 45, and the arguments to which they are appended).

one form TeR-T-. This is particularly apparent in seṭ roots
TeR-H- [H = ə], where the aorist in the older languages
regularly has the second state form TR-eH-: Gk. ἔτλη, ἔβλη,
ἔπλητο.[43]

Designating it *dr-éu̯- as opposed to *dr-éy̯-, Benveniste
nonetheless clearly saw in this given manifestation of state II
another instance of a functional correlation with state I, in
this case *dér-y̯-: from the vantage point of hindsight, paradigmatic relationships of the type {nominative dā́ru : genitive
dróḫ} conceal, beneath the stage of grammaticalization, a
pristine phase with a nominal opposition {fundamental
*dér-y̯- : derivational *dr-éy̯-}:

> Les noms dérivés [italics supplied] *dr-éu-, *pk-éu-, *gn-éu-,
> *sn-éu- apparaissent soit en composition, soit comme mots
> indépendants, soit enfin mêlés, comme cas faibles, à la flexion
> des thèmes I qui fournissent les cas forts: ainsi skr. sā́nu, g. abl.
> snóḫ, dā́ru, g. abl. dróḫ [cross-reference here to Origines 54]. Au
> point de vue indo-européen, il s'agit d'un thème indépendant,
> apte à recevoir . . . des éléments de dérivation.[44]

[43] Celtic Verb I 100; an example of CₑC-(C-)/CC-ₑ(C-): *ségh-... > ἔχ(ει),
*sgh-ét > (ἔ)σχε. Cf. also Kuryłowicz, Apophonie 131. For more on the theme
II type *gʷléə₁- vs. the theme I type *gʷélə₁- (as in Epic aorist βλη- vs. e.g.
Arcadian present δελ-), cf. Schwyzer, GG I 743. Against the argument that
βλη-C- should be derived exclusively from *gʷlā-C- (< *gʷ]ə₁-C-), never from
*gʷlē-C- (< *gʷleə₁-C-), we can cite K. Strunk, Nasalpräsentien und Aoriste
(Heidelberg 1967) 40–45 et passim. But there is also a built-in criterion for
determining whether a given instance of the base βλη- is to be derived from
*gʷleə₁- or from *gʷ]ə₁-: once granted that the productive aorist passive
formant -θη- can be traced back etymologically to the stative formant *-dh-
plus a constituent suffix *-eə₁- which has broken away from its radical locus
(cf. Kuryłowicz, Apophonie 131–134, especially n. 35 therein), it follows that
instances of identity between the desinences of residual base βλη- and productive base -θη- reveal in the former the ancestral pattern CReə₁- from which the
latter had been generated. Hence e.g. ξυμ-βλή-την vs. -θή-την (e.g. δηρινθήτην,
Π 756), βλή-μεναι vs. -θή-μεναι (e.g. διακρινθήμεναι, Γ 98), ἀπο-βλῆ-ι vs. -θῆ-ι
(e.g. ἰανθῇ, χ 59). However, in a collocation like Λ 410 ἑστάμεναι κρατερῶς,
ἤ τ' ἔβλητ' ἤ τ' ἔβαλ' ἄλλον, the specifically passive (not just residual intransitive)
context and the middle desinence suggest parallelism with the type (ἔ)κτατο
"was killed," so that we may reconstruct here a ø-grade *gʷ]ə₁-C-. Ultimately,
(ἔ)βλητο was ousted by the etymologically pleonastic (ἐ)βλήθη.
[44] Benveniste, Origines 179.

The mentioned derivational elements capable of being attached to state II (CC-ϵC'-) involve the basic pattern *-ϵC-, and the suffixation of such a morpheme to a base in state II seems to have been accompanied by the reduction of the immediately preceding ϵ-grade to ø-grade:[45]

CC-$\acute{\epsilon}$C'- + $\acute{\epsilon}$C $\Rightarrow$ CC-C'-$\acute{\epsilon}$C-.

For example:

*dr-$\acute{\epsilon}$u̯- + $\acute{e}$s $\Rightarrow$ *dr-u̯-$\acute{e}$s- (Greek δρυός)
*dr-$\acute{\epsilon}$u̯- + $\acute{e}$n $\Rightarrow$ *dr-u̯-$\acute{e}$n- (Avestan *drvan-*)
*ə̯u̯-$\acute{e}$d- + $\acute{e}$n $\Rightarrow$ *ə̯u̯-d-$\acute{e}$n- (Sanskrit *udán-*).[46]

The resulting structure CC-C'-ϵC- will here be designated state II$_2$. With the addition of another morpheme, again of the pattern *-ϵC-, the same process is repeated, resulting in state II$_3$:

CC-C'-$\acute{\epsilon}$C- + $\acute{\epsilon}$C $\Rightarrow$ CC-C'-C-$\acute{\epsilon}$C-.

For example:

*dr-u̯-$\acute{e}$n- + $\acute{e}$s $\Rightarrow$ *dr-u̯-n-$\acute{e}$s- (Sanskrit *drúṇaḥ*)
*ə̯u̯-d-$\acute{e}$n- + $\acute{e}$s $\Rightarrow$ *ə̯u̯-d-n-$\acute{e}$s- (Sanskrit *udnáḥ*).[47]

The grammaticalization inherent in the attested paradigmatic forms δρυός, *drúṇaḥ*, and *udnáḥ* (all genitive singular) recalls the previous discussion of the IE suffix *-ϵs-,[48] where an attempt was made to show that this morpheme ultimately

---

[45] The term ø-grade is not meant here or elsewhere to imply the phonetic reality of a segment like [CC] as opposed to e.g. [CeC]; rather, it designates a condition which ultimately caused in the IE dialects the variously attested reflexes showing the absence of interconsonantal thematic vocalism in a given slot.

[46] Herewith a transformational interpretation of the data supplied in *Origines* 179 f.

[47] *Ibid.*

[48] Cf. § 3, § 4.

took several different directions of specialization, and that the attested IE dialects are thus left with areas of distribution revealing both maintenance, albeit restricted, of suffixal status (hence ἐs-stems of the type γένος/genus/jánaḥ) as well as innovation in the expanded development of desinential functions (hence *-ἐs of the nominative plural and genitive singular). In the context of this evaluation of an original IE morpheme *-ἐs-, it is finally possible to account directly for an original pattern like *dréu̯-s (... > e.g. Sanskrit dróḥ) in terms of Benveniste's theory of the IE root. According to the latter scheme, when a so-called constituent suffix $+\acute{e}C'$ is applied to a fundamental radical pattern CéC-, the pristine structures designated as states I and II emerge:

$$C\acute{e}C\text{-} + \acute{e}C' \Rightarrow \text{(I)} \ C\acute{e}C\text{-}C'\text{-}$$
$$\text{(II)} \ CC\text{-}\acute{e}C'\text{-}.$$

In view of this formulation, it would seem to follow that if a derivative formation like *dr-u̯-és (... > e.g. Greek δρυός) is designated as existing in state II_2, then *dr-éu̯-s (... > e.g. Sanskrit dróḥ) would be the corresponding derivative in state I_2; indeed, state II_n could be expected to have a corresponding state I_n. This extension of an accentual/apophonic mechanism from constituent to non-constituent suffixal patterns can be symbolized with the following proportion:

(I) $C\acute{e}C\text{-}C'\text{-}$: (II) $CC\text{-}\acute{e}C'\text{-}$ = (I_n) ...$\acute{e}C\text{-}C\text{-}$: (II_n) ...$C\text{-}\acute{e}C\text{-}$.

For such a scheme to match the attested state of affairs, it is important to maintain that while it is possible to formulate a chain of foundations like

(II) $CC\text{-}\acute{e}C\text{-} \rightarrow (II_2) \ CC\text{-}C'\text{-}\acute{e}C\text{-} \rightarrow (II_3) \ CC\text{-}C'\text{-}C\text{-}\acute{e}C\text{-} \rightarrow ...$
e.g. *dr-éu̯- → *dr-u̯-én- → *dr-u̯-n-és,

it does not necessarily follow that $(I) \rightarrow (I_2) \rightarrow (I_3) \rightarrow \ldots$
also. Instead, the hierarchy seems to be this:

$$C\acute{e}C\text{-} \rightarrow \begin{cases} (I) \ C\acute{e}C\text{-}C'\text{-} \\ \downarrow \\ (II) \ CC\text{-}\acute{e}C'\text{-} \rightarrow \end{cases} \begin{cases} (I_2) \ CC\text{-}\acute{e}C'\text{-}C\text{-} \\ \downarrow \\ (II_2) \ CC\text{-}C'\text{-}\acute{e}C\text{-} \rightarrow \end{cases}$$

$$\begin{cases} (I_3) \ CC\text{-}C'\text{-}\acute{e}C\text{-}C\text{-} \\ \downarrow \\ (II_3) \ CC\text{-}C'\text{-}C\text{-}\acute{e}C\text{-} \rightarrow \ldots \end{cases}$$

For example:

$$*d\acute{e}r\text{-} \rightarrow \begin{cases} (I) \ *d\acute{e}r\text{-}u\text{-} \\ \downarrow \\ (II) \ *dr\text{-}\acute{e}u\text{-} \rightarrow (I_2) \ *dr\text{-}\acute{e}u\text{-}s \\ \qquad\qquad\quad \mapsto (II_2) \ *dr\text{-}u\text{-}\acute{e}s \\ \qquad\qquad\quad \mapsto (II_2) \ *dr\text{-}u\text{-}\acute{e}n\text{-} \rightarrow (II_3) \ *dr\text{-}u\text{-}n\text{-}\acute{e}s. \end{cases}$$

The purpose of such formulations is basically this: to show presently that Benveniste's intuitive conclusions about the structural permutations of the IE root can be applied also to the earliest phases of the IE suffix, and even to the IE desinence. What is more, I propose as a general principle that the earliest IE suffixal and desinential configurations should be explained in terms of original emanations from radical states I and II. Actually, Benveniste's *Origines* already contains several strong hints that lead to such an interpretation. To wit, it is clearly inferred therein (1) that the original constituent suffix seen in $(C\acute{e}C)\text{-}C'\text{-}$ and $(CC)\text{-}\acute{e}C'\text{-}$ spreads beyond this radical frame as productive formant, either simplex $(+\epsilon C)$ or complex $(+\epsilon C + \epsilon C\ldots)$, of new derivative categories,[49] and (2) that many such non-constituent suffixes can thereupon become specialized as

[49] Cf. e.g. *Origines* 160: the originally *radical* (thus constituent) element *-$\epsilon\vartheta$- of $CC\text{-}\epsilon\vartheta$ can spread within *n*-infix verbs with e.g. base $CC\text{-}n\text{-}\epsilon\vartheta_2$, so that *-nā- ($<$ *-n$\epsilon\vartheta_2$-) ultimately becomes a productive predesinential verbal

desinences by the process of grammaticalization.[50] However, the very onset of grammaticalization eventually came to destroy the original apophonic mechanism whereby structural foundations like $\{...\text{-}C_1\text{-}\epsilon C_2 \to ...\text{-}C_1\text{-}C_2\text{-}\epsilon C_3\}$ had been operative;[51] and after such an apophonic breakdown, the addition of any new suffixal segment $+\epsilon C$ to a previous string could no longer automatically exert a rearrangement of quantitative gradation in that string: in fact, double and even multiple ϵ-grade now became possible. That and intra-paradigmatic leveling helped wipe out in the IE dialects most traces of the old apophony, so that evaluations of this phenomenon have to be drawn from such synchronically anomalous configurations as Sanskrit *dấru/dróh*. Occasionally, however, we may discern the survival of an alternating pattern like state I_n/state II_n even within the paradigm of productive categories. Thus in Sanskrit *r*-stem and *n*-stem nominals, the locative is reflected as *-ari, -ani* and the dative as *-re, -ne* (e.g. *dātari, takṣaṇi* and *dātre, takṣṇe*):[52]

$$... + \epsilon r + \epsilon\underset{\sim}{i} \Rightarrow (I_n) \; *\text{-}\epsilon r\text{-}\underset{\sim}{i} > \text{-}ari$$
$$(II_n) \; *\text{-}r\text{-}\epsilon\underset{\sim}{i} > \text{-}re$$
$$... + \epsilon n + \epsilon\underset{\sim}{i} \Rightarrow (I_n) \; *\text{-}\epsilon n\text{-}\underset{\sim}{i} > \text{-}ani$$
$$(II_n) \; *\text{-}n\text{-}\epsilon\underset{\sim}{i} > \text{-}ne.$$

Judging from the already-proposed foundation $\{I_n \to II_n\}$, I surmise that the original grammaticalized function of $+\epsilon\underset{\sim}{i}$ had been locative; then the derivative variant $*\text{-}\epsilon\underset{\sim}{i}$ (II_n) of

---

formant, capable of being attached even to complex bases which would have been previously incongruous: hence e.g. Greek verbs in *-νημι*, where the *-η-* conceals a former radical element. Cf. also Strunk, *Nasalpräsentien* (n. 43) 56–59 *et passim*.

[50] Cf. e.g. *Origines* 173, where a very important survey is taken of some IE-inherited verbal desinences and of the underlying suffixes which had produced them: where too we see that some of the latter are still attested as actual suffixes in nominal categories, specialized as desinences only in verbal categories.

[51] Cf. § 7 *infra*.

[52] Cf. Kuryłowicz, *Inflectional Categories* 195 f.

*-i̯ (I$_n$) could have later extracted a specialized dative function from an original absence of dative/locative distinction, thus relegating through this functional split the residual locative function to the primary form *-i̯.[53] Here, then, the case-differentiation is achieved by the specialization of one state as opposed to the other. A similar mechanism is the addition of another morpheme to the desinence-segment *-εC, with the result again being case-differentiation: hence when there evolved within the IE genitive desinence +εs a functional split between ablative and genitive, the ablative developed a more characterized +εt + εs; resolved as *-t-εs (state II$_n$), the latter is seen in e.g. Vedic secondary new ablative śīrṣa-táḥ (< *...n̥-t-és) vs. the simplex primary old genitive śīrṣṇ-áḥ (< *...n-és); we may also compare the Latin type caelitus, funditus, etc. The possible objection remains, however, that positing + εt + εs cannot be justified until a configuration in state I$_n$ (*-εt-s) is found as parallel to state II$_n$ (*-t-εs). I propose that an extant category corresponding to just such a pattern is the Hittite ablative desinence -az = /-ats/,[54] a remnant of state I$_n$ (*-εt-s), vs. the simplex genitive -aš = /-as/. The synchronic function of +εt in early IE could be described as a reinforcing formant introduced before instead of after the main formant +εC which is to be characterized. The combination +εt + εs just proposed involved the reinforcement of an eventual desinence +εs, but we must keep in mind that the

---

[53] That the locative, not dative, is primary appears to be corroborated by the fact that locative desinences, unlike the dative, are sometimes etymologically missing: in e.g. Sanskrit par-út (vs. Greek πέρ-υσ-ι), the configuration of the old nominal phrase (later to become an adverb) is still attested without the derivative suffix that was to become grammaticalized as locative desinence.

[54] Cf. E. H. Sturtevant, *A Comparative Grammar of the Hittite Language* (Philadelphia 1933) § 196; however, unlike here, Sturtevant segments -z- = /-ts/, as if this were ø-grade of *-tos; the preceding -a- he derives from *-ō-. For still another explanation of Hittite -az, cf. E. Benveniste, "Études hittites et indo-européennes," *Bulletin de la Société de Linguistique de Paris* 50 (1954) 32 ff.

latter formant also survived productively in the pristine non-grammaticalized function of adjectival suffix, only later to be resegmented in such a way that while *-ε- persisted as derivative-formant, *-s of the nominative (as well as e.g. a restructured *-m of the accusative) became sole desinence-marker[55]: hence such adjectival formations as deverbative śru-tá-ḥ in Sanskrit, κλυ-τό-s in Greek, (in-)cli-tu-s in Latin, etc.; so also denominative barbā-tu-s again in Latin, brada-tъ in Old Slavonic, barzdó-ta-s in Lithuanian, etc.[56] In the residual Greek type ἄγνως "unknown/unknowing" vs. ἄγνωτος "unknown," we see an original state I_n nominative *-ετ-s in functional opposition to the prevailing state II_n nominative *-t-ες,[57] later resegmented as *-tε-s. In sum, just as there existed a reinforced derivative (*-t-ες) of *-ες, structurally paralleling a reinforced desinence (*-t-ες) of *-ες, so also the ultimate dative/locative desinence +εi̯ had not just a simplex derivative counterpart +εi̯, the so-called i-stem nominals,[58] but also the reinforced structure +εt +εi̯, leading to nomina actionis in *-t-εi̯-.[59] Since this discussion is meant to be heuristic rather than exhaustive, I mention other such cases of suffixal reinforcement by +εt

---

55 Cf. § 6.
56 For a clear summary of the range of adjectival *-to-, cf. Meillet, Introduction 268 f; Meillet's structural insight prompts him to list *-et- side by side with *-to-, *-er- with *-ro-, *-ter- with *-tro-, etc. On p. 269, he designates *-ko- as "la forme thématique" of *-ek-. Likewise van Wijk, Genetiv Singular, passim.
57 Cf. E. Benveniste, Noms d'agent et noms d'action en indo-européen (Paris 1948) 168, on the type ἀγν-ώς (< *-ōts). The lengthened grade of the nominative is here irrelevant (cf. § 8); what matters is that *-ēt-s corresponds to state I_n, and that there is a functional distinction between this and the configuration in state II_n, *-t-ες: "passif/individualisant" for the latter, "actif/moins individualisé . . ." for the former. As for Hittite -at-, formant of abstract nouns, cf. E. Benveniste, Hittite et indo-européen (Paris 1962) 89: the same segmentation, *-et-, can be detected in Sanskrit srav-át-, Latin teg-et-, Gothic mit-aþ-s. The prevalence of the suffix -at- in Hittite as opposed to other IE languages might be structurally relevant to the etymology just proposed for the Hittite ablative desinence -az.
58 Further discussion in § 8.
59 Cf. Benveniste, Noms d'agent et noms d'action (n. 57), passim.

only in passing: *nomina actionis* in *-t-εμ-, *nomina agentis* in
*-t-εr-, comparatives in *-t-εr-ε- (vs. residual *-εr-ε- as in
Latin *sup-er-u-s*),[60] etc. This much observed about +εt, we
are ready to review Benveniste's definition of the term
enlargement:

> Nous opérerons constamment avec les termes de "suffixe" et
> d' "élargissement", bien que le même élément puisse être l'un
> ou l'autre. Nous distinguons un suffixe d'un élargissement d'une
> manière purement formelle: le suffixe est caractérisé par sa
> forme alternante (*-et-/-t-*, *-en-/-n-*, *-ek-/-k-*, etc.), l'élargissement
> par sa forme fixe et consonantique (*-t-*, *-n-*, *-k-*, etc.). Cette
> distinction, qui est capitale, sera ici substituée à la notion de
> "déterminant de racine" ("Wurzeldeterminativ") dont on a
> fait un usage inconsidéré.[61]

While this statement is to be upheld, one proposed corollary
on the basis of the discussion preceding is this: an enlargement is a suffix +εC which had lost its thematic vocalism
*-ε- and thereupon fails to exert any further apophonic
pressure on other sequences of +εC to which it is added.
Such an elaboration on Benveniste's basic formulation implies
that enlargements and original non-constituent suffixes
involve variant diachronic levels, and that the former can be
explained historically in terms of the latter. Thus e.g. the
*-t- in IE-inherited *-t-os as found in the attested dialects
is indeed synchronically an infixed enlargement; but diachronically, a case can be made that it is a derivational suffix
+εt. In other words, there is to have arisen a metastasis
of *-t-, from derivational suffix *-εt- with ø-grade to differentiating infix with no apophonic implication.

§6. The just-posited sequence of structural foundations
in the pattern {state II → state II$_2$ → ...} may supplement
Kuryłowicz's cogent schema for tracing back the original

---

[60] *Ibid.* For the conflation of the types *-t-εr-C (I$_n$) and *-t-r-εC (II$_n$) as
*-tεrεC, cf. § 8.
[61] *Origines* 148.

locus of diffusion in the relation of the IE formant *-o- to
*-ā-:

The relation -o-:-ā-, which seems to be fundamental in all
speculations upon the [IE] gender, could, just like the relation
between the -e/o- aorist and the -ā- (or -ē-) aorist,[62] be traced back
to the replacement of state II of the root (TRo₂) by the younger
state II' (TR̥₂ó). The verbal adjectives of the structure TRā
(< TRo₂) were renewed by the more recent form TR̥o (<
TR̥₂ó), the former being gradually restricted to the function of an
abstract noun. ... The proportion TR̥o:TRā gave rise to
*lukó:*lukā́, etc.[63]

[62] Cf. also Kuryłowicz, *Apophonie* 131–134; cf. especially n. 35 therein, for
this crucial statement: "Il ne faut pas confondre le η suffixal de δαμ-η avec le η
faisant partie de la forme radicale II (βλη). Après la chute des ₂ intervocaliques
la voyelle longue de la forme II, cessant d'être sentie comme partie intégrante
de la racine, est appréciée comme un élément suffixal détachable."

[63] Kuryłowicz, *Inflectional Categories* 217. Actually, the functional split
between *-o- and *-ā- takes two directions:
(1) substantival/pronominal masculine *-o- vs. feminine *-ā-
(2) adjectival animate *-o- vs. abstract substantival *-ā-; the latter *-ā-
incidentally acquires feminine gender from formal identity with the substantival/pronominal feminine *-ā-.
By contrast, formal identity of the abstract suffix *-es with the adjectival
suffix *-es is no longer perceived once the latter becomes resegmented (cf. § 6);
hence the residual gender, neuter (⇐ inanimate) of the former, as in the type
γέν-ος; hence also the relatively late consonant-stem inflection of the type
γέν-ος, as even seen from the general lack of quantitative apophonic interplay
in the suffix: e.g. γένος/γένους < *genos/*geneses.
The abstract substantival suffix *-ā- (ø-grade *-ə₂-) could become grammaticalized as plural desinence *-ā-(/*-ə₂-), through the intermediacy of
specialization as collective-marker (type πάτρᾱ). Relevant here is the already-mentioned proposition (§ 3) that the abstract suffix *-es was grammaticalized
as marker of the animate nominative plural, and that this desinence could
become formally differentiated from the original suffix by restriction of e-
grade to the former and o-grade to the latter: hence such a qualitative apophonic
opposition as between abstract γέν-ος and plural φρέν-ες in Greek. On the
other hand, grammaticalization of *-ā-(/*-ə₂-) as marker of the inanimate
nominative/accusative plural could entail a quantitative apophonic opposition:
e.g. in Greek, full-grade abstract suffix *-ā- (type γον-ή) vs. ø-grade plural
desinence *-ə₂- (type ζῷα). There are attested instances where the two types
of ending still coexist on the same base: e.g. ἡνίᾱ/ἡνίᾰ (cf. Schwyzer, *GG* I
582). For a discussion of how the original abstract-marker *-ā-(/*-ə₂-) may have
spread from adjectival to substantival bases (whence the opportunity for whole-sale desinential specialization), cf. chap. ii n. 78.

I propose that the mentioned functional displacement of state II CR-$\acute{\epsilon}$ə- by what is now symbolized as CR-ə-$\acute{\epsilon}$- was preceded by the actual derivation of the latter from the former: CR-$\acute{\epsilon}$ə- $+\acute{\epsilon}$s, $+\acute{\epsilon}$m, etc. ⇒ state II_2 (Kuryłowicz's state II′) C$\mathring{R}$-ə-$\acute{\epsilon}$s, C$\mathring{R}$-ə-$\acute{\epsilon}$m, etc. Thus: state II CR-$\acute{\epsilon}$ə- → state II_2 C$\mathring{R}$-ə-$\acute{\epsilon}$C, with the final -ϵC of state II_n ultimately shifting into ...ϵ-C, so that only -C remains with desinential function; hence the segmentation C$\mathring{R}$-ə-$\acute{\epsilon}$-. Meanwhile, CR-$\acute{\epsilon}$ə- $+\acute{\epsilon}$s, $+\acute{\epsilon}$m, etc. ⇒ state I_2 CR-$\acute{\epsilon}$ə-s, CR-$\acute{\epsilon}$ə-m, etc., > CR-$\acute{a}$-s, CR-$\acute{a}$-m, etc., accompanied by the evolution of the state I_n suffixes *-s, *-m, etc. from originally derivational to desinential function. With C_d representing the ultimately desinential components like *-s, *-m, etc., the $\bar{a}$-stem and the ϵ-stem nominals of the attested IE languages can be characterized thus etymologically:

state I_n: ...ϵC_d, resegmented as ...ϵ-C_d
state II_n: ...ϵə-C_d > ...$\bar{a}$-C_d.

An important result is that where function requires ø-desinence, there may ensue the loss of -C_d in various paradigmatic categories of what are now thematic-stem formations in *-ϵ-C_d, on the model of athematic-stem counterparts. Hence e.g. the generation of such ø-desinence thematic forms as the vocative in *-ϵ.

§7. The phenomenon of quantitative apophony, as described until now, had involved the alternation of ϵ-grade and ø-grade between root and suffix, with the presence of either grade in one slot presupposing the generation of its opposite in the other slot. Such an equilibrium could be operative in the context of a remote stage of IE, before grammaticalization of certain suffixes had yet set in. Nevertheless, even such an early apophonic system already contained a built-in mechanism for its own ultimate self-destruction, as also for the evolution of a newer system. The

source of disruption must have involved the combining of
productive suffixes with a base (either simplex—hence a
root—or complex) which was no longer motivated, that is,
having no living relationship to any formal alternate by way
of quantitative apophony. As a case in point, we note that an
inanimate-marking suffix *-r originally presupposed a
base with ϵ-vocalism:

...ø... $+$ r $\Rightarrow$ ...ø $+$ $\acute{\epsilon}$... $+$ r $=$ ...$\acute{\epsilon}$...r

e.g.

*ən-ø-k-t- $+$ r $\Rightarrow$ *ən-ø $+$ $\acute{\epsilon}$-k-t- $+$ r $=$ *ən$\acute{\epsilon}$ktr, as in $\nu\acute{\epsilon}\kappa\tau\alpha\rho$.[64]

But if the base, having become unmotivated, had lost the
apophonic alternation {...ϵ.../...ø...}, then an already-
existing ϵ-vocalism within this base could no longer be
appreciated as such, but rather, as a functional (though not
formal) ø-vocalism, having no rôle in the constitution of
new derivations. Thus since e.g. *-r in the above configuration automatically confers ϵ-grade on the base, the result
can be the following:

...ϵ... $+$ r $\Rightarrow$ ...ϵ $+$ ϵ... $+$ r $=$ ...$\bar{\epsilon}$...r

e.g.

*sn-ϵ-u̯- $+$ r $\Rightarrow$ *sn-ϵ $+$ ϵ-u̯- $+$ r $=$ *sn$\acute{\epsilon}$u̯r, as in Avestan
snāvar.[65]

Such instances provided mere formal precedent for the new
phase of IE quantitative apophony, wherein the actual
alternation of ø-grade and ϵ-grade in base and suffix was
no longer obligatory. As for the impetus leading to general
rather than selective adaptation of new productive formations with double or multiple ϵ-grade, it has already been
ascribed here to the process of grammaticalization. A

[64] Cf. Benveniste, *Origines* 18, 154 f; for *ə₂n$\acute{\epsilon}$ksə₂, cf. Latin *noxa* (cf. also
Kuchean 3rd singular *neksa*); for state I of the root, cf. Hittite *ḥenk-an* "plague"
and Greek ἀν-άγκ-η.
[65] For other attestations of the type *sn$\acute{\epsilon}$u̯r, cf. Benveniste, *Origines* 182 f
et passim.

crucial factor is that while a derivative category is a marked member founded by its unmarked correlate, the same situation does not necessarily hold for inflectional categories. Granted, when an ending$_a$ and an ending$_b$ had still been suffixes, the formations which they constituted might have been under a derivational hierarchy, such as form A→ form B. Hence a proportion like

(1) word$_1$ + ending$_a$: word$_1$ + ending$_b$ = word$_2$ + ending$_a$: word$_2$ + new ending$_b$.

But with the advent of grammaticalization, there is now the possibility of a proportion like

(2) word$_1$ + ending$_a$: word$_2$ + ending$_a$ = word$_1$ + ending$_b$: word$_2$ + new ending$_b$,[66]

provided that word$_2$ is semantically subordinate to word$_1$.[67] With the type (1), a mechanism of the original apophonic pattern could be maintained, as e.g. in the following nominal proportion:

(1) X-t-er : X-t-r-es = Y-t-er : Y-t-r-es.

With the type (2), however, *-t-er has already been restructured as suffix *-t-er- + nominative desinence ø, and *-t-r-es as suffix *-t-r- + e.g. genitive desinence *-es; hence

(2) X-t-er : Y-t-er = X-t-r-es : Y-t-er-es.

Proportion (2), then, exerts merely an additive process in the creation of Y-t-er-es; whereas the apophonic structure of X-t-r-es reveals an original foundation {X-t-er → derivative X-t-r-es}, the relationship between Y-t-er and Y-t-er-es is now simply that between constituents of one paradigm. And within the context of a paradigm, opposition between suffixal e-grade (*-t-er-) and ø-grade (*-t-r-) loses its relevance, since this apophonic mechanism had served as marker of a derivational rather than inflectional relationship.

---

[66] New ending$_b$ may have entailed replacement of an old ending $_x$.
[67] Cf. Kuryłowicz, *Inflectional Categories* 38.

For an example where a later-extinct derivational foundation {X-t-er → X-t-r-es} survived formally under the guise
of an inflectional relationship {nominative singular →
genitive singular}, we can cite the type πατήρ[68]/πατρός;
the suffixal apophony {*-ter- : *-tr-} is here apparent. But
with the advent of proportion (2), suffixal apophony is
subject to becoming wiped out in motivated forms of the
type ἀπάτωρ:

(2) X-t-er : Y-t-er = X-t-r-es : Y-t-er-es
   πατήρ : ἀπάτωρ = πατρός : ἀπάτορος.

An example of Y-t-r-es is the type δαι-τρός, a residue from
proportion (1): it was generalized as a derivative nominal,
with *-es becoming singular nominative-marker; on the
other hand, the type δαί-τορος (of δαί-τωρ; cf. Δαίτορα,
Θ275)[69] illustrates the pattern resulting from proportion (2)
and serving as inflectional paradigm-constituent, with *-es
becoming singular genitive-marker. Other such contrasts
might include pairs like

inflectional ὑμένος (genitive of ὑμήν) and derivational ὕμνος
inflectional λιμένος (genitive of λιμήν) and derivational λίμνη.[70]

In sum, because of the onset of grammaticalization, obligatory alternation of ø-grade and ε-grade in base and suffix
broke down within motivated categories: the old apophonic
mechanism, marker of derivation, had simply become ruined
by the incipient inflectional system. Hence a new layer of
derivations, in the era when desinences coexisted with suffixes, could generate ε-grade in both base and suffix instead

---

[68] The original pair would have been reconstructed as *-tér/*-trós for Common Greek (that the *-t- in this entry may belong etymologically to the root is
formally irrelevant here), if it were not for the IE secondary morphological
lengthening of *-e- in the nominative as underlying case-marker (for which cf.
§ 8); actually, the old nominative -τερ is attested, though relegated to the
secondary function of vocative (cf. again § 8).

[69] Cf. Frisk, GEW s.v. δαίομαι.

[70] Cf. Schwyzer, GG I 524 f.

of exclusively in one; indeed, double or multiple ϵ-grade could become an actual characteristic of motivated derivational categories.

§8. While IE quantitative apophony in its older phase had both additive $(+\epsilon)$ and subtractive $(-\epsilon = \emptyset)$ mechanisms, the new phase is left with only the former of the two. We have also seen from the type *sn$\bar{e}$ur ($>$ Avestan *snāvar*) that the additive mechanism of e.g. double ϵ-grade can be manifested not just contiguously in different slots (...ϵ...ϵ...) but also simultaneously in the same slot (...$\epsilon + \epsilon$... $>$ ...$\bar{\epsilon}$...).[71] As a further example, the earlier animate adjective-formant suffix and later desinence in the split functions of (1) animate nominative-marker *par excellence* and (2) animate/inanimate genitive-marker, namely $+\epsilon$s,[72] can exert the following formal developments in the base:

$$(C)C\epsilon C(...) + \epsilon s \Rightarrow \begin{cases} (C)C\bar{\epsilon}C(...)s\ a \\ (C)C\epsilon C(...)\epsilon s\ \beta. \end{cases}$$

State a, $(C)C\bar{\epsilon}C(...)C$, would be a secondary reflex of state I_n, while state β, $(C)C\epsilon C(...)C$, which is an unchanged result of the juxtaposition $(C)C\epsilon C(...) + \epsilon C$, corresponds to an original state II_n, lacking the latter's basic subtractive transformation.[73] Then the following type of distribution is possible:

$$*p\acute{e}d + \acute{e}s \Rightarrow \begin{cases} \text{state } a \text{ nominative } *p\bar{e}d\text{-s}; > \text{e.g. Dorian } \pi\acute{\omega}s \\ \text{state } \beta \text{ genitive } *p\epsilon d\text{-}\acute{e}s; > \text{e.g. Dorian } \pi o\delta\acute{o}s. \end{cases}$$

$$*\underset{\sim}{u}\acute{e}k^w + \acute{e}s \Rightarrow \begin{cases} \text{state } a \text{ nominative } *\underset{\sim}{u}\bar{e}k^w\text{-s}; > \text{e.g. Latin } u\bar{o}x \\ \text{state } \beta \text{ genitive } *\underset{\sim}{u}\epsilon k^w\text{-}\acute{e}s; \text{e.g. Homeric } (F)o\pi\acute{o}s. \end{cases}$$

As for those entries where state β instead of state a is generalized for the formant of the animate nominative singular, no such formal split can be utilized, so that a mechanism for

[71] Cf. § 7.
[72] Cf. § 3, § 4, § 5.
[73] The common structural source of what are here designated as states a and β is noted by van Wijk, *Genetiv Singular* (*passim*).

forming a genitive singular is not immediately available.[74] The actual formulation of state β can also account for such relatively recent IE formations as seen in the Greek inanimate nominative/accusative πέδον,[75] or the animate/inanimate nominative φορός/φορόν.[76] Then too, the same configuration of state β is evident in such Sanskrit genitives as mádhvaḥ (< *medhu̯es) and ávyaḥ (< *ə₃eu̯i̯es), which Kuiper cogently analyzes[77] as chronologically later than the genitival types seen in Sanskrit dróḥ (< *dréu̯s),[78] dyóḥ (< *di̯éu̯s), and diváḥ (< *diu̯és). An ensemble like *diu̯és, attested in Sanskrit diváḥ, Greek Δι(F)ός, etc., can be characterized as being in state II₂; the newer formation in state β, *deiu̯es, is attested in such nominatives as Lithuanian diẽvas (cf. the Finnish loanword taivas "sky"), Latin deus/dīuos (paradigmatically-conditioned nominative variants), Old Icelandic Týr (< Common Germanic *teiwaz), etc.; the other variation in state β, *di̯eu̯es, can be seen in Old Latin diouos.[79] As for the formulation of state a, such types as *péd-s/*ped-és could influence formations like *di̯-éu̯-s/ *di-u̯-és, where the apophonic pattern still betrays the old derivational relationship {I₂ *di̯-éu̯-s → II₂ *di-u̯-és}. But now an inflectional relationship has taken over; consequently, just as paradigm-constituents like genitive *ped-és (Greek ποδός) and dative *ped-éi̯ (Latin pedī) presuppose a

[74] Hence the structural ambiguity of {nominative *-es : genitive *-es}; cf. again § 4.

[75] An earlier IE phase, when the root-vocalism had still been subject to subtractive apophony, can still be seen in such residual forms as Greek ἐπι-βδ-α, Sanskrit upa-bd-á-, Avestan fra-bd-a-, vs. the type *ped-em, reflected as Greek πέδον, Sanskrit padám Avestan paδəm, Hittite pedan, etc.

[76] To be contrasted is the earlier subtractive apophonic pattern still seen in δί-φρ-ος (cf. also φευκτός vs. residual φυκτός); for the new state a counterpart of the state β type φορός, namely the type φώρ, cf. n. 84 infra.

[77] Vedic noun-inflexion 7.

[78] The corresponding form in state β: *deru̯es, > e.g. Greek δουρός.

[79] Cf. Leumann, LG 267. The present terminology can also be applied to suffixes: e.g. state IIₙ *-i̯os vs. state βₙ *-ei̯os.

nominative paradigm-constituent *péd-s (Dorian πώς), so also the original derivatives of state II *di̯-eu̯-(Latin diū),[80] e.g. the now-genitive *di-u̯-és (Sanskrit diváḥ) and now-dative *di-u̯-éi̯ (Greek ΔιϜει),[81] presuppose a new nominative *di̯éu̯-s (Sanskrit dyáuḥ) replacing the old potential *di̯éu̯-s; the latter is attested as the Vedic genitive dyóḥ (cf. also Avestan dyaoš), with its function expectedly stemming from a pristine derivational relationship {I₂ *di̯éu̯s ← II *di̯eu̯}.[82] Eventually, the lengthened ε-grade of nominatives like *di̯éu̯s is reinterpreted as not just an accessory of the singular nominative case, but as a prime constituent thereof, iso-functional with the nominative desinence *-s. Thus besides a generalization throughout e.g. suffixal formations in *-eu̯- (hence nominative *-ēu̯s/ genitive *-u̯es, as still seen in the Avestan type -bāz-āuš/ -bāz-vō),[83] the same morphological characteristic of lengthened ε-grade is also extended into the nominative of radical and suffixal formations in *-er-, *-en-, *-es-, etc., where s-desinence had not ever even been introduced to mark the nominative; hence the generation of lengthened grade in e.g. the nominative types φώρ,[84] πατήρ, πειθώ (< *peithōi).[85]

[80] Also Old Irish -díu, as in indíu "today"; on both Latin diū and Old Irish -díu, cf. C. Watkins, "The Indo-European word for 'day' in Celtic and related topics," Trivium 1 (1966) 102–120, esp. 111, 117; *di̯eu̯ is better designated as "indefinite case," rather than "suffixless locative"; cf. Watkins, "IE word for 'day' " 113.

[81] As in Cypriote ti-we-i-pi-lo-se = Διϝειφιλος; q.v. in O. Masson, ed., Les inscriptions chypriotes syllabiques (Paris 1961) 352.

[82] As also locative dyávi (< *di̯éu̯-i ← *di̯eu̯); the type diví is modeled on e.g. diváḥ, by paradigmatic leveling. A point of interest is that the genitives in dyóḥ and diváḥ seem to be formulaically distributed in the Rigvedic corpus: dyóḥ after short vowel, diváḥ elsewhere: cf. F. Edgerton, "The Indo-European Semivowels," Language 19 (1943) 98 and n. 37.

[83] From *-āuš/*-vas < *-ēu̯s/*-u̯es; cf. Kuiper, Vedic noun-inflexion 44 passim.

[84] Hence this is an indirect state a reflex of state β φορός; cf. n. 76 supra and van Wijk, Genetiv Singular 10 ff, where a list of such pairs is given: e.g. Latin rōs/Sanskrit rásaḥ.

[85] From this period onward, an inanimate abstract suffix *-es can develop an animate derivative with nominative in *-ēs: e.g. γέν-ος → εὐγεν-ής. By now the original adjective-suffix *-es, historically identical with the abstract

Meanwhile, the old nominative structure, seen in e.g. πάτερ and πειθοῖ, became relegated to the secondary function of vocative.[86] But the actual locus of diffusion for doubled ε-grade in the nominative is to be found in formations where the nominative singular had indeed been characterized by the desinence *-s, originally +εs exerting a formation in state α.[87] Isolating the original relationship from the attested evidence is indeed elusive, especially since motivated suffixal combinations tended to lose the old apophonic mechanism, as already seen in the contrast of ἀπάτ-ορ-ος with πατ-ρ-ός. There can even occur later the generalization of the lengthened ε-grade of the nominative singular throughout the paradigm: hence δο-τ-ήρ/δο-τ-ῆρ-ος. Examples of the already-mentioned Avestan type -bāz-āuš/-bāz-vō are comparatively rare; even in the latter case, paradigmatic pressure had generated a genitive -bāz-āuš besides -bāz-vō.[88]

---

suffix, had become resegmented as thematic-stem formant *-ε- + nominative desinence *-s. But as for the nominative plural formant of thematic-stem nominals, namely *-ōs as in Gothic *wulf-os*, it may well be formally kindred to the likewise new animate suffix with nominative *-ēs, derived from the mentioned inanimate abstract suffix *-εs. The following indirect genetic proportion is implied: adjective-formant *-εs : athematic nominative plural *-εs = new adjective-formant *-ēs : thematic nominative plural *-ēs.

[86] For a basic discussion of this distribution, cf. Kuryłowicz, *Apophonie* 143. For the Greek intonation of the nominative/vocative, cf. *idem*, *Accentuation* 130.

[87] Otherwise explained by Kuryłowicz, *Apophonie* 143; cf. the relevant discussion by C. Watkins in his review of *Apophonie*, *Language* 34 (1958) 386 f. An impetus towards the present interpretation has been Watkins' following intuitive statement (387): "one cannot separate the question of lengthening in the nominative singular from that of the morpheme -s (also absent in the vocative)."

[88] For a detailed discussion, cf. Kuiper, *Vedic noun-inflexion* 44. I suggest that the mechanism made available for this type of leveling involved the original possibility of two derivational structures from a basic form like *djéu (Latin *diū*):

II *djéu → {I₂ *djéus, as in Sanskrit *dyóḥ* / II₂ *diyés, as in Sanskrit *diváḥ*.

At a stage when *-éus/*-ués were already paradigm-constituents, the replacement of *-ués by a residual *-eus could then lead to this leveling: *-éus/ *-eus ⇒ *-éus/*-éus; cf. Old Persian *dahyāuš/dahyāuš*.

Perhaps most representative of such archaic paradigms still revealing the old quantitative apophony is the Hittite group in -aiš/-iyaš:

zaḫḫaiš/zaḫḫiyaš
ḫurtaiš/ḫurtiyaš
lengaiš/lenkiyaš
maniyaḫḫaiš/maniyaḫḫiyaš
šagaiš/šakiyaš, etc.[89]

But here too, the forces of grade-leveling are operative under the surface, with the result that genitive doublets like linkiyaš/lingayaš are attested.[90] Sometimes the actual result of leveling may reveal chronologically different phases within the original apophonic structure of the respective paradigm. For example, nominal categories showing the distribution *-ús/*-u̯és as seen in Sanskrit masculine paśúḥ/paśváḥ (vs. neuter páśu)[91] seem to point towards a paradigmatic stage where *-éu̯s/*-u̯és had not yet been transformed into *-éu̯s/*-u̯és; leveling of the latter type, on the other hand, could result in *-ū́s/*-u̯és, as seen in e.g. χέλū̄ς[92]/χέλυος,

---

[89] Kuiper, Vedic noun-inflexion 59 f. Diphthongal restoration (or possibly preservation) in nominative -aiš may be due to the paradigmatic pressure of constituents like -iyaš.

[90] Q.v. in J. Friedrich, Hethitisches Wörterbuch (Heidelberg 1952) s.v. lingāi-: cf. also Kuiper, Vedic noun-inflexion 59 f.

[91] Cf. paśúḥ : páśu with vṛṣṇíḥ : vṛ́ṣṇi; once *-éu̯s/*-u̯és and *-éis/*-i̯és are leveled into *-ús/*-u̯és and *-ís/*-i̯és respectively, there is an opportunity for formal confusion with those neuters in *u̯u and *u̯i which later shifted to the animate category by means of simply an added desinence *-s: e.g. animate mádhu-ḥ vs. inanimate mádhu. With the genesis of an animate declensional type *u̯us/*-éu̯s and *u̯is/*-éis, old genitives *-u̯és *-i̯és could be replaced by new *-éu̯s *-éis, as in Sanskrit -eḥ -oḥ, Oscan -eis -ous, Lithuanian -iẽs -aũs, Gothic -ais -aus, Greek -εις (for citations, cf. Schwyzer, GG I 572). As for the rare Greek type Ποσει-δῶν (Ionic)/Ποτει-δᾶν (Doric), it may show a residual vocative in *-ei detached at an early stage from a paradigm like *poteis/*potios (cf. Kuiper, Vedic noun-inflexion 66), later leveled to *potis/*potios as in the attested Ionic πόσις/πόσιος. For a discussion of *ποτει and of the vocatives of i-stems and u-stems in general, cf. Watkins, "The IE word for 'day' in Celtic" (n. 80) 114 ff and n. 38.

[92] Metrically attested in e.g. Hymn to Hermes 33; cf. Schwyzer, GG I 571; also Kuiper, Vedic noun-inflexion 48.

as also apparently in nouns with suffix -τύς/-τύος.[93] Then too, leveling can produce a formal split to accompany an already-existing functional one; hence e.g. the following opposition in Greek:

{*-ús (masculine singular adjective) : *-éus (> *-éus; masculine singular substantive)}:

{adjective βαρύς: substantive ἱερεύς}.

Meanwhile, formal syncretism is maintained in slots like the feminine singular {adjective βαρεῖα[94]: substantive ἱέρεια}.[95]

§9. On the basis of the arguments assembled up to this point, what has already been implied in § 1 can now be formulated explicitly: the adjectival suffix + εἰ in the configuration of inanimate nominative/accusative singular *-i (state I_n) could become grammaticalized as locative singular desinence once it acquired a primarily adverbial function.[96] The crucial factor is probably that a basic

---

[93] E.g. ἐδητύς/ἐδητύος; cf. Schwyzer, *GG* I 506 f; Benveniste, *Origines* 71 f; Kuiper, *Vedic noun-inflexion* 53.

[94] The accent is imposed by paradigmatic pressure from the masculine in -ύς: with adjectives, the relationship of masculine to feminine is inflectional, while with substantives, it is only derivational; cf. Kuryłowicz, *Accentuation* 119.

[95] In both types, -εια < *-εμῖα.

[96] Cf. n. 53 and the discussion to which it is appended. Granted, the full-grade dative *-ei, a functional specialization of ø-grade locative *-i, had been produced by an old apophonic mechanism originally operative on derivational categories: e.g., the etymological interdependence of gradation for suffix + desinence in the Sanskrit locative/dative type -ari/-re (< *-ɘr-i̯/*-r-ei̯) does indeed reflect an original gradation for suffix + suffix, namely state I_n/state II_n. But this does not mean that we must therefore try to find reasons for a separate grammaticalization of *-ei besides *-i: rather, we may say that the grammaticalized morpheme *-i inherited an appohonic foundation from its derivational phase, state I_n → state II_n = *-ɘC-i̯ → *-C-ei̯, later leveled simply to *-i → *-ei. An ultimate locative/dative functional split can thereupon inherit such formal variants, with the primary function of locative being assigned to the primary form *-i. In some IE languages, of course, such a split is not perpetuated: hence e.g. standard Attic-Ionic consonant-stem dative singular -ι, not -ει (though there are still sporadic instances of -ει: cf. e.g. n. 81).

formant of compound adjectives in IE languages is the
i-stem;[97] thus Y- → X-Y-i-, where -Y- = a substantive
with athematic stem, -X- = the first constituent of a compound adjective, and -i- = i-stem;[98] for example, the simplex athematic-stem substantive μην- generates the compound
adjective διχό-μην-ι-ς.[99] Isovalent with i-stem compound
adjectives were thematic-stem (= o-stem) compound adjectives of the type X-Y-o-, such as διχό-μην-o-ς; thus any
restriction of inanimate nominative/accusative singular
X-Y-i to secondary adverbial function may well be due
to a prevalence of o-stem over i-stem in the primary function
of compound adjective-marker. Given such a prevalence, then
from the adverbial context of a compound collocation X-Y-i
might arise, through decomposition into Y-i, the grammaticalization of the latter into the locative case of a substantive
Y-.[100]

What, then, is the status of the type διχο-μήν-ι-ο-ς?
Aside even from compounds, the o-stem has been inherited

---

[97] I.e., with an original derivative suffix +ej, in a residual, non-grammaticalized, category. Henceforth all IE nominal formations with suffixal constituent
+ej will be designated simply as i-stems, even if the *-e- had not yet been
paradigmatically leveled out from e.g. an original nominative singular *-ei-s;
cf. n. 91.

[98] For details about such compounds from the IE standpoint, cf. Schwyzer,
GG I 450, d. 1. Even Greek adjectives like τρόχις, στρόφις, τρόφις, ἴδρις,
εὖνις could all have been at one time components of compound nominal
formations, only later to become simplex entities as well. Types like κυδι-
and ἀργι-, as in ἀργι-κέραυνος and κυδι-άνειρα, are just as adjectival (from
the historical standpoint) as κυδρός, ἀργ(ρ)ός. As Benveniste concludes, "il
s'agit donc d'une seule et même formation en *-ei- usitée au début ou en fin de
composés et qui a tendu à devenir la forme de composition par excellence"
(*Origines* 80).

[99] The introduction of an enlargement -δ- into the actual declension of this
nominal type (e.g. genitive διχομήνιδος) is a Greek innovation; cf. also chap.
iii n. 197.

[100] In Benveniste's words, as already cited, "des thèmes élargis en *-i a
été extraite, en partant des emplois adverbiaux qui ont dû constituer le premier
contingent des 'locatifs', une finale -i qui a tendu à spécifier une détermination
de temps ou de lieu."—*Origines* 99.

from IE as a general adjective-formant,[101] but so also the *i*-stem.[102] When both types have become specialized as substantives,[103] one option for the perpetuation of adjectival function with these formants is the fusion of the two into one morpheme,[104] *-(i)i̯o- or *-ei̯o-;[105] in fact, such fusion can occur even without the precondition just mentioned,[106] and we have already observed instances of etymological isomorphism not only between *-o- and *-i̯o- vs. *-i- and *-i̯o-, but also between *-o-/-ā- and *-i̯o-/-i̯ā-.

[101] Cf. chap. ii § 8 and chap. iv § 6.

[102] Cf. Benveniste, *Origines* 35 ff; in fact, the *i*-stem has even prevailed over the *o*-stem in some IE languages, as in Luwian: "C'est un des traits les plus saillants de la morphologie nominale luwi que la tendance à généraliser le vocalisme suffixal *-i-* aux dépens de *-a-*, et à faire de *-i-* une véritable voyelle thématique. La majorité des thèmes nominaux du luwi sont en *-i-* contre *-a-* du hittite, qu'ils soient substantifs ou adjectifs."—Benveniste, *Hittite et indo-européen* (n. 34) 27.

[103] For a selective discussion of the typology {adjective ⇒ substantive}, cf. chap. ii § 8 and § 12.

[104] Cf. chap. ii n. 11.

[105] State II_n and state β_n respectively (cf. § 6 and § 8; also n. 56 and van Wijk, *Genetiv Singular* 15, 21 ff), from the etymological standpoint of a stage before desinential resegmentation (as discussed in § 6). For a list of attested substantivized *o*-stems with corresponding adjectival *i̯o*-stems, cf. J. W. Poultney, "Some Indo-European morphological alternations," *Language* 43 (1967) 874 f.

[106] For the replacement of e.g. *neu̯-o- (as in Greek *νέος*) by *neu̯-i̯o- (as in Gothic *niujis*) in the original adjectival function (cf. Poultney, "Alternations" [n. 105] 875), we may again apply Kuryłowicz's axiom I, quoted in chap. i n. 5.

WORD INDEX

ALBANIAN

ban, 41
dal/del, 40
flas/flet, 40
hap, 41
ngox/ngex, 40
njof/njef, 40
njoh/njeh, 40
zââ/zêê, 40

ANATOLIAN

(Hittite unlabelled)

ḫawi-(Luwian), 152n1
ḫenkan, 173n64
ḫurtaiš, 180
lengaiš, 180
maniyaḫḫaiš, 180
paprizzi kuiš, 43–44n121
pedan, 177n75
šagaiš, 180
dammešḫiškizzi kuiš, 44n121
zaḫḫaiš, 180

BALTIC

(Lithuanian unlabelled)

akáitė, 85
akìs, 85
akmenyčia, 86n127
akmuõ, 86n127
aknas (Latvian), 94
álnis (Latvian), 54
antrãdienis, 52
árti, 51n6
àš/èš, 94, 95
assaran (Old Prussian), 94n155
aswinan (Old Prussian), 94n155
ašvà/ešvà, 94n155
atsargà, 64n45

barzdótas, 169
bažnýčia, 86n127
bevaĩkė, 60
bevaĩkis, 52, 60
bìtė, 59n36
bitìs, 59n36
bobvedỹs, 53
brãlis (Latvian), 97n161
brólis, 97n161
dadzis (Latvian), 97
dagà, 65, 67
dagė, 65, 67
dagỹs, 97
dainà, 56
dainė̃, 56
dangà, 67, 68
dègti, 65, 67n59, 97n164
deiwas (Old Prussian), 160
dèlbti, 69
deñgti, 67
dìdis etc., 49, 79–84
didùs, 82, 84
dieváitė/dieváičia, 86
dieváitis, 86
diẽvas/diẽvo, 160, 177
dìlba, 69
dõras/dorà, 72
dúonkubilis, 52
ẽknos/ãknos, 94, 95
élnias/élnis, 54
ércikaičia, 85
ẽžeras, 94n155
ẽdžia, 70
ẽdžios, 67, 68
ẽsti, 67, 70
gaida, 64n46
gaidas, 53, 64n46
gaidỹs, 53, 54, 64, 96n160
gaĩlestis/gaĩlas, 160
ganýti, 68
geĩtas/geltà, 72

takṣnī́, 116
dámiya-, 42
dā́ru/dróḥ, 155, 156, 158, 162, 163,
  165, 167, 177
divyá-, 47
dúrya-, 42
devī́, 119
dáivya-, 47
dyáuḥ/dyóḥ/diváḥ, 124n84, 177, 178,
  179n88
drúṇa-, 164
návya-, 10
pátnī, 116, 119
padám, 177n75
parút, 168n53
paśú-/páśu, 180
pṛthvī́, 116
prátiardhi-, 52
matí-, 153, 154
mádya-, 42
mádhu-, 154, 155, 156, 158, 177,
  180n91
mártiya-, márta-, 48n138
mādáyati, 23
mṛtá-, 48n138
mṛtyú-, 48n138
medya-, 46
yoktár-, 124n84
rása-, 178n84
ruváti, 90
rócate, 22
rocáyati, 21, 22
várdhati/várdhate, 21
vardháyati, 21
vṛṣṇí-/vṛ́ṣṇi, 180n91
śīrṣṇá-, 168
śīrṣatá-, 168
śrāmya-, 46
śrutá-, 169
satyá-, 44
sárasvatī, 43n121
satī́, 116
sā́nu/snóḥ, 155, 163
sīvya-, 46
súvar, 47
sūnu-, 154
sū́rya-, 47
stáriḥ, 116
sravát-, 169n57

IRANIAN

(Avestan unlabelled)

išya-, 41
uvāmaršiyu- (Old Persian), 48n138
xšāy-, 43n121
xšāyaθiya- (Old Persian), 43n121
šāh (New Persian), 43n121
dahyāuš (Old Persian), 179n88
dǝ̄ng, 154
dyaoš, 178
drvan-, 164
paδǝm, 177n75
-bāzāuš/-bāzvō, 178, 179
frabda-, 177n75
marǝta-/mǝrǝta-, 48n138
martiya-, marta- (Old Persian),
  48n138
märd/murd (New Persian), 48n138
mǝrǝθyu-, 48n138
Μαζάρης < mazdara-, 127
vāstrya-, 48
vairya-, 41
snāvar, 173, 176
zǝvištya-, 48
Harauvatiya- (Old Persian), 43n121
haiθya-, 44
hašiya- (Old Persian), 43n121
xᵛǝ̄ng, 154

ITALIC

(Latin unlabelled)

acupedius, 31n80
adāgium, 32
aeteis/aíttíúm (Oscan), 112n36
agrestis/ager, 159
aiō, ais/aīs, 30n79, 32, 32n83, 32n85
Aius Locútius/Loquēns, 32
alius, 12, 30
amiciō, amicīre, amicuī/amixī, amictus, 20, 31–32n82
amictus/amiectus, 31–32n82
arborius, 31n80
āstūtus/āstūtia, 72
audiō, audīre, 33

SUBJECT INDEX

SUBJECT INDEX

div-verbs (Sanskrit), 44–46
Dorian: a definition, 128, 140
Dozuhnen: *pasakos*, 83

East-Thessalian: relevance to definition of Aiolian, 128
Edalion Bronze, 142n172
Edgerton's Converse, 3n1, 4, 6, 9
Elbing Glossary: its orthographic
system, 50, 100
"enlargements" (IE), 170

f-future (Old Irish), 16, 17
figura etymologica, 59n34
free variation, 57

gemination, 30–31, 39, 102–112, 116,
117, 123, 124n85, 125, 131, 134,
140
gender: masculine/feminine vs. animate, 61–63, 171n63; suppression
of masculine vs. feminine distinction in Greek adjectives, ancient
and modern (e.g. Calabrian), 62–
63n41, n42
gerundives (Sanskrit), 44
Godlewa: *dainos* and *pasakos*, 77
"grammaticalization", 157, 161, 163,
164, 167, 168n53, 171n63, 172, 173,
174, 175, 181, 182
Greek: nominals/verbals in -αν-/-ν-,
6n7, 8; nominals in -ειος, -αιος, 141

Hesiod, 61
heteroclisis, 156, 157, 158
Hittite: abstract substantives in -*ašti*,
160n34; thematic-stem genitives in
-*aš*, 161; ablatives in -*az*, 168,
169n57
homorganic off-glides, from vocalic
*i or *u, 4, 5, 6, 8, 41–48
hypercorrection, 60n36, 133, 136

iambic shortening (Latin), 33n86
iio-stem vs. *iiā*-stem, 60–61, 63, 65,
79, 183
inflection vs. derivation, 44–46, 86,
156–162, 163, 165, 168n53, 169,
172–181

intensive vs. attenuative verbs, 23n62
intervocalic *s* (Greek), 134
intonational displacement, 71
iterative vs. causative verbs, 21–26,
34–36

Kambyses: his death, 48n138
Klein: *Compendium*, 89; *Grammatica*,
83, 89
Kuryłowicz's axiom I, 5n5, 119n68,
141n167, 183n106; axiom IV, 6n7,
79n101, 85, 120n74, 178–179;
axiom V, 82n112

labiopalatal glides, 143n174
laryngeals (IE), 163n43, 171n62;
disappearance thereof, 4, 5, 6
Latin: nominals in -*eus/-ea*, 12; in
-*ius/-ia*, 12, 30–32
Lesbian: relevance to definition of
Aiolian, 128
levelling(paradigmatic), 18–19,28–29,
37, 54–56, 57–59, 74–83, 86,
96n160, 106–112, 115n46, 118–119,
123, 135–136, 167, 178n82, 178–182
light vs. heavy syllables, 3, 3n3, 5, 6,
7, 8, 25, 33, 34, 35, 36, 38, 42, 46,
47, 50, 102
Linear B: omission of syllable-coda,
133n132; alternations of orthographic mechanisms, 142–144, 145,
146–147, 147–148n187; possible
dialectal inconsistencies in scribal
hands, 147, 149–150
Lithuanian: nominals in -*klas* vs.
-*klis*, 53; -*ysta* vs. -*ystė*, 56; -*imas*
or -*ymas*, 68, 73, 73n83; -*ýbė*, 72,
73n83; -*ùs* (feminine -*ì/-iõs*), 75–79,
82–84; comparatives in -*èsnis*,
-*èsnė/-èsni*, -*esnýji*, -*esnióji*, 73–79;
superlatives in -*iáusias*, 52
Lucretius, 68–69

magic and poetry, 10–11n16
Messenian Phera, 151
metathesis, 126–127, 130, 135
metrical preservation of archaisms,
25n67, 41–48, 62n42, 107, 108,
116–117, 134, 180n92

198